WILDSTORM

REVELATIONS

Writers: Scott Beatty
with Christos Gage
Artist: Wes Craig
Colors: Jonny Rench
Letters: Wes Abbott

Collected Edition and Original Series covers
by Ivan Reis and Richard Friend
Covers colored by Randy Mayor [#1-2, 4].
Carrie Strachan [#3], Jonny Rench [#5]
and Tony Aviña [#6]

Jim Lee, Editorial Director
John Nee, Senior VP—Business Development
Ben Abernathy, Editor
Kristy Quinn, Assistant Editor
Ed Roeder, Art Director
Paul Levitz, President & Publisher
Georg Brewer, VP—Design & DC Direct Creative
Richard Bruning, Senior VP—Creative Director
Patrick Caldon, Executive VP—Finance & Operations
Chris Caramalis, VP—Finance
John Cunningham, VP—Marketing
Terri Cunningham, VP—Managing Editor
Alison Gill, VP—Manufacturing
David Hyde, VP—Publicity
Hank Kanalz, VP—General Manager, WildStorm
Paula Lowitt, Senior VP—Business & Legal Affairs
MaryEllen McLaughlin, VP—Advertising & Custom Publishing
Gregory Noveck, Senior VP—Creative Affairs
Sue Pohja, VP—Book Trade Sales
Steve Rotterdam, Senior VP—Sales & Marketing
Cheryl Rubin, Senior VP—Brand Management
Jeff Trojan, VP—Business Development, DC Direct
Bob Wayne, VP—Sales

WILDSTORM REVELATIONS published by WildStorm Productions. 888 Prospect St. #240,
La Jolla, CA 92037. Compilation and sketches Copyright © 2008 WildStorm Productions, an
imprint of DC Comics. All Rights Reserved. WildStorm and logo, all characters, the distinctive
likenesses thereof and all related elements are trademarks of DC Comics. Originally
published in single magazine form as WILDSTORM REVELATIONS #1-6 © 2008
WildStorm Productions, an imprint of DC Comics.

The stories, characters, and incidents mentioned in this magazine are entirely fictional.
Printed on recyclable paper. WildStorm does not read or accept unsolicited submissions
of ideas, stories or artwork. Printed in Canada.

DC Comics, a Warner Bros. Entertainment Company.

ISBN: 978-1-4012-1867-6

Cover Sketches
by Ivan Reis

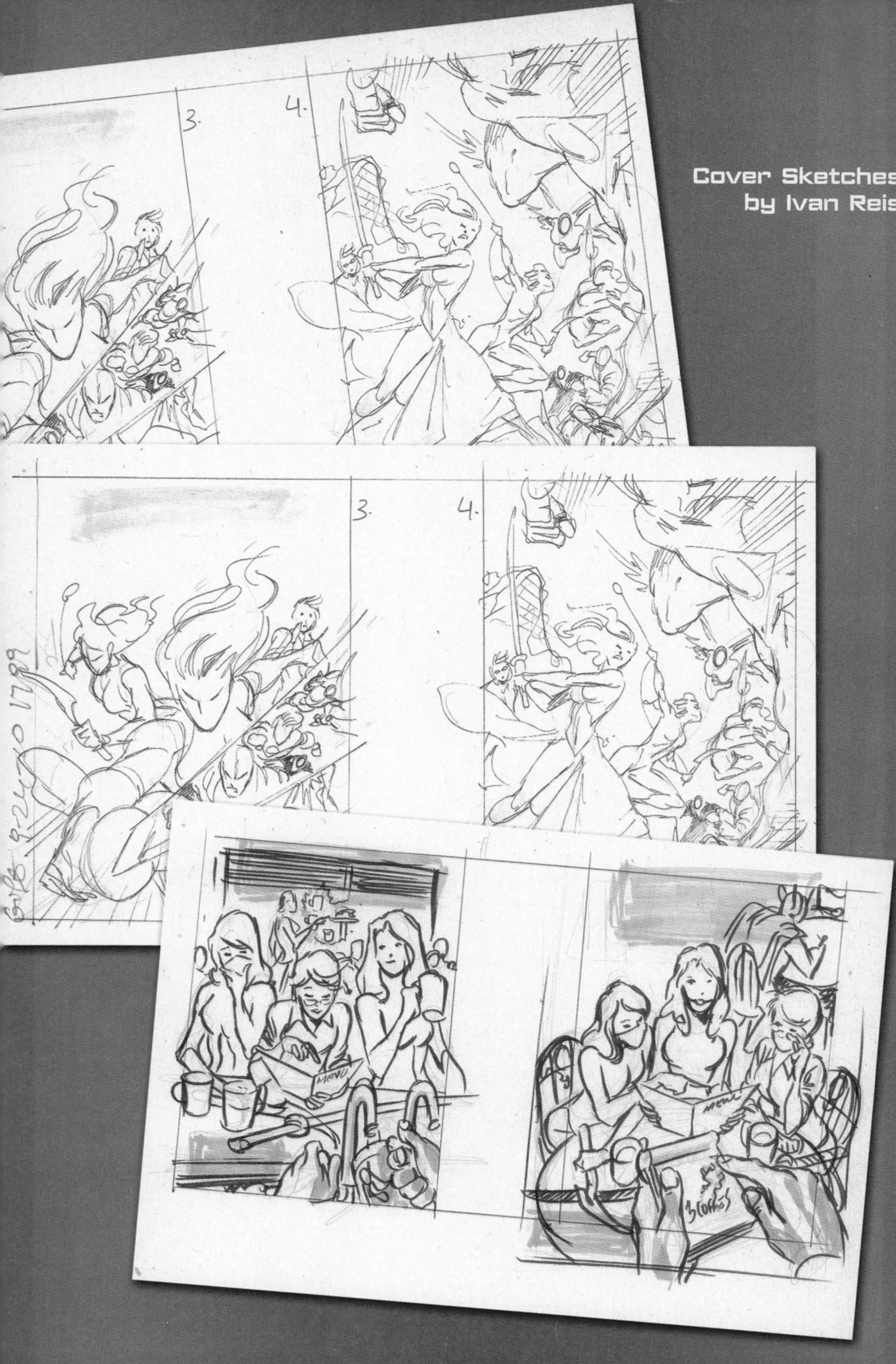
3.
4.
3.
4.
MENU
MENU

ARMAGEDDON IS COMING TO THE WILDSTORM UNIVERSE.

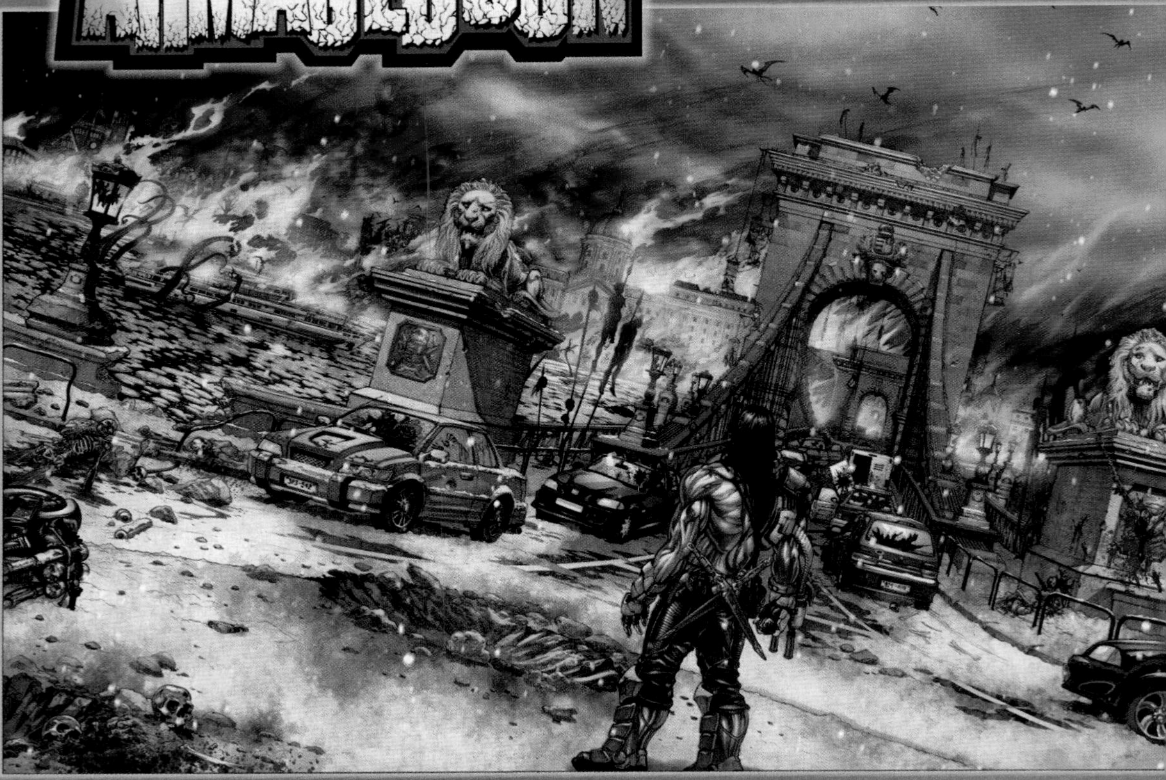

Or is it? Our trio of heroines are asking themselves this question and more as they set out to thwart the coming destruction. But what set them on this quest?

In the recent WILDSTORM ARMAGEDDON, Void appeared to various WildStorm heroes and transported them to a not-too-distant future where the world was in ruin and humanity dead—but what caused this apocalypse? Accounts from the few survivors in this future wasteland were remarkably similar—a sudden appearance of "new" super-humans followed by a massive, destructive battle that led to a global cataclysm. Void implored every hero to stop Armageddon, but each one had a different reaction to what they'd seen. Only the disgraced Coda warrior Nemesis was given any real piece of the puzzle...but is it a wild goose chase?

REVELATIONS offers the first step in cracking this code of destruction—but is the future set in stone or can it be altered?

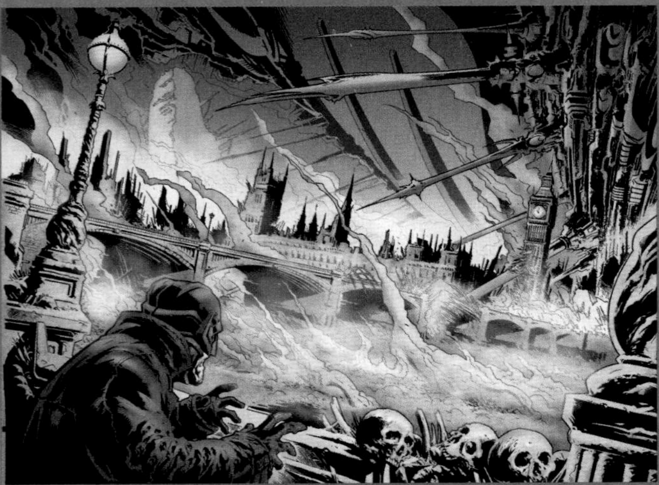

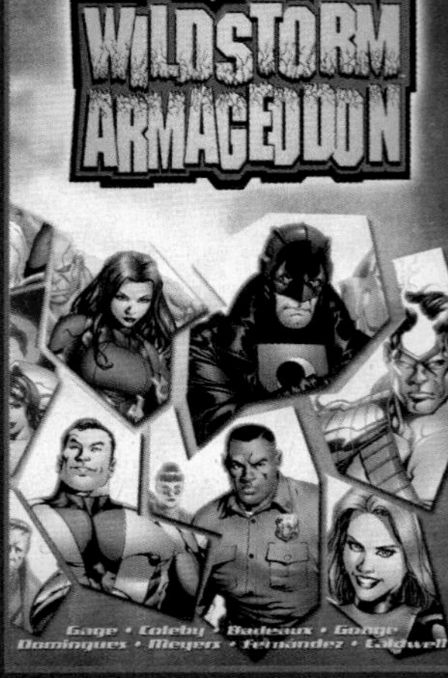
WILDSTORM
ARMAGEDDON

Chapter 1

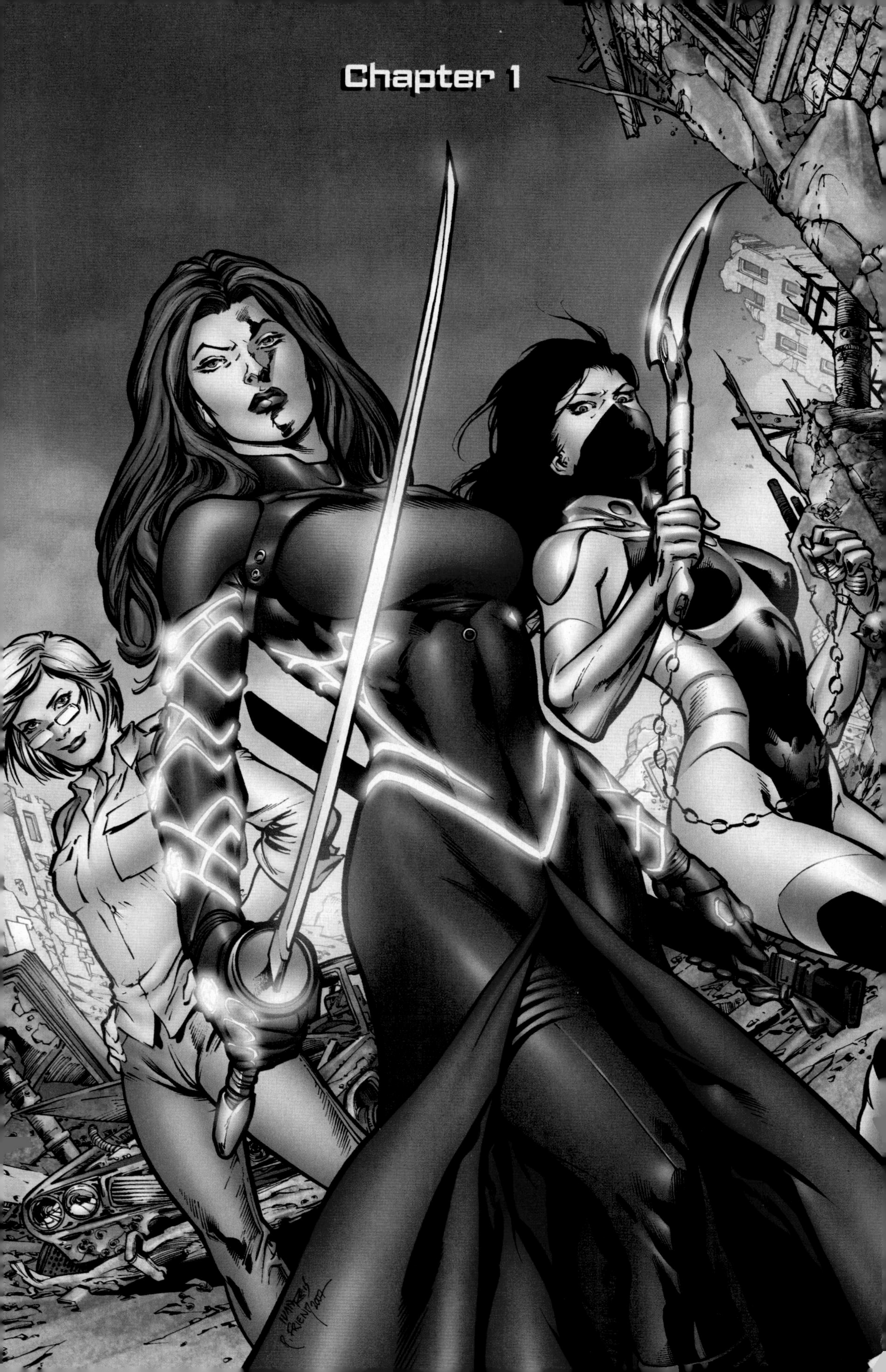

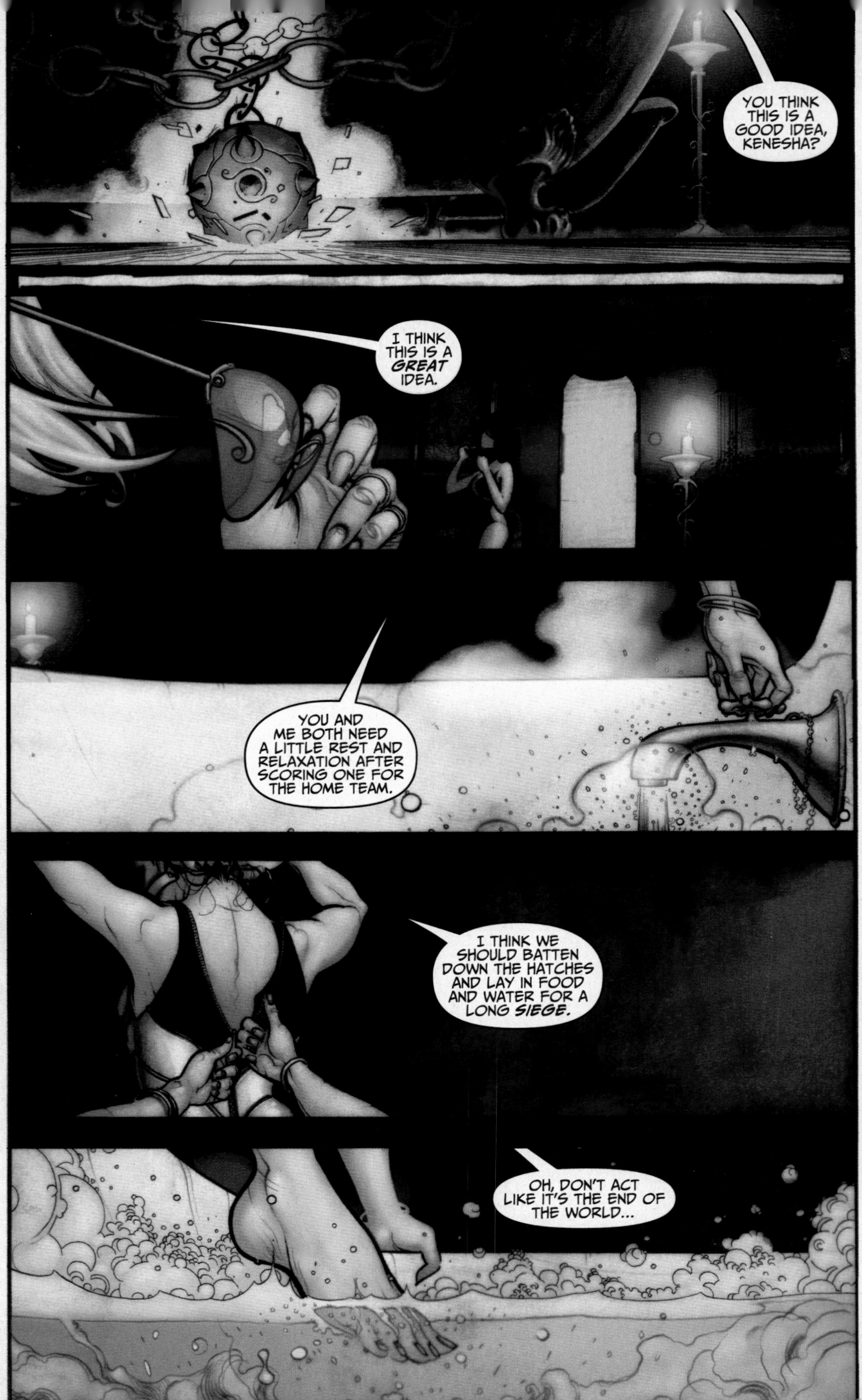
YOU THINK THIS IS A GOOD IDEA, KENESHA?
I THINK THIS IS A GREAT IDEA.
YOU AND ME BOTH NEED A LITTLE REST AND RELAXATION AFTER SCORING ONE FOR THE HOME TEAM.
I THINK WE SHOULD BATTEN DOWN THE HATCHES AND LAY IN FOOD AND WATER FOR A LONG SIEGE.
OH, DON'T ACT LIKE IT'S THE END OF THE WORLD...

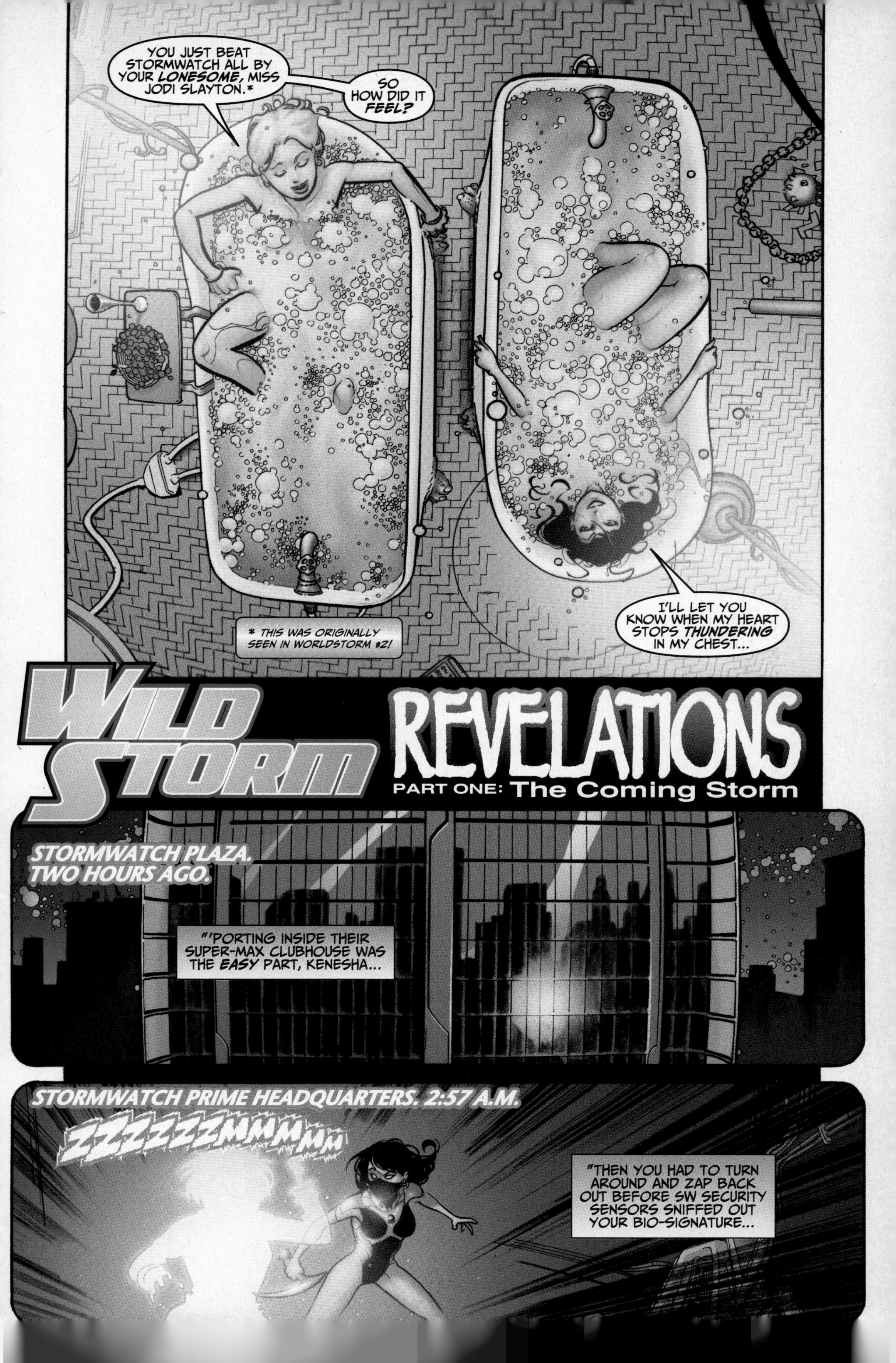
YOU JUST BEAT STORMWATCH ALL BY YOUR LONESOME, MISS JODI SLAYTON.*
SO HOW DID IT FEEL?
I'LL LET YOU KNOW WHEN MY HEART STOPS THUNDERING IN MY CHEST...
* THIS WAS ORIGINALLY SEEN IN WORLDSTORM #2!
WILD STORM
REVELATIONS
PART ONE: The Coming Storm
STORMWATCH PLAZA. TWO HOURS AGO.
"'PORTING INSIDE THEIR SUPER-MAX CLUBHOUSE WAS THE EASY PART, KENESHA...
STORMWATCH PRIME HEADQUARTERS. 2:57 A.M.
ZZZZZZMMMMMM
"THEN YOU HAD TO TURN AROUND AND ZAP BACK OUT BEFORE SW SECURITY SENSORS SNIFFED OUT YOUR BIO-SIGNATURE...

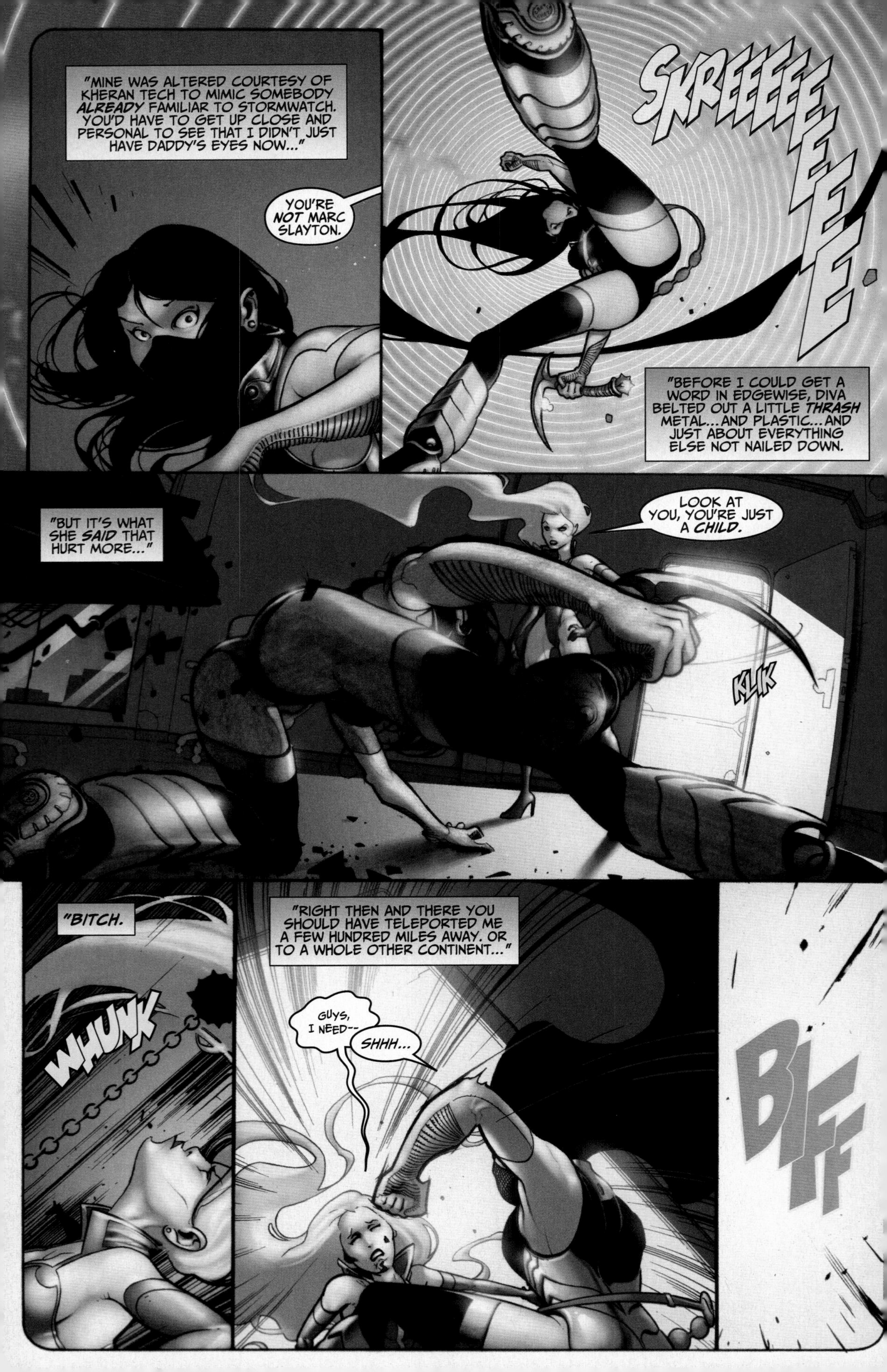
"MINE WAS ALTERED COURTESY OF KHERAN TECH TO MIMIC SOMEBODY ALREADY FAMILIAR TO STORMWATCH. YOU'D HAVE TO GET UP CLOSE AND PERSONAL TO SEE THAT I DIDN'T JUST HAVE DADDY'S EYES NOW..."
YOU'RE NOT MARC SLAYTON.
SKREEEEEEEEE
"BEFORE I COULD GET A WORD IN EDGEWISE, DIVA BELTED OUT A LITTLE THRASH METAL...AND PLASTIC...AND JUST ABOUT EVERYTHING ELSE NOT NAILED DOWN.
"BUT IT'S WHAT SHE SAID THAT HURT MORE..."
LOOK AT YOU, YOU'RE JUST A CHILD.
KLIK
"BITCH.
WHUNK
"RIGHT THEN AND THERE YOU SHOULD HAVE TELEPORTED ME A FEW HUNDRED MILES AWAY. OR TO A WHOLE OTHER CONTINENT..."
GUYS, I NEED--
SHHH...
BIFF

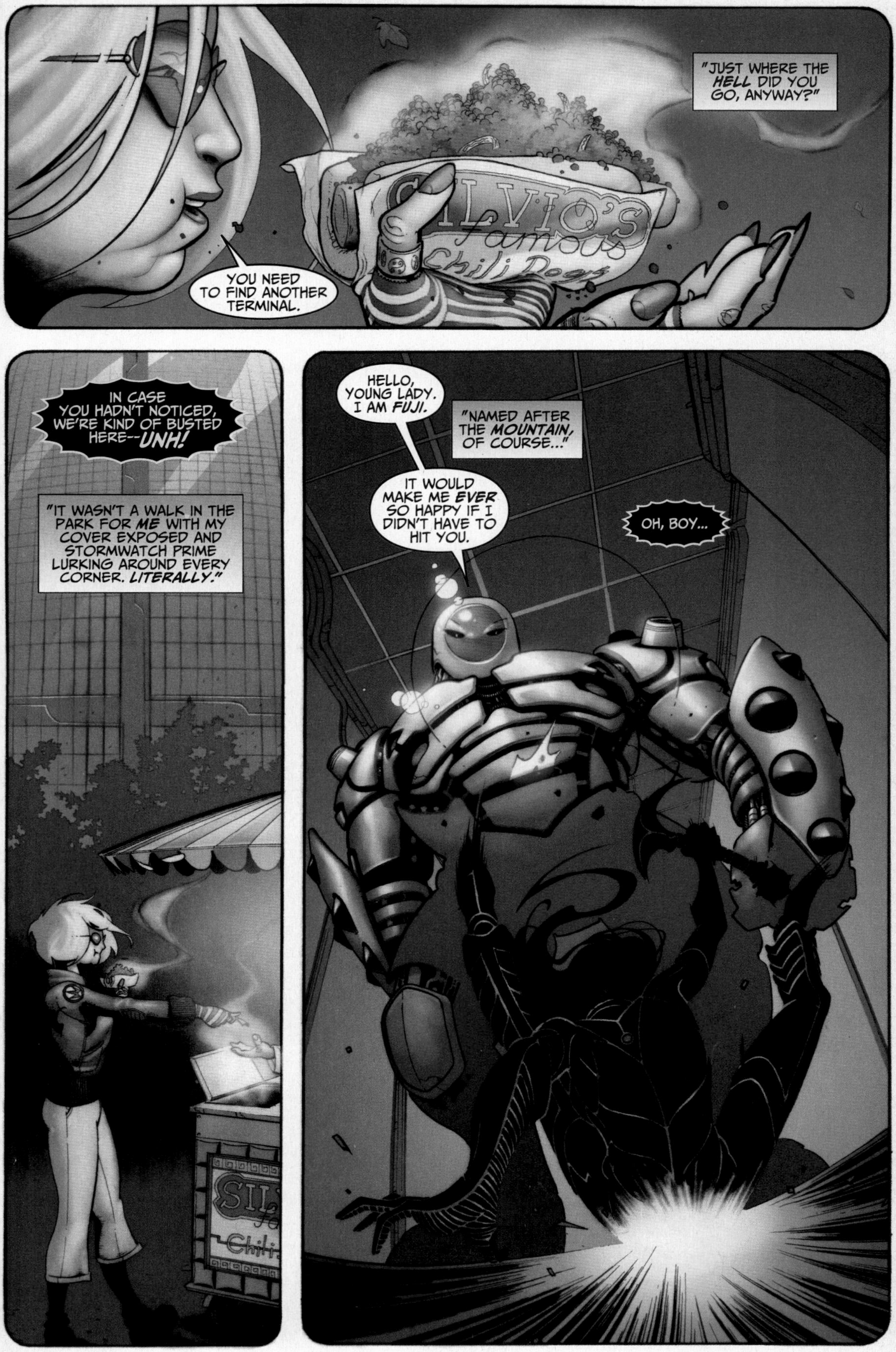
"JUST WHERE THE HELL DID YOU GO, ANYWAY?"
YOU NEED TO FIND ANOTHER TERMINAL.
SILVIO'S Famous Chili Dogs
IN CASE YOU HADN'T NOTICED, WE'RE KIND OF BUSTED HERE--UNH!
"IT WASN'T A WALK IN THE PARK FOR ME WITH MY COVER EXPOSED AND STORMWATCH PRIME LURKING AROUND EVERY CORNER. LITERALLY."
HELLO, YOUNG LADY. I AM FUJI.
"NAMED AFTER THE MOUNTAIN, OF COURSE..."
IT WOULD MAKE ME EVER SO HAPPY IF I DIDN'T HAVE TO HIT YOU.
OH, BOY...

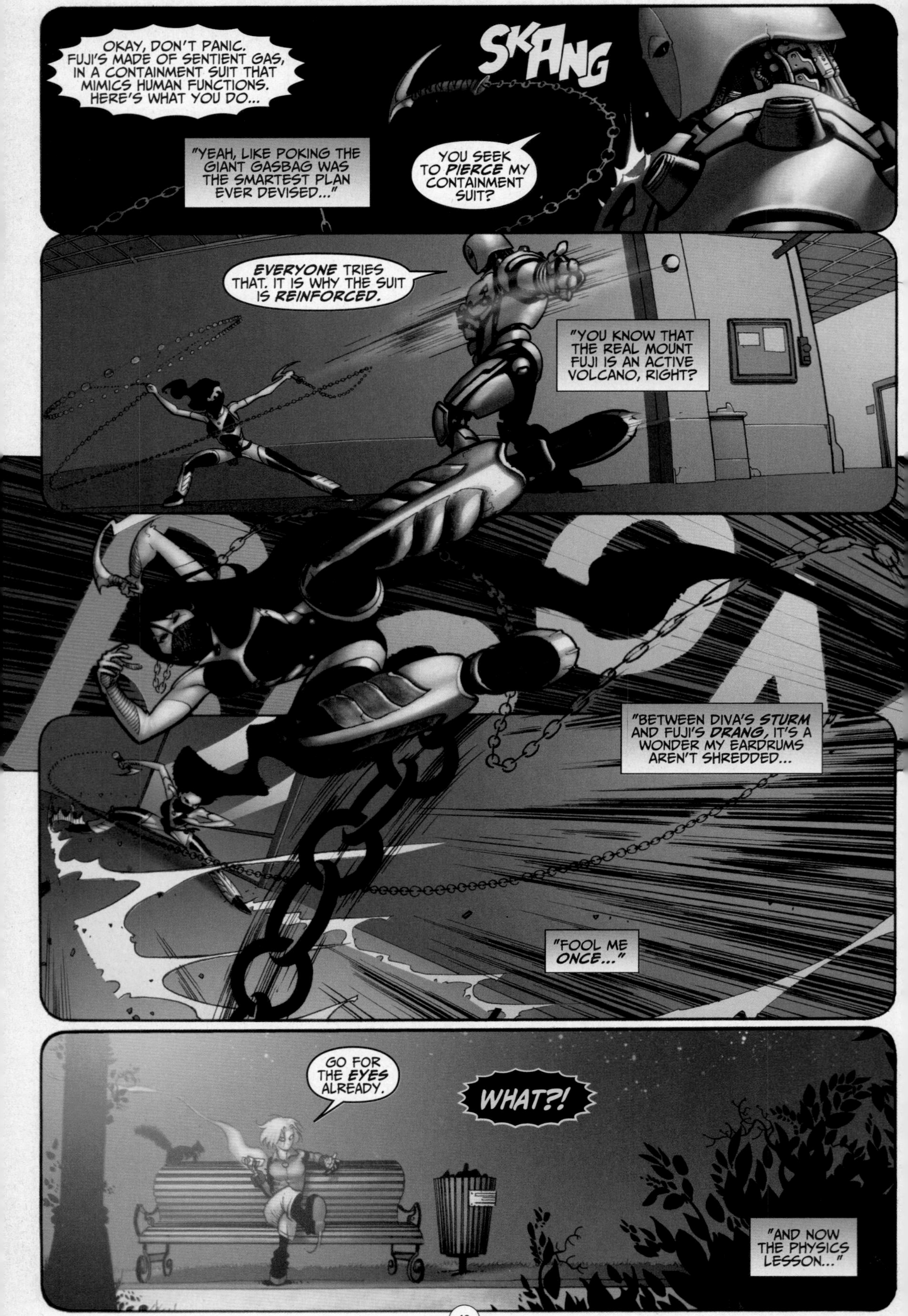
OKAY, DON'T PANIC. FUJI'S MADE OF SENTIENT GAS, IN A CONTAINMENT SUIT THAT MIMICS HUMAN FUNCTIONS. HERE'S WHAT YOU DO...
SKANG
"YEAH, LIKE POKING THE GIANT GASBAG WAS THE SMARTEST PLAN EVER DEVISED..."
YOU SEEK TO PIERCE MY CONTAINMENT SUIT?
EVERYONE TRIES THAT. IT IS WHY THE SUIT IS REINFORCED.
"YOU KNOW THAT THE REAL MOUNT FUJI IS AN ACTIVE VOLCANO, RIGHT?
"BETWEEN DIVA'S STURM AND FUJI'S DRANG, IT'S A WONDER MY EARDRUMS AREN'T SHREDDED...
"FOOL ME ONCE..."
GO FOR THE EYES ALREADY.
WHAT?!
"AND NOW THE PHYSICS LESSON..."

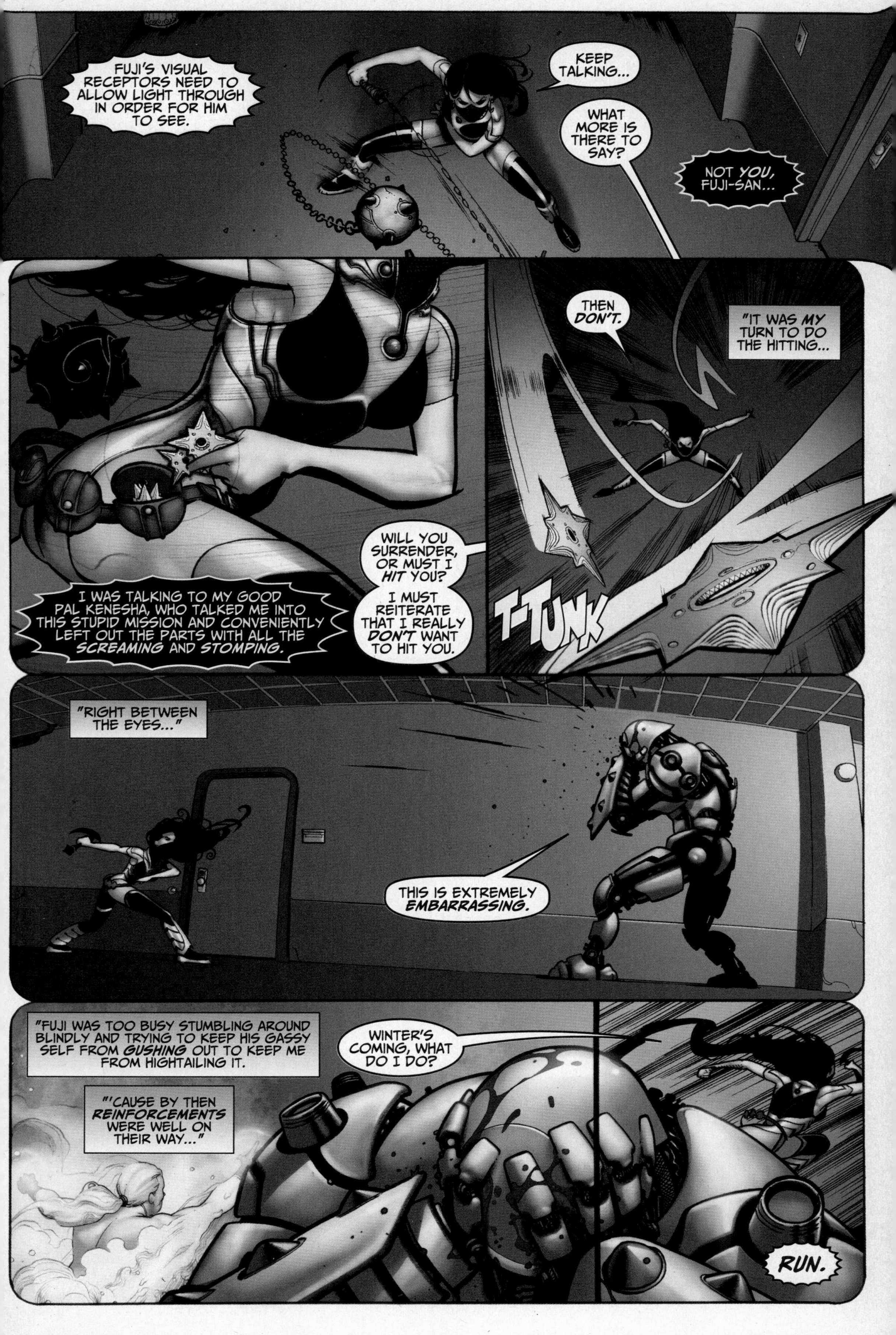
FUJI'S VISUAL RECEPTORS NEED TO ALLOW LIGHT THROUGH IN ORDER FOR HIM TO SEE.
KEEP TALKING...
WHAT MORE IS THERE TO SAY?
NOT YOU, FUJI-SAN...
I WAS TALKING TO MY GOOD PAL KENESHA, WHO TALKED ME INTO THIS STUPID MISSION AND CONVENIENTLY LEFT OUT THE PARTS WITH ALL THE SCREAMING AND STOMPING.
WILL YOU SURRENDER, OR MUST I HIT YOU?
I MUST REITERATE THAT I REALLY DON'T WANT TO HIT YOU.
THEN DON'T.
"IT WAS MY TURN TO DO THE HITTING...
T-TUNK
"RIGHT BETWEEN THE EYES..."
THIS IS EXTREMELY EMBARRASSING.
"FUJI WAS TOO BUSY STUMBLING AROUND BLINDLY AND TRYING TO KEEP HIS GASSY SELF FROM GUSHING OUT TO KEEP ME FROM HIGHTAILING IT.
"'CAUSE BY THEN REINFORCEMENTS WERE WELL ON THEIR WAY..."
WINTER'S COMING, WHAT DO I DO?
RUN.

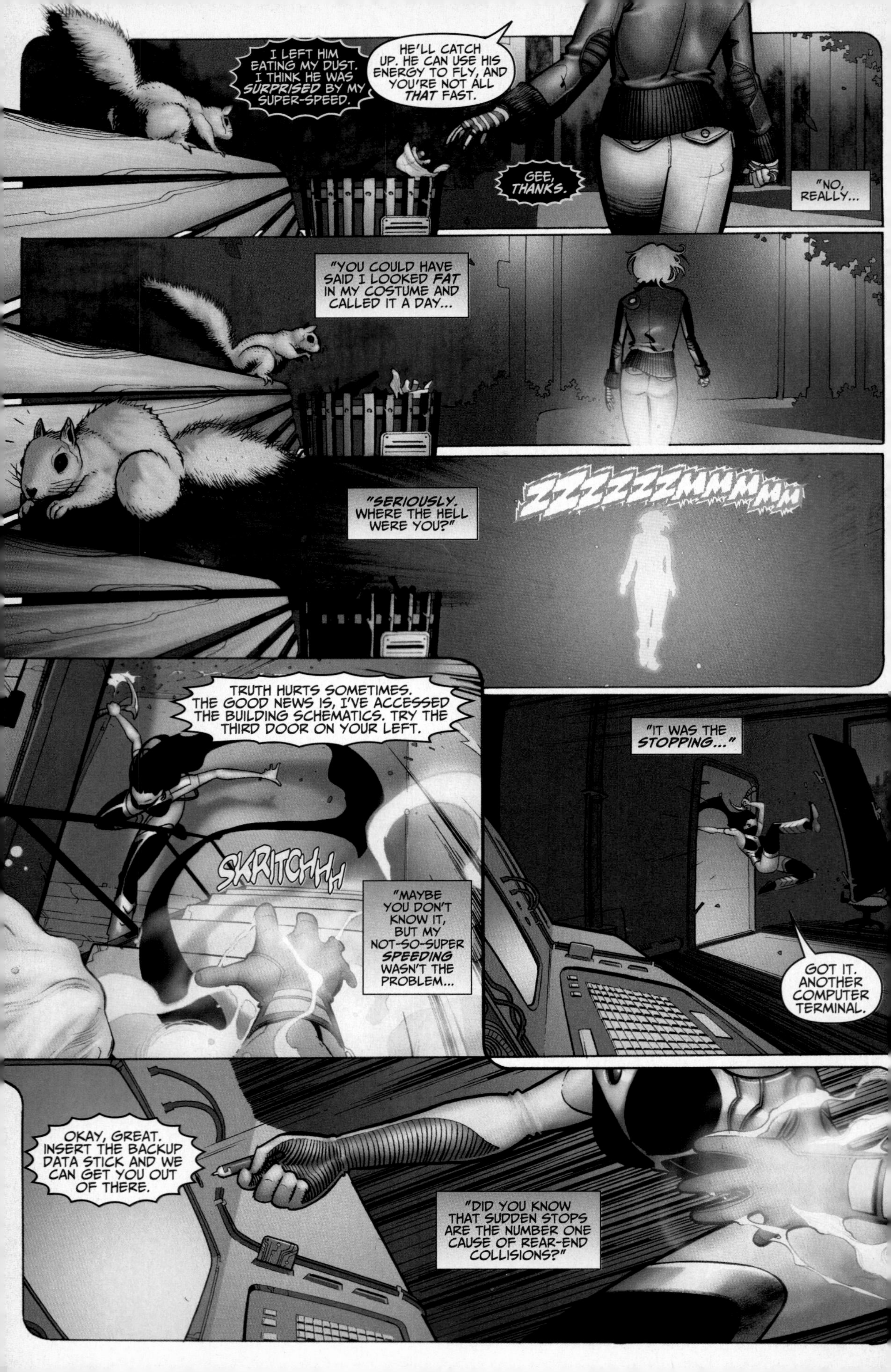

I LEFT HIM EATING MY DUST. I THINK HE WAS SURPRISED BY MY SUPER-SPEED.
HE'LL CATCH UP. HE CAN USE HIS ENERGY TO FLY, AND YOU'RE NOT ALL THAT FAST.
GEE, THANKS.
"NO, REALLY...
"YOU COULD HAVE SAID I LOOKED FAT IN MY COSTUME AND CALLED IT A DAY...
"SERIOUSLY. WHERE THE HELL WERE YOU?"
ZZZZZZMMMMMM
TRUTH HURTS SOMETIMES. THE GOOD NEWS IS, I'VE ACCESSED THE BUILDING SCHEMATICS. TRY THE THIRD DOOR ON YOUR LEFT.
SKRITCHHH
"MAYBE YOU DON'T KNOW IT, BUT MY NOT-SO-SUPER SPEEDING WASN'T THE PROBLEM...
"IT WAS THE STOPPING..."
GOT IT. ANOTHER COMPUTER TERMINAL.
OKAY, GREAT. INSERT THE BACKUP DATA STICK AND WE CAN GET YOU OUT OF THERE.
"DID YOU KNOW THAT SUDDEN STOPS ARE THE NUMBER ONE CAUSE OF REAR-END COLLISIONS?"

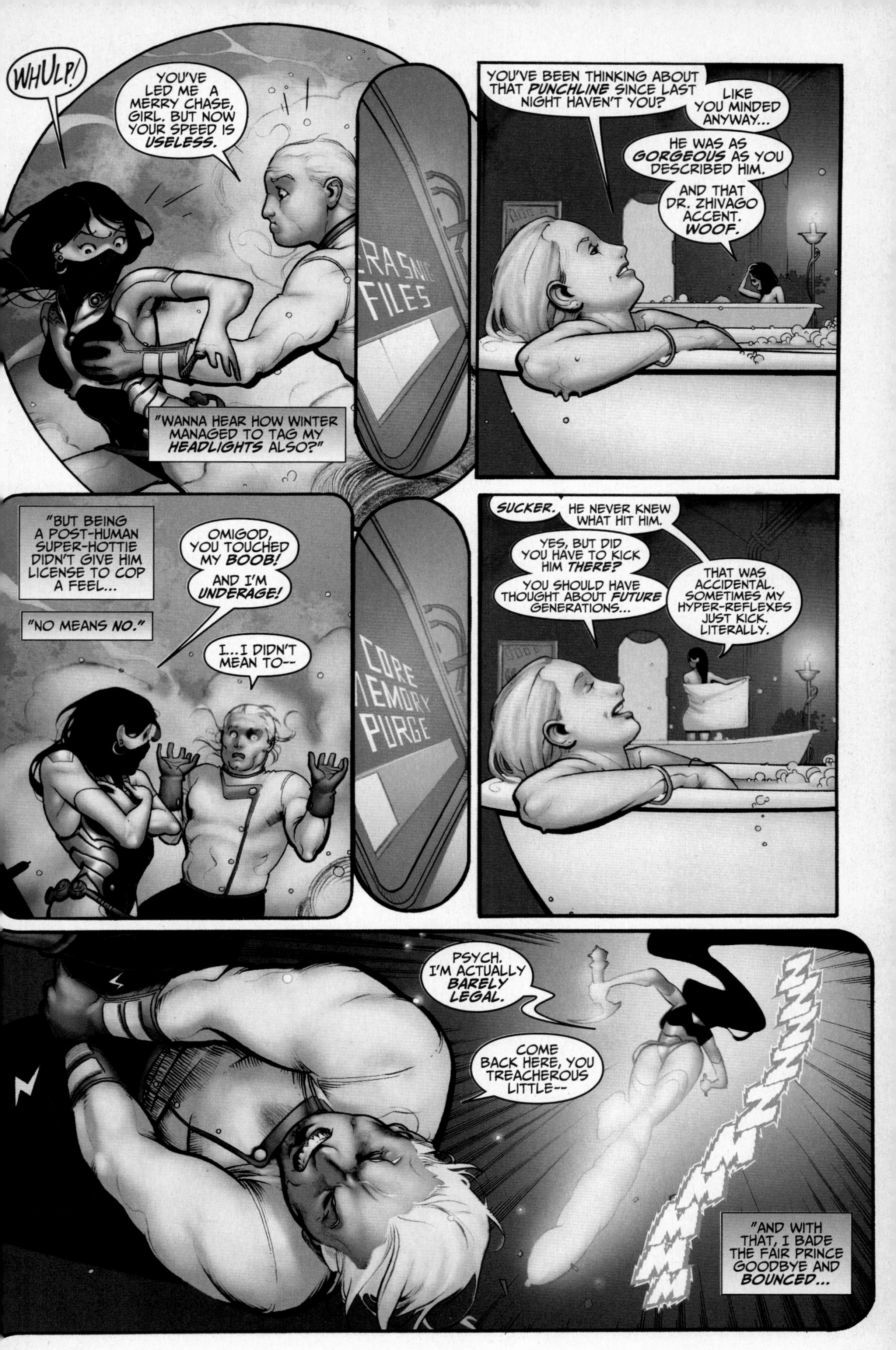
WHULP!
YOU'VE LED ME A MERRY CHASE, GIRL. BUT NOW YOUR SPEED IS USELESS.
ERASING FILES
"WANNA HEAR HOW WINTER MANAGED TO TAG MY HEADLIGHTS ALSO?"
YOU'VE BEEN THINKING ABOUT THAT PUNCHLINE SINCE LAST NIGHT HAVEN'T YOU?
LIKE YOU MINDED ANYWAY...
HE WAS AS GORGEOUS AS YOU DESCRIBED HIM.
AND THAT DR. ZHIVAGO ACCENT. WOOF.
"BUT BEING A POST-HUMAN SUPER-HOTTIE DIDN'T GIVE HIM LICENSE TO COP A FEEL...
"NO MEANS NO."
OMIGOD, YOU TOUCHED MY BOOB!
AND I'M UNDERAGE!
I...I DIDN'T MEAN TO--
CORE MEMORY PURGE
SUCKER.
HE NEVER KNEW WHAT HIT HIM.
YES, BUT DID YOU HAVE TO KICK HIM THERE?
YOU SHOULD HAVE THOUGHT ABOUT FUTURE GENERATIONS...
THAT WAS ACCIDENTAL. SOMETIMES MY HYPER-REFLEXES JUST KICK. LITERALLY.
PSYCH. I'M ACTUALLY BARELY LEGAL.
COME BACK HERE, YOU TREACHEROUS LITTLE--
"AND WITH THAT, I BADE THE FAIR PRINCE GOODBYE AND BOUNCED...

SO IS IT ANY WONDER WHY MY HEART'S GOING *PITTER-PATTER* ON A SEISMIC SCALE?

I MADE SOME DANGEROUS NEW *ENEMIES* TONIGHT. MY FUTURE'S *SCREWED.*

RELAX. THEY'RE BASICALLY HEROES. THEY *DON'T* HOLD GRUDGES.

BY DOWNLOADING THAT VIRUS AND WIPING STORMWATCH'S DATABASES, WE KEEP OUR *SECRETS* SECRET FOR PHASE TWO.

GREAT. PHASE TWO...

I'M HUNGRY. YOU WANT ANYTHING?

I'LL SCREAM FOR ICE CREAM!

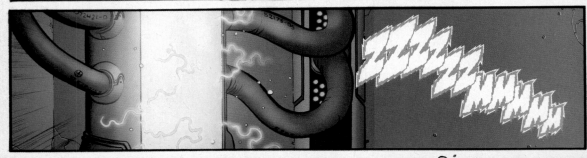

ZZZZZZZZZMMMMM

ZERT.

14

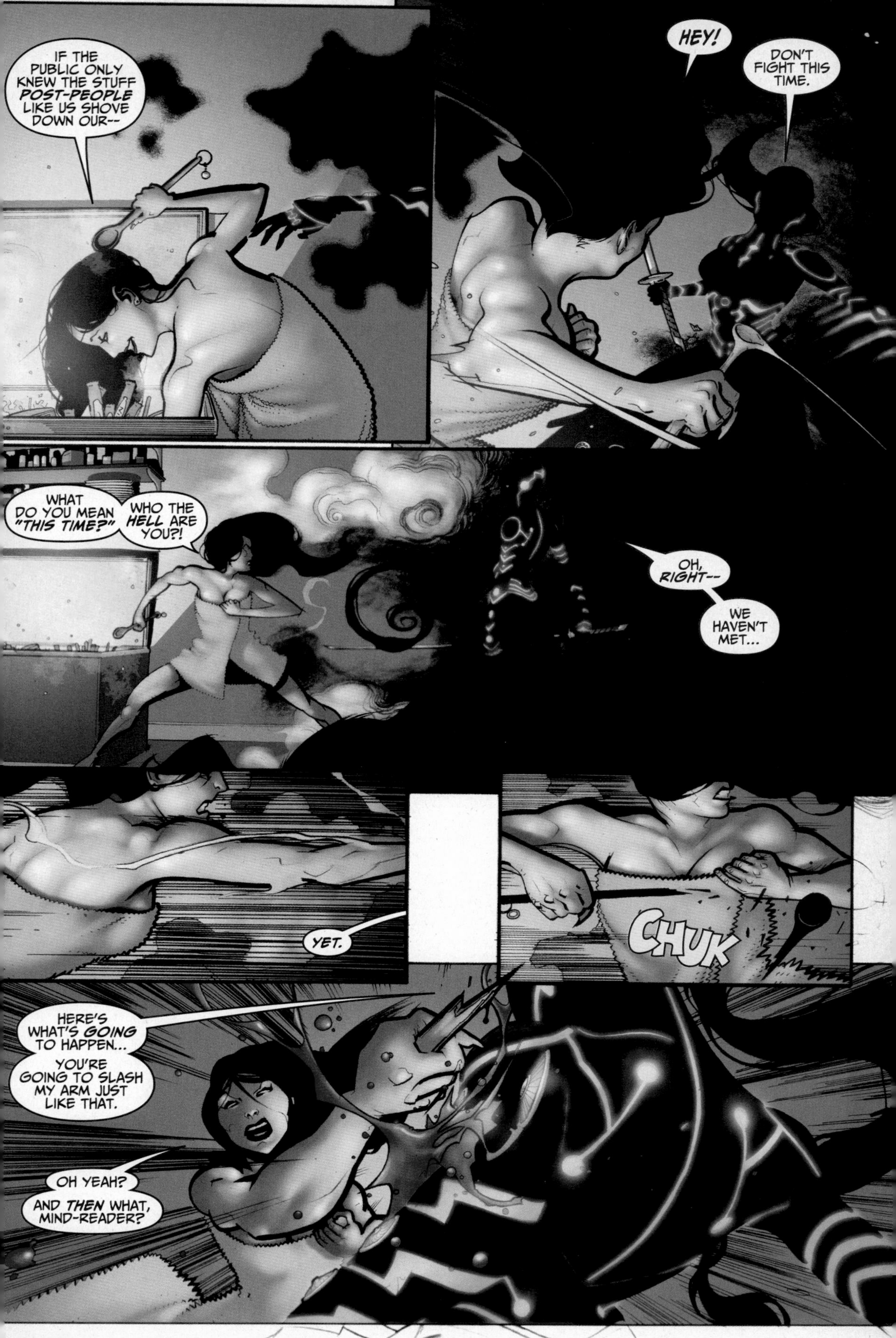
IF THE PUBLIC ONLY KNEW THE STUFF POST-PEOPLE LIKE US SHOVE DOWN OUR--
HEY!
DON'T FIGHT THIS TIME.
WHAT DO YOU MEAN "THIS TIME?"
WHO THE HELL ARE YOU?!
OH, RIGHT--
WE HAVEN'T MET...
YET.
CHUK
HERE'S WHAT'S GOING TO HAPPEN...
YOU'RE GOING TO SLASH MY ARM JUST LIKE THAT.
OH YEAH?
AND THEN WHAT, MIND-READER?

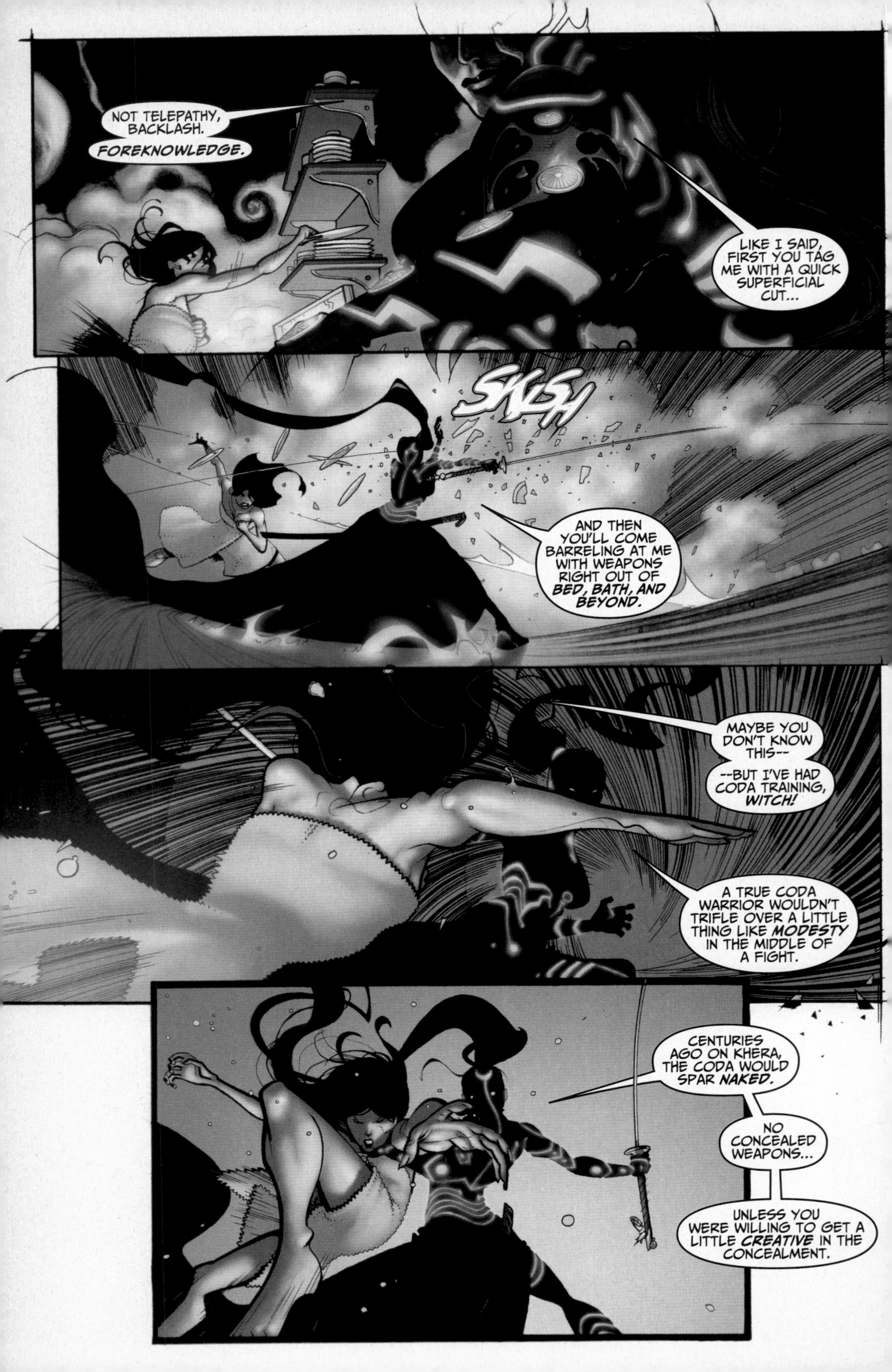
NOT TELEPATHY, BACKLASH.
FOREKNOWLEDGE.
LIKE I SAID, FIRST YOU TAG ME WITH A QUICK SUPERFICIAL CUT...
SKSH
AND THEN YOU'LL COME BARRELING AT ME WITH WEAPONS RIGHT OUT OF BED, BATH, AND BEYOND.
MAYBE YOU DON'T KNOW THIS--
--BUT I'VE HAD CODA TRAINING, WITCH!
A TRUE CODA WARRIOR WOULDN'T TRIFLE OVER A LITTLE THING LIKE MODESTY IN THE MIDDLE OF A FIGHT.
CENTURIES AGO ON KHERA, THE CODA WOULD SPAR NAKED.
NO CONCEALED WEAPONS...
UNLESS YOU WERE WILLING TO GET A LITTLE CREATIVE IN THE CONCEALMENT.

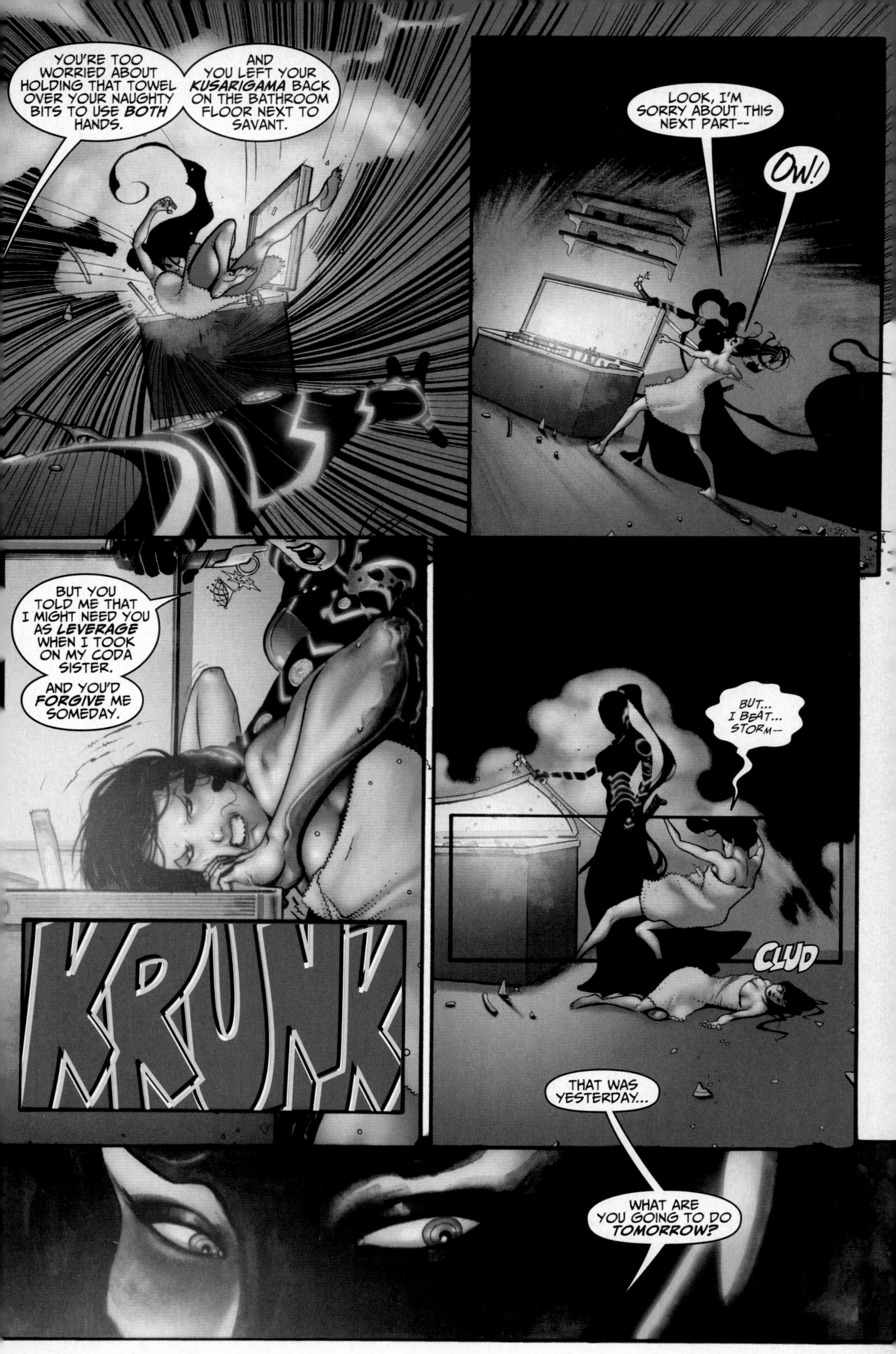
YOU'RE TOO WORRIED ABOUT HOLDING THAT TOWEL OVER YOUR NAUGHTY BITS TO USE BOTH HANDS.
AND YOU LEFT YOUR KUSARIGAMA BACK ON THE BATHROOM FLOOR NEXT TO SAVANT.
LOOK, I'M SORRY ABOUT THIS NEXT PART--
OW!
BUT YOU TOLD ME THAT I MIGHT NEED YOU AS LEVERAGE WHEN I TOOK ON MY CODA SISTER.
AND YOU'D FORGIVE ME SOMEDAY.
KRUNK
BUT... I BEAT... STORM--
CLUD
THAT WAS YESTERDAY...
WHAT ARE YOU GOING TO DO TOMORROW?

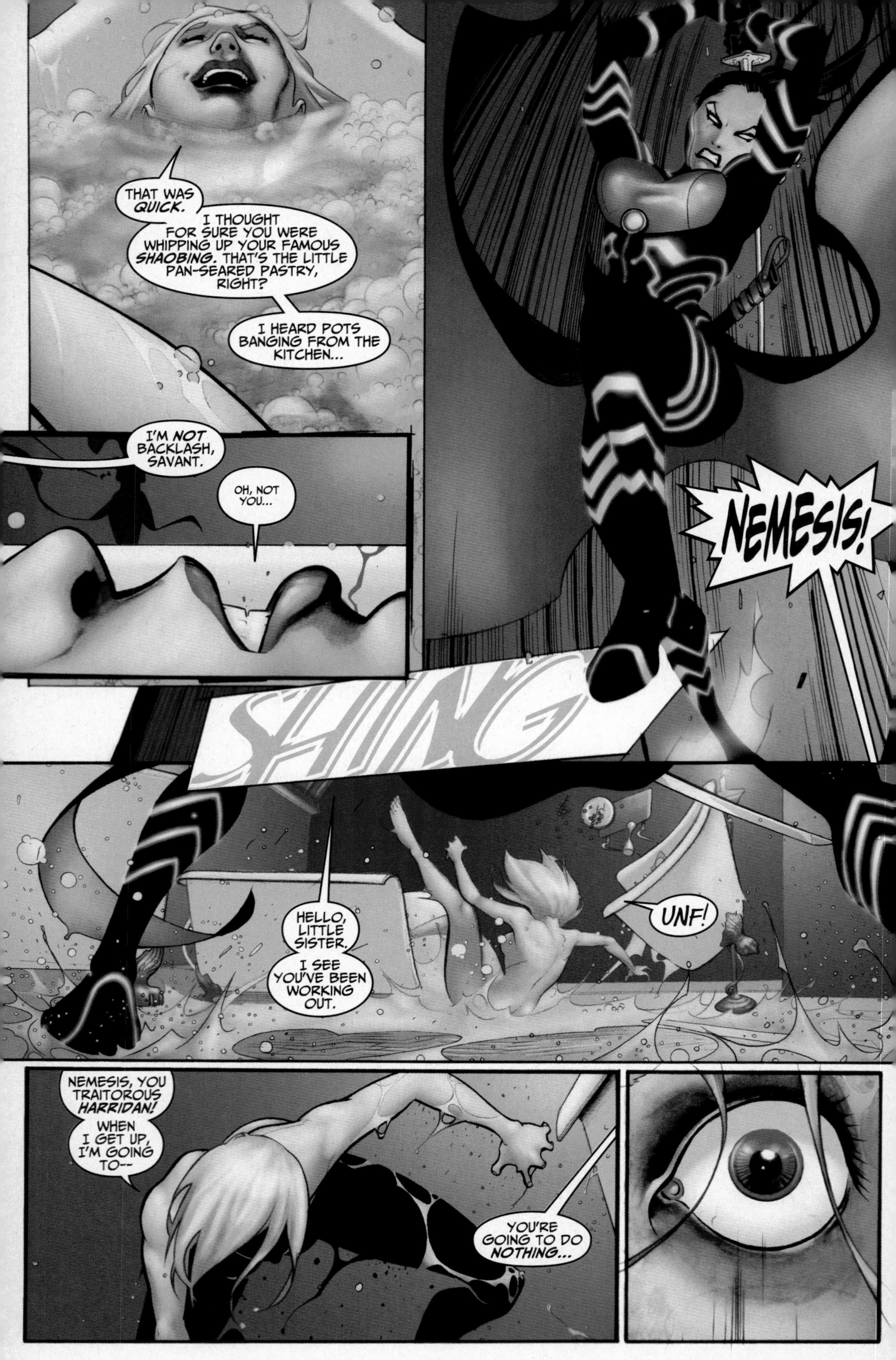

THAT WAS QUICK.
I THOUGHT FOR SURE YOU WERE WHIPPING UP YOUR FAMOUS SHAOBING. THAT'S THE LITTLE PAN-SEARED PASTRY, RIGHT?
I HEARD POTS BANGING FROM THE KITCHEN...
I'M NOT BACKLASH, SAVANT.
OH, NOT YOU...
NEMESIS!
SHING
HELLO, LITTLE SISTER.
I SEE YOU'VE BEEN WORKING OUT.
UNF!
NEMESIS, YOU TRAITOROUS HARRIDAN!
WHEN I GET UP, I'M GOING TO--
YOU'RE GOING TO DO NOTHING...

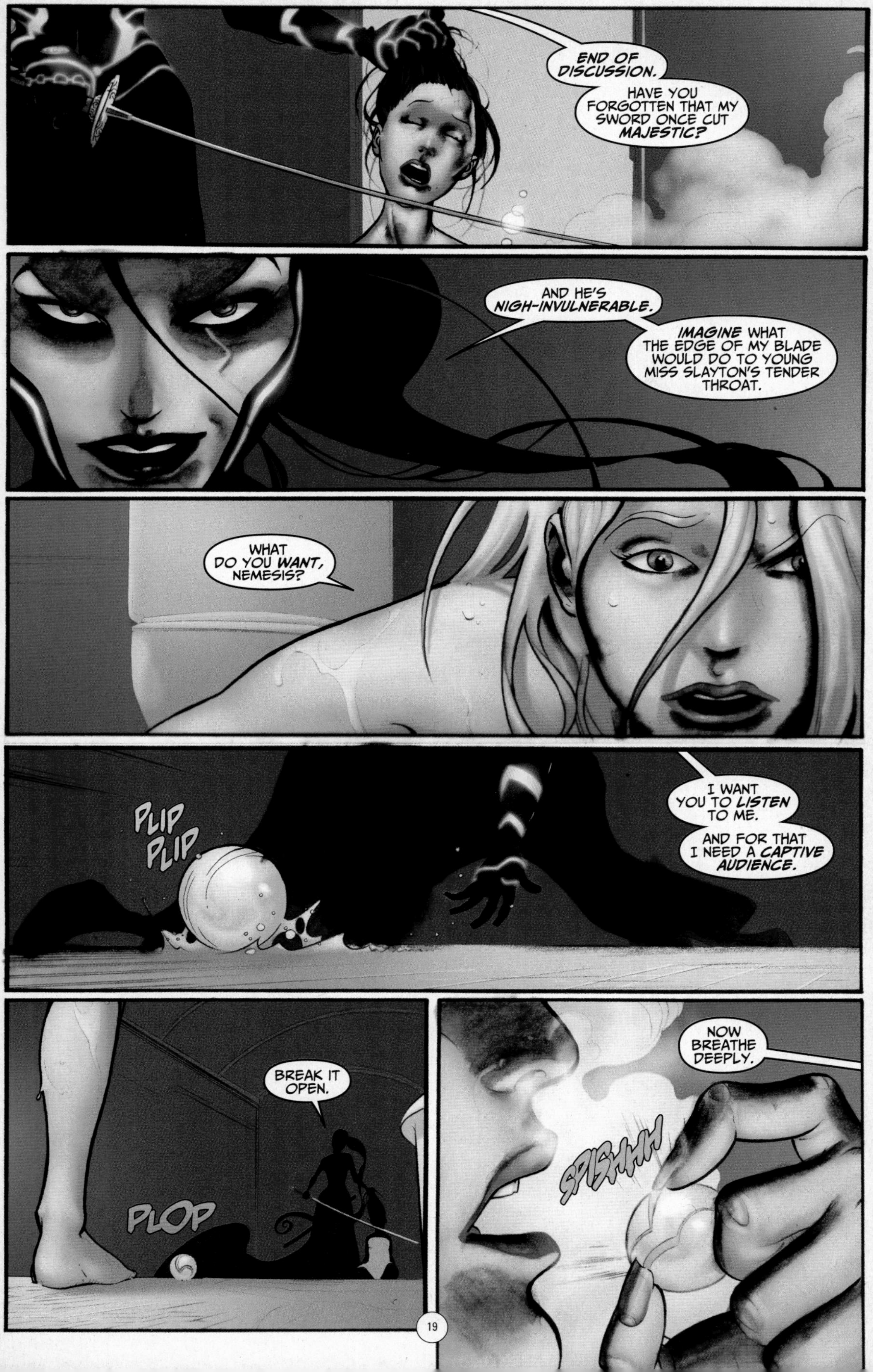

END OF DISCUSSION.
HAVE YOU FORGOTTEN THAT MY SWORD ONCE CUT MAJESTIC?
AND HE'S NIGH-INVULNERABLE.
IMAGINE WHAT THE EDGE OF MY BLADE WOULD DO TO YOUNG MISS SLAYTON'S TENDER THROAT.
WHAT DO YOU WANT, NEMESIS?
PLIP PLIP
I WANT YOU TO LISTEN TO ME.
AND FOR THAT I NEED A CAPTIVE AUDIENCE.
BREAK IT OPEN.
PLOP
NOW BREATHE DEEPLY.
SPISHHH

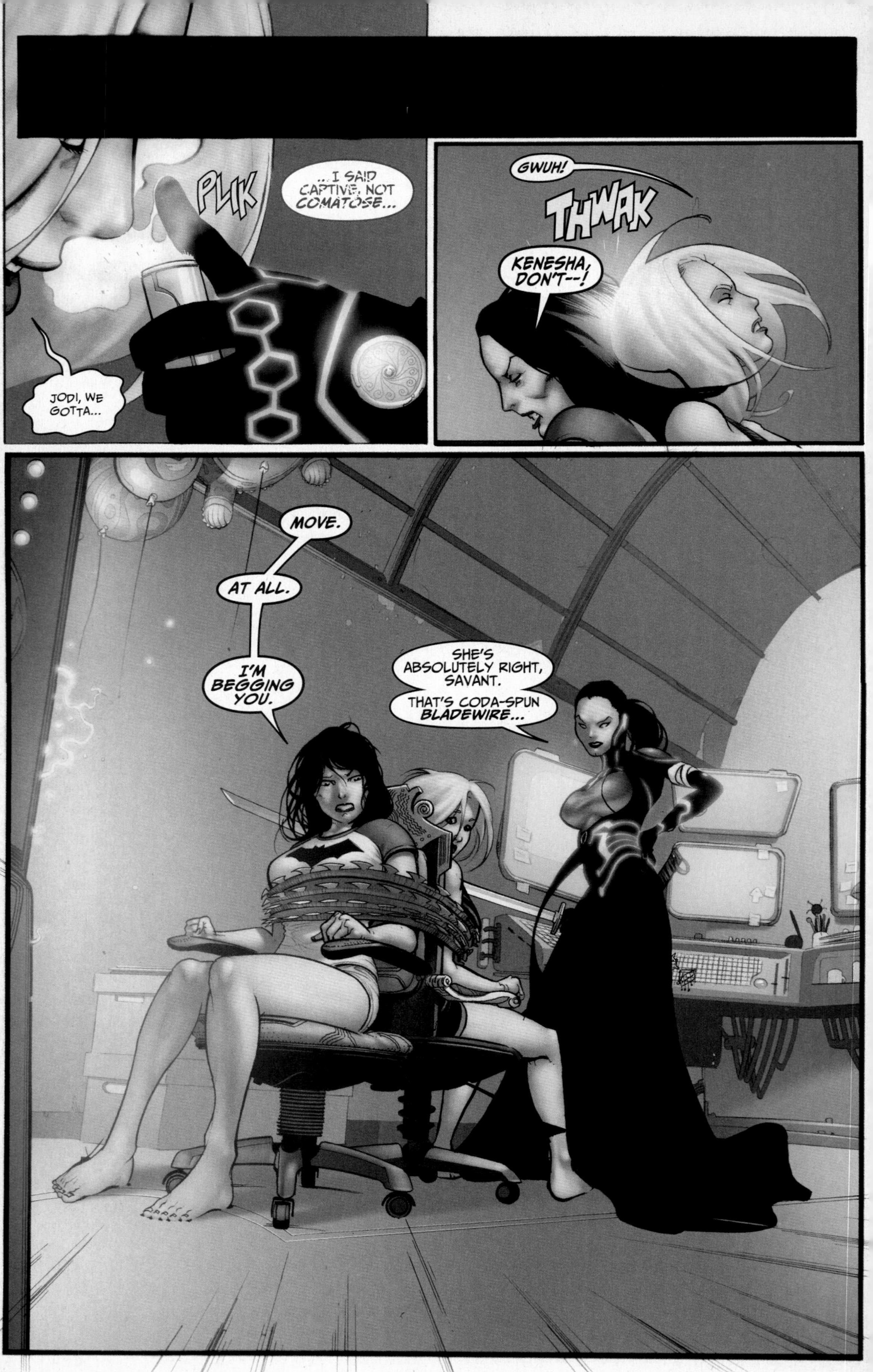
[redacted]
PLIK
...I SAID CAPTIVE, NOT COMATOSE...
JODI, WE GOTTA...
GWUH!
THWAK
KENESHA, DON'T--!
MOVE.
AT ALL.
I'M BEGGING YOU.
SHE'S ABSOLUTELY RIGHT, SAVANT.
THAT'S CODA-SPUN BLADEWIRE...

AND IT'LL SLICE US TO RIBBONS IF **WE** SO MUCH AS **WIGGLE** OUR EYEBROWS CROSSWISE.

SO YOU **WEREN'T** KIDDING ABOUT WANTING A "CAPTIVE AUDIENCE."

AND YOU EVEN TOOK THE TIME TO DRESS US. YOU'RE GETTING DOWNRIGHT **CHARITABLE** IN YOUR OLD AGE, CHARIS.

SO JUST **HOW** DID YOU MANAGE TO HACK YOUR WAY INTO OUR TELEPORT MATRIX?

ASK **BACKLASH**... SHE GAVE ME THE SECURITY CODES.

NO WAY!

SHE'S **LYING**, KENESHA! I DIDN'T GIVE HER ANY CODES! I DON'T EVEN KNOW **WHO** THE HELL SHE IS!

SHE'S **CHARIS OF THE ADRASTEA.** THINK OF HER AS A FREELANCE TROUBLEMAKER. NOBODY I KNOW **LIKES** OR **TRUSTS** HER.

AND I'M AWARE THAT YOU'VE NEVER MET BEFORE **TONIGHT.**

NO, BUT SHE **WILL**...

IN THE **NEAR FUTURE,** THAT IS. IT'S A **LITERAL** PARADOX, SO DON'T THINK TOO HARD ON IT.

I NEED YOU BOTH TO BE **OPEN-MINDED** SO YOU CAN BEGIN TO UNDERSTAND AND BELIEVE SOMETHING VITALLY **IMPORTANT.**

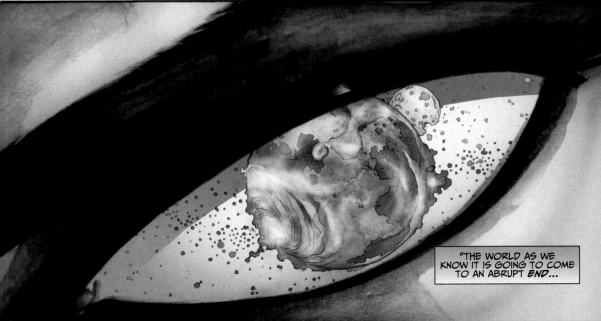

"THE WORLD AS WE KNOW IT IS GOING TO COME TO AN ABRUPT **END**...

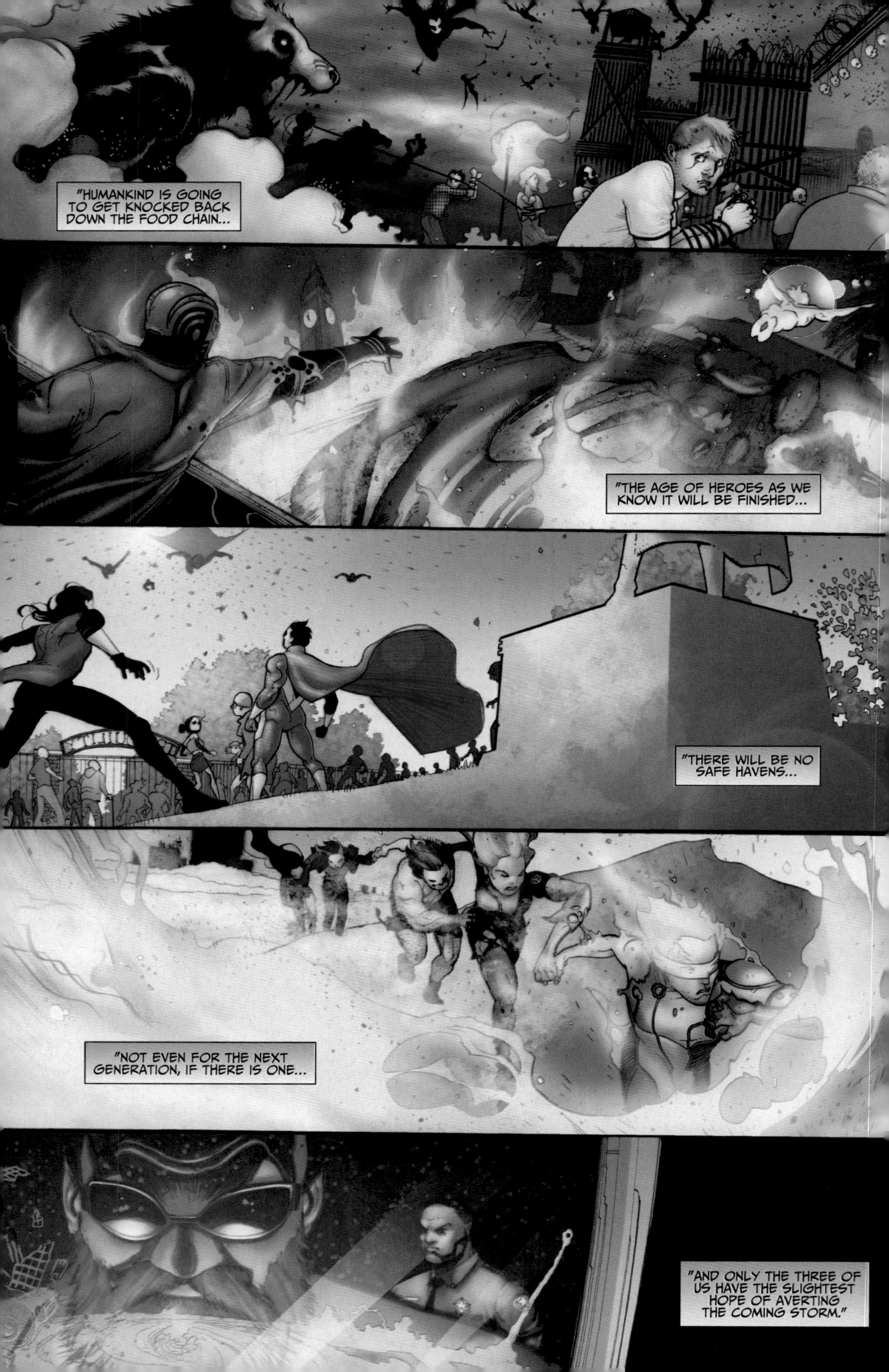
"HUMANKIND IS GOING TO GET KNOCKED BACK DOWN THE FOOD CHAIN...
"THE AGE OF HEROES AS WE KNOW IT WILL BE FINISHED...
"THERE WILL BE NO SAFE HAVENS...
"NOT EVEN FOR THE NEXT GENERATION, IF THERE IS ONE...
"AND ONLY THE THREE OF US HAVE THE SLIGHTEST HOPE OF AVERTING THE COMING STORM."

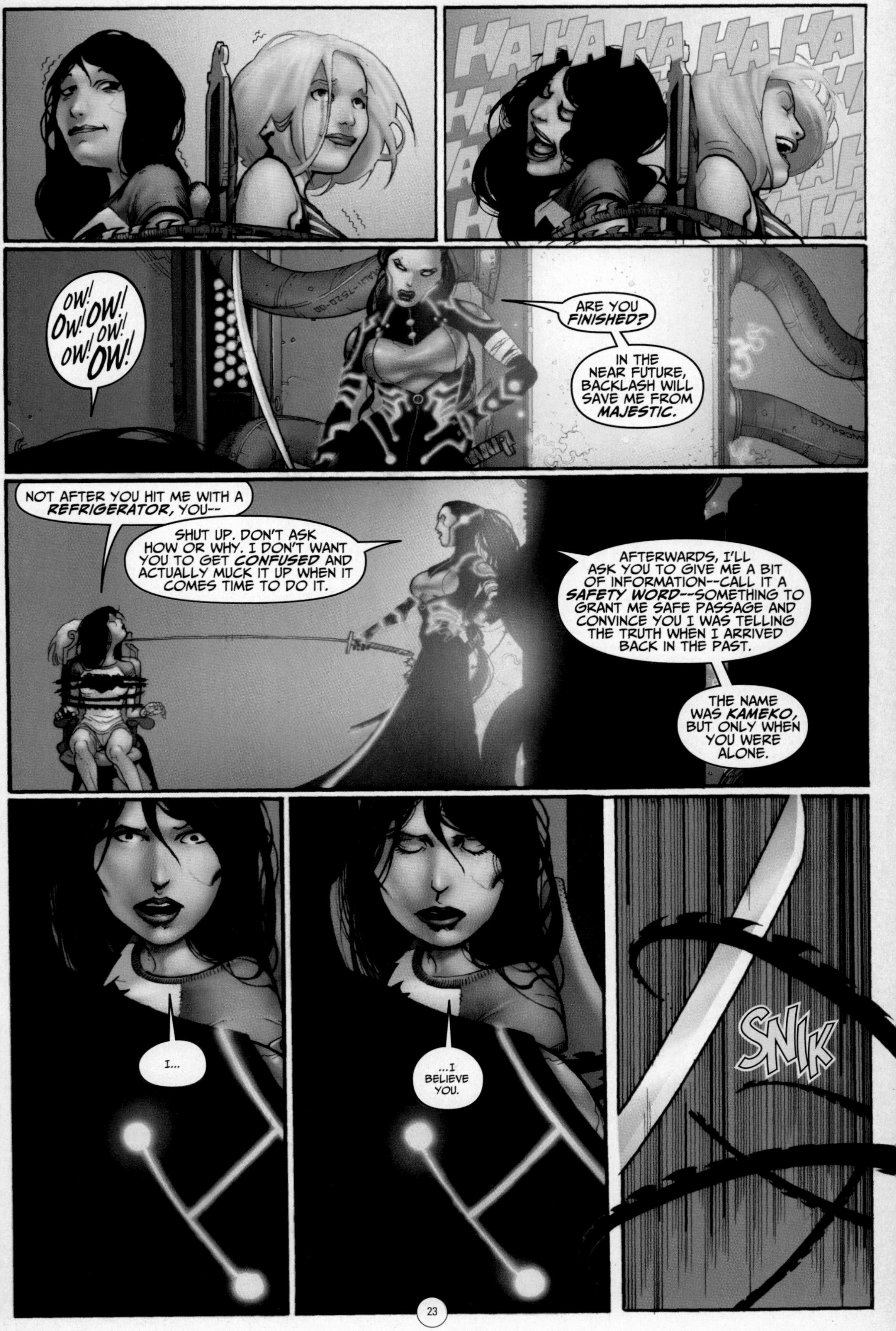
HA HA HA HA HA HA HA HA HA HA HA HA HA
OW! OW! OW! OW! OW! OW! OW!
ARE YOU FINISHED?
IN THE NEAR FUTURE, BACKLASH WILL SAVE ME FROM MAJESTIC.
NOT AFTER YOU HIT ME WITH A REFRIGERATOR, YOU--
SHUT UP. DON'T ASK HOW OR WHY. I DON'T WANT YOU TO GET CONFUSED AND ACTUALLY MUCK IT UP WHEN IT COMES TIME TO DO IT.
AFTERWARDS, I'LL ASK YOU TO GIVE ME A BIT OF INFORMATION--CALL IT A SAFETY WORD--SOMETHING TO GRANT ME SAFE PASSAGE AND CONVINCE YOU I WAS TELLING THE TRUTH WHEN I ARRIVED BACK IN THE PAST.
THE NAME WAS KAMEKO, BUT ONLY WHEN YOU WERE ALONE.
I...
...I BELIEVE YOU.
SNIK

WHAT'S *KAMEKO,* JODI?

LATER.

TELL US YOUR PLAN, NEMESIS.

IS THERE A *PLAN,* NEMESIS? OR ARE YOU FLYING BY THE SEAT OF YOUR LEATHER BREECHES, JUST LIKE *ALWAYS?*

JUST HOW IS THE WORLD SUPPOSED TO END? IN FIRE? OR WILL IT BE ICE?

WE KILL IT.

US.

THE GOOD GUYS ARE GOING TO DESTROY EARTH.

THAT'S UTTERLY *RIDICULOUS.*

IS IT? FUTURE-BACKLASH'S DETAILS WERE *SKETCHY* AT BEST...

THIS WORLD IS FULL OF POST-HUMANS AND PLAIN HUMANS *CONSPIRING* TO KEEP THEM IN CHECK.

EARTH DIES BECAUSE OF ONE TOO MANY OF EITHER. OR *BOTH.*

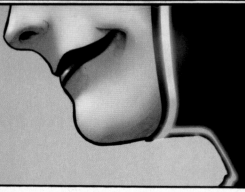

SOMETHING HAPPENS TO UNRAVEL IT ALL.

KNOWING THAT AND *ONLY* THAT, I FIGURED WE SHOULD START RIGHT AT THE *TOP* AND WORK OUR WAY DOWN.

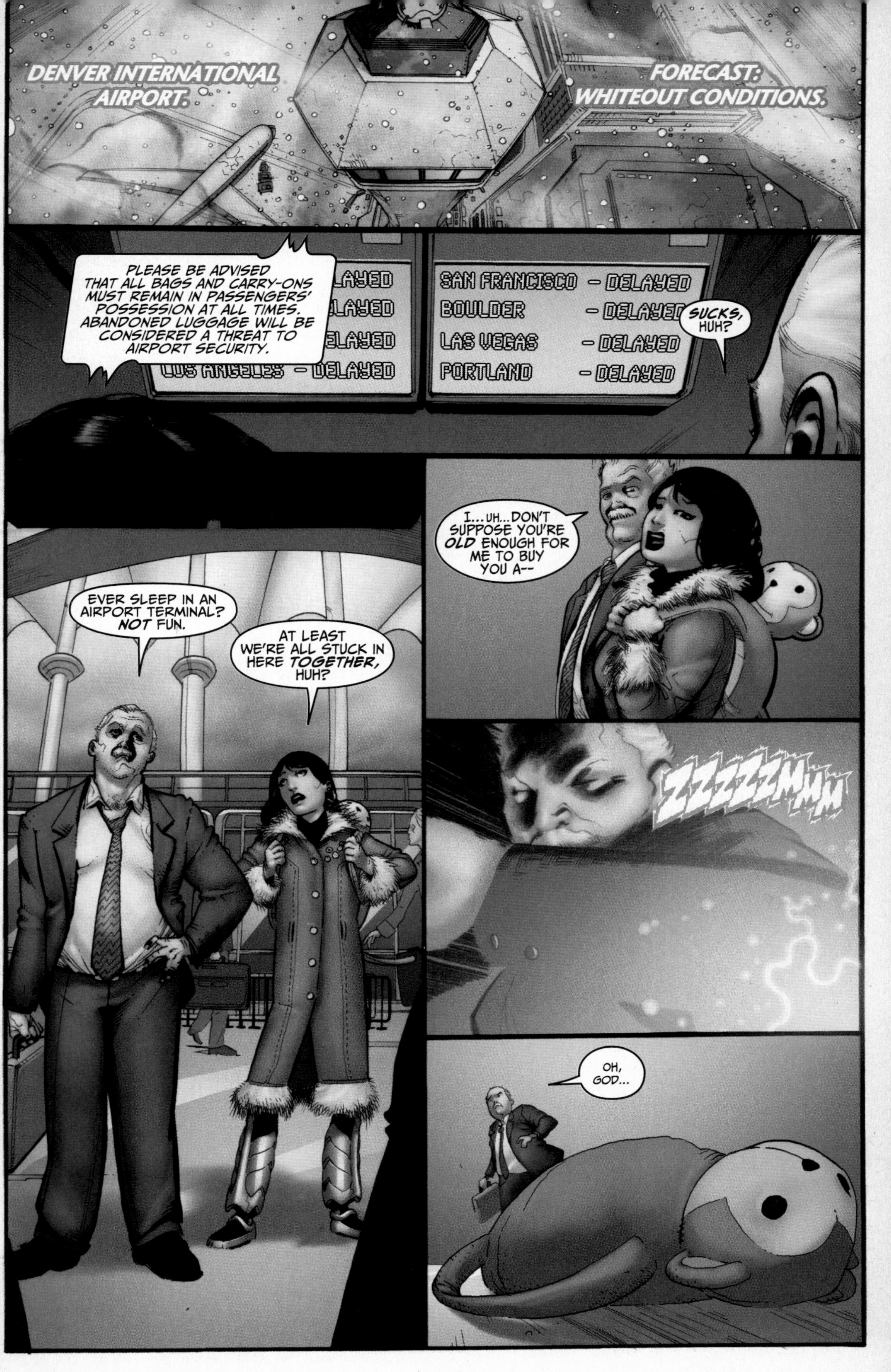
DENVER INTERNATIONAL AIRPORT.
FORECAST: WHITEOUT CONDITIONS.
PLEASE BE ADVISED THAT ALL BAGS AND CARRY-ONS MUST REMAIN IN PASSENGERS' POSSESSION AT ALL TIMES. ABANDONED LUGGAGE WILL BE CONSIDERED A THREAT TO AIRPORT SECURITY.
LOS ANGELES - DELAYED
SAN FRANCISCO - DELAYED
BOULDER - DELAYED
LAS VEGAS - DELAYED
PORTLAND - DELAYED
SUCKS, HUH?
EVER SLEEP IN AN AIRPORT TERMINAL? NOT FUN.
AT LEAST WE'RE ALL STUCK IN HERE TOGETHER, HUH?
I...UH...DON'T SUPPOSE YOU'RE OLD ENOUGH FOR ME TO BUY YOU A--
ZZZZZMMM
OH, GOD...

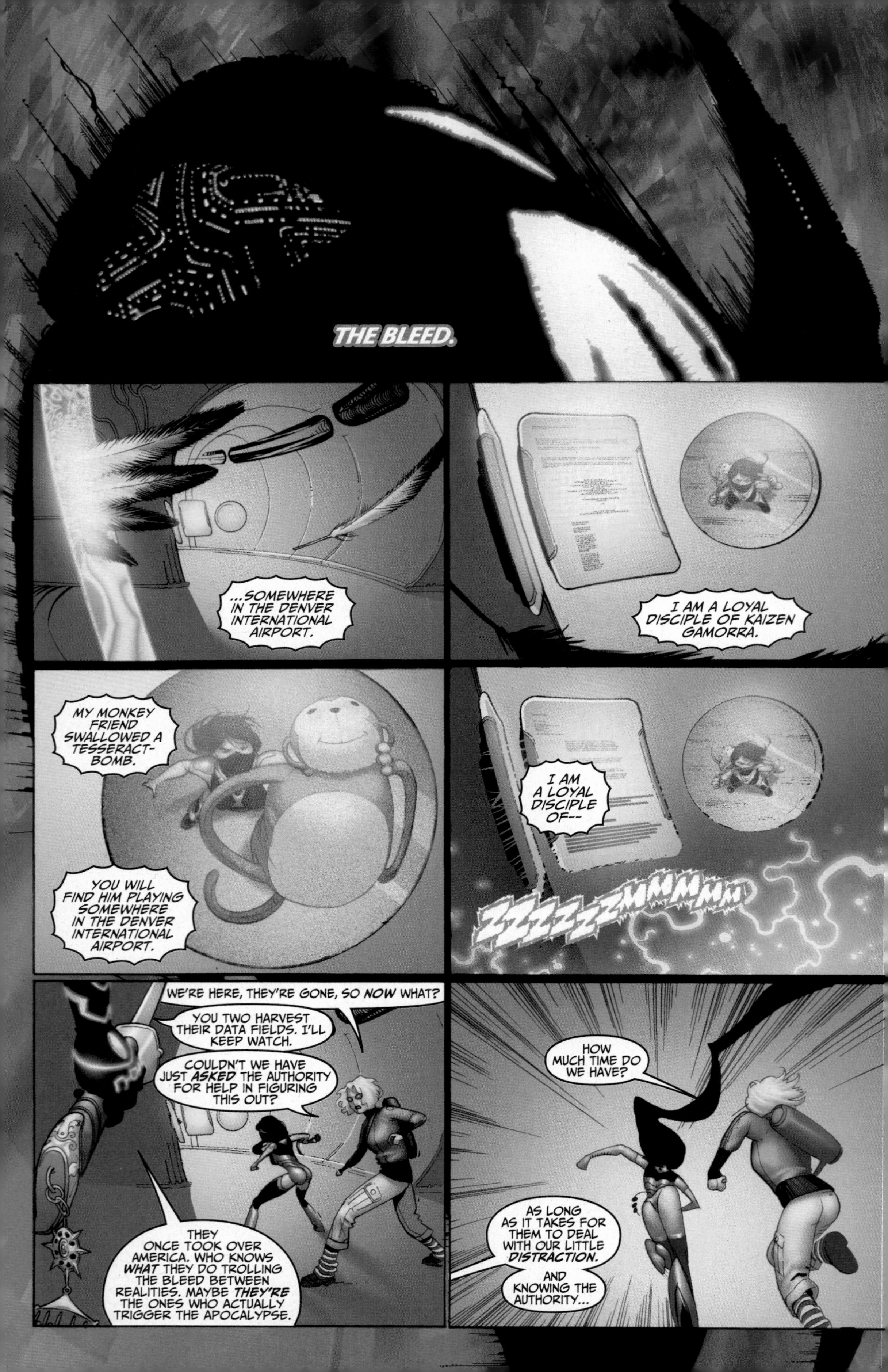
THE BLEED.
...SOMEWHERE IN THE DENVER INTERNATIONAL AIRPORT.
I AM A LOYAL DISCIPLE OF KAIZEN GAMORRA.
MY MONKEY FRIEND SWALLOWED A TESSERACT-BOMB.
YOU WILL FIND HIM PLAYING SOMEWHERE IN THE DENVER INTERNATIONAL AIRPORT.
I AM A LOYAL DISCIPLE OF--
ZZZZZZZMMMMMM
WE'RE HERE, THEY'RE GONE, SO NOW WHAT?
YOU TWO HARVEST THEIR DATA FIELDS. I'LL KEEP WATCH.
COULDN'T WE HAVE JUST ASKED THE AUTHORITY FOR HELP IN FIGURING THIS OUT?
THEY ONCE TOOK OVER AMERICA. WHO KNOWS WHAT THEY DO TROLLING THE BLEED BETWEEN REALITIES. MAYBE THEY'RE THE ONES WHO ACTUALLY TRIGGER THE APOCALYPSE.
HOW MUCH TIME DO WE HAVE?
AS LONG AS IT TAKES FOR THEM TO DEAL WITH OUR LITTLE DISTRACTION.
AND KNOWING THE AUTHORITY...

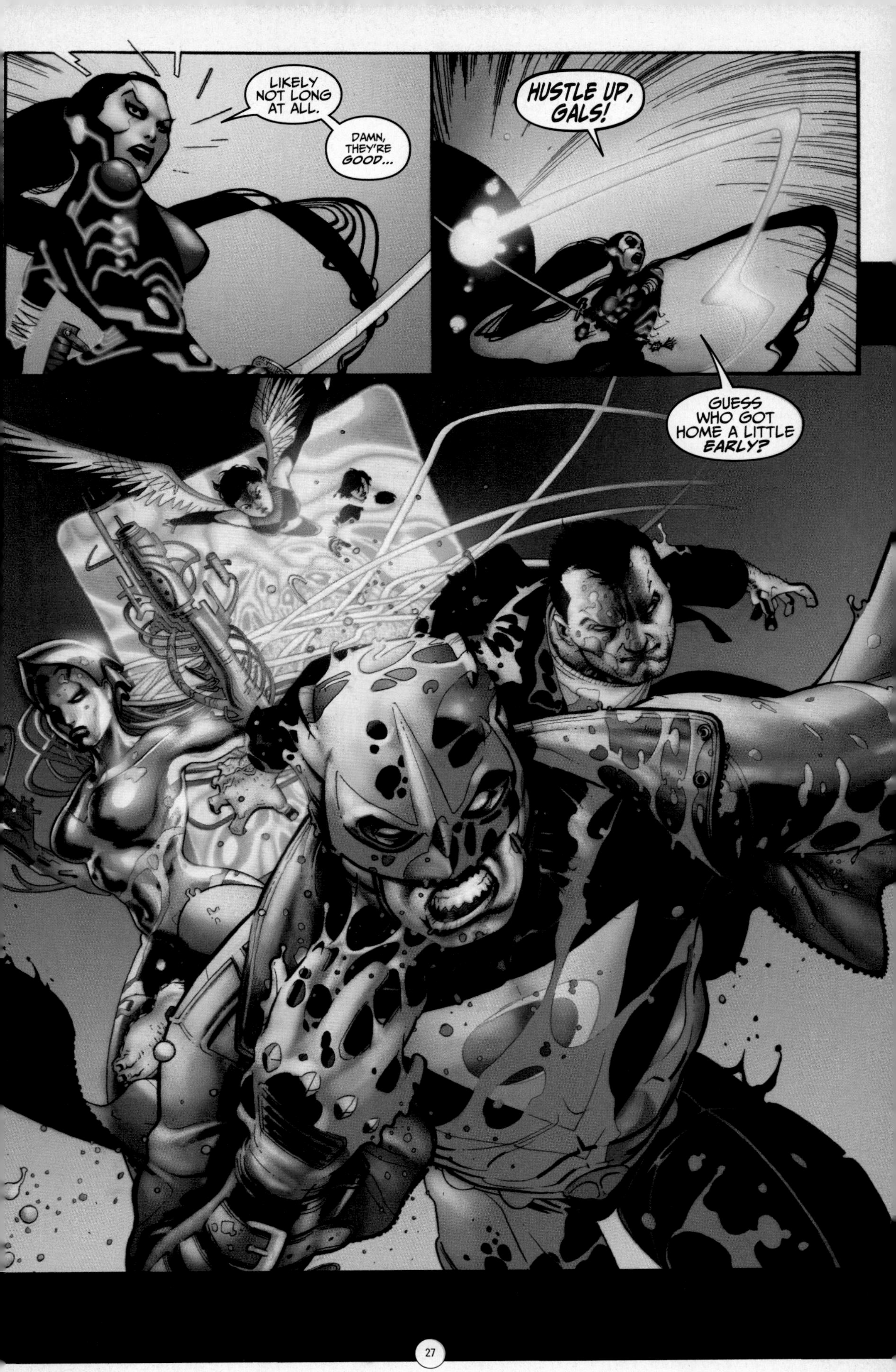
LIKELY NOT LONG AT ALL.
DAMN, THEY'RE GOOD...
HUSTLE UP, GALS!
GUESS WHO GOT HOME A LITTLE EARLY?

Chapter 2

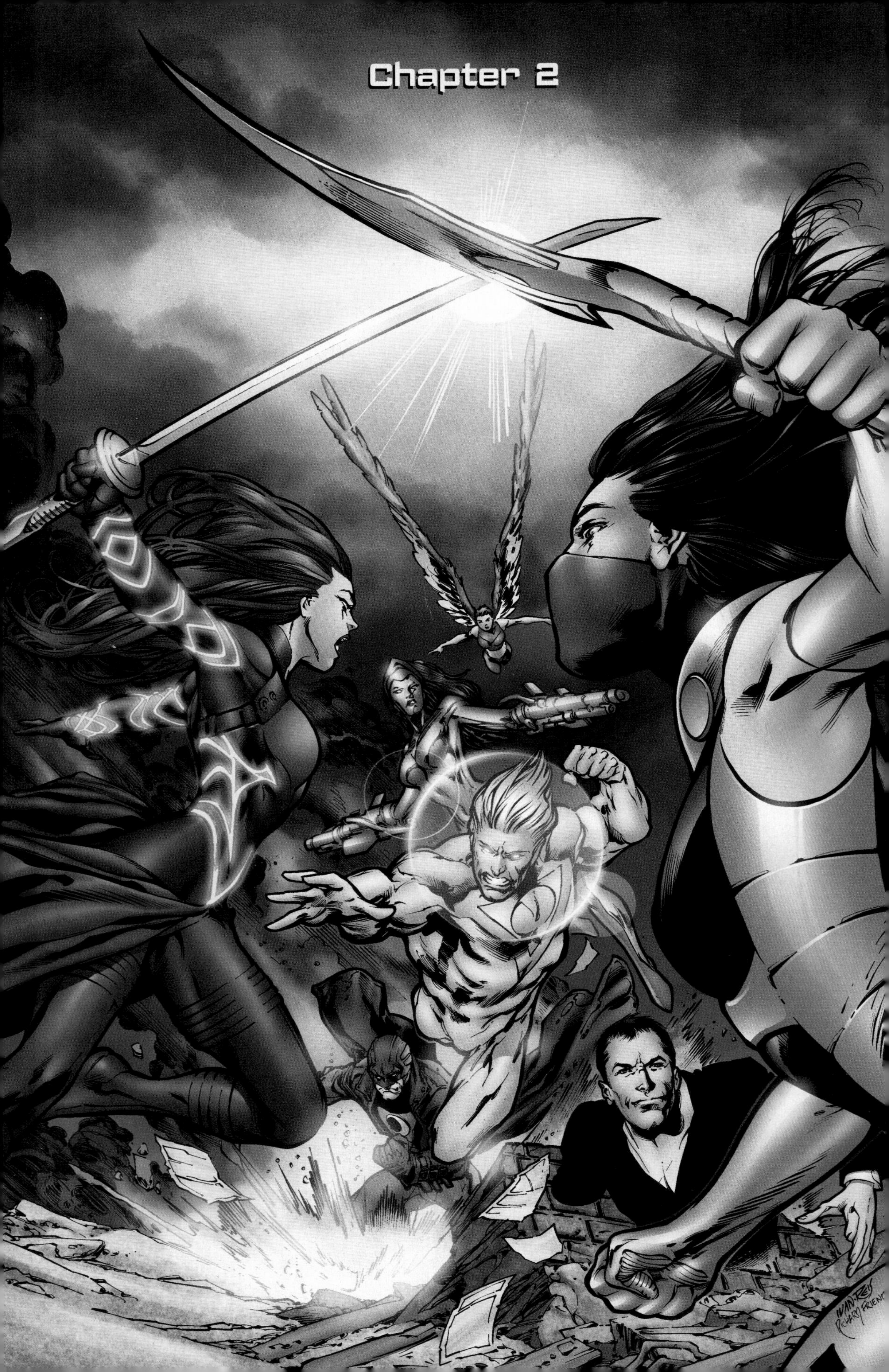

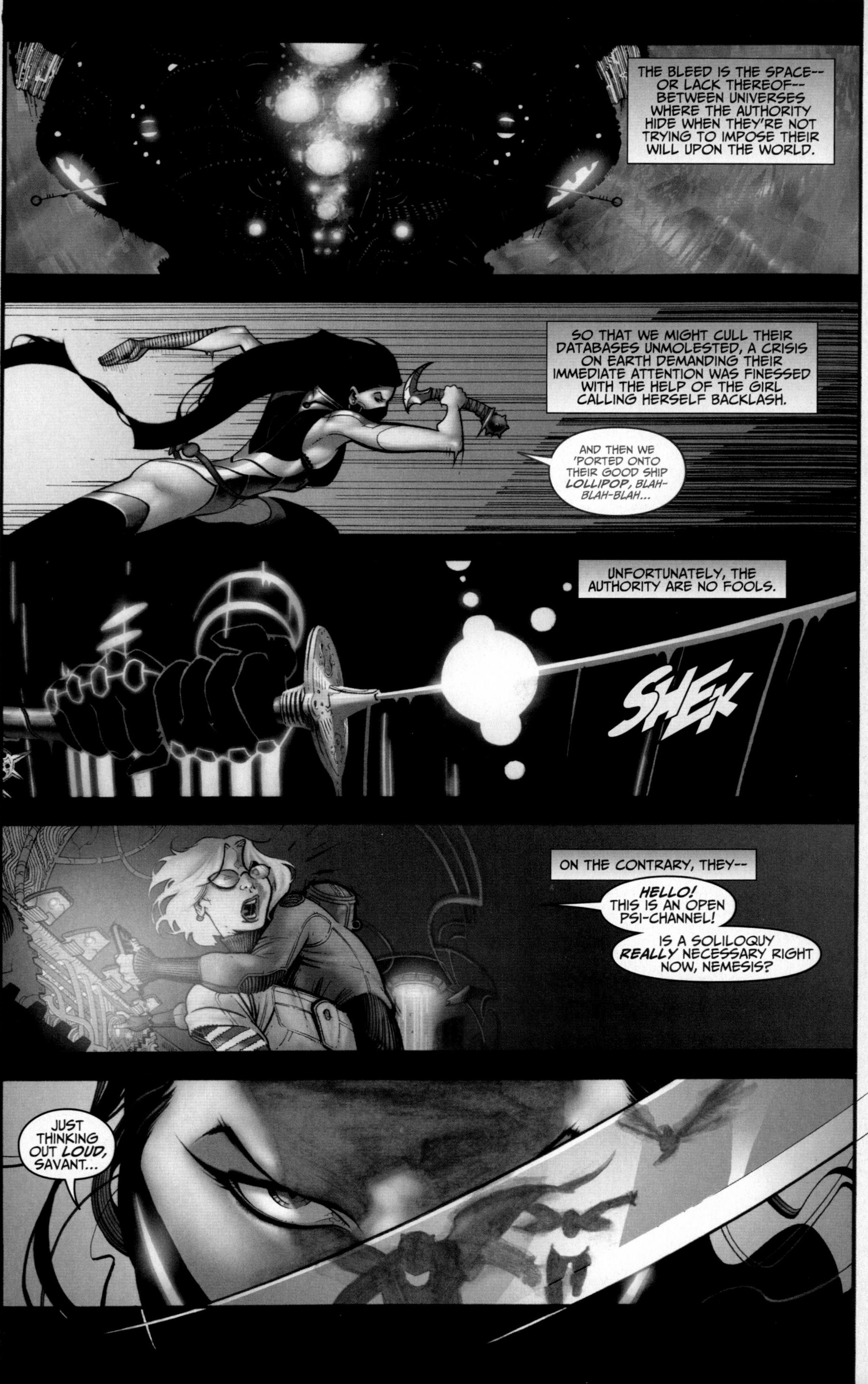

THE BLEED IS THE SPACE-- OR LACK THEREOF-- BETWEEN UNIVERSES WHERE THE AUTHORITY HIDE WHEN THEY'RE NOT TRYING TO IMPOSE THEIR WILL UPON THE WORLD.
SO THAT WE MIGHT CULL THEIR DATABASES UNMOLESTED, A CRISIS ON EARTH DEMANDING THEIR IMMEDIATE ATTENTION WAS FINESSED WITH THE HELP OF THE GIRL CALLING HERSELF BACKLASH.
AND THEN WE 'PORTED ONTO THEIR GOOD SHIP LOLLIPOP, BLAH-BLAH-BLAH...
UNFORTUNATELY, THE AUTHORITY ARE NO FOOLS.
SHEK
ON THE CONTRARY, THEY--
HELLO! THIS IS AN OPEN PSI-CHANNEL!
IS A SOLILOQUY REALLY NECESSARY RIGHT NOW, NEMESIS?
JUST THINKING OUT LOUD, SAVANT...

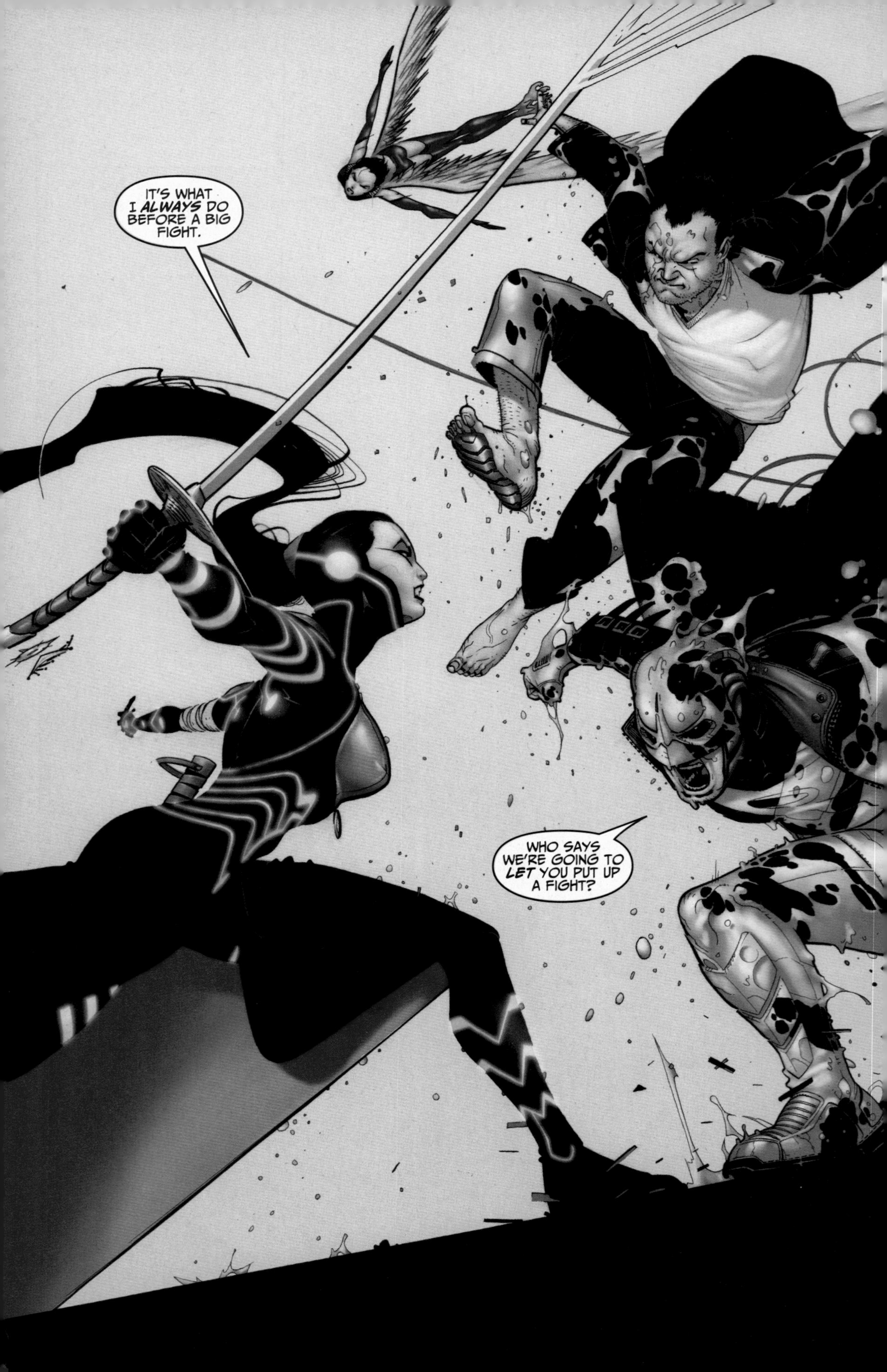
IT'S WHAT I ALWAYS DO BEFORE A BIG FIGHT.
WHO SAYS WE'RE GOING TO LET YOU PUT UP A FIGHT?

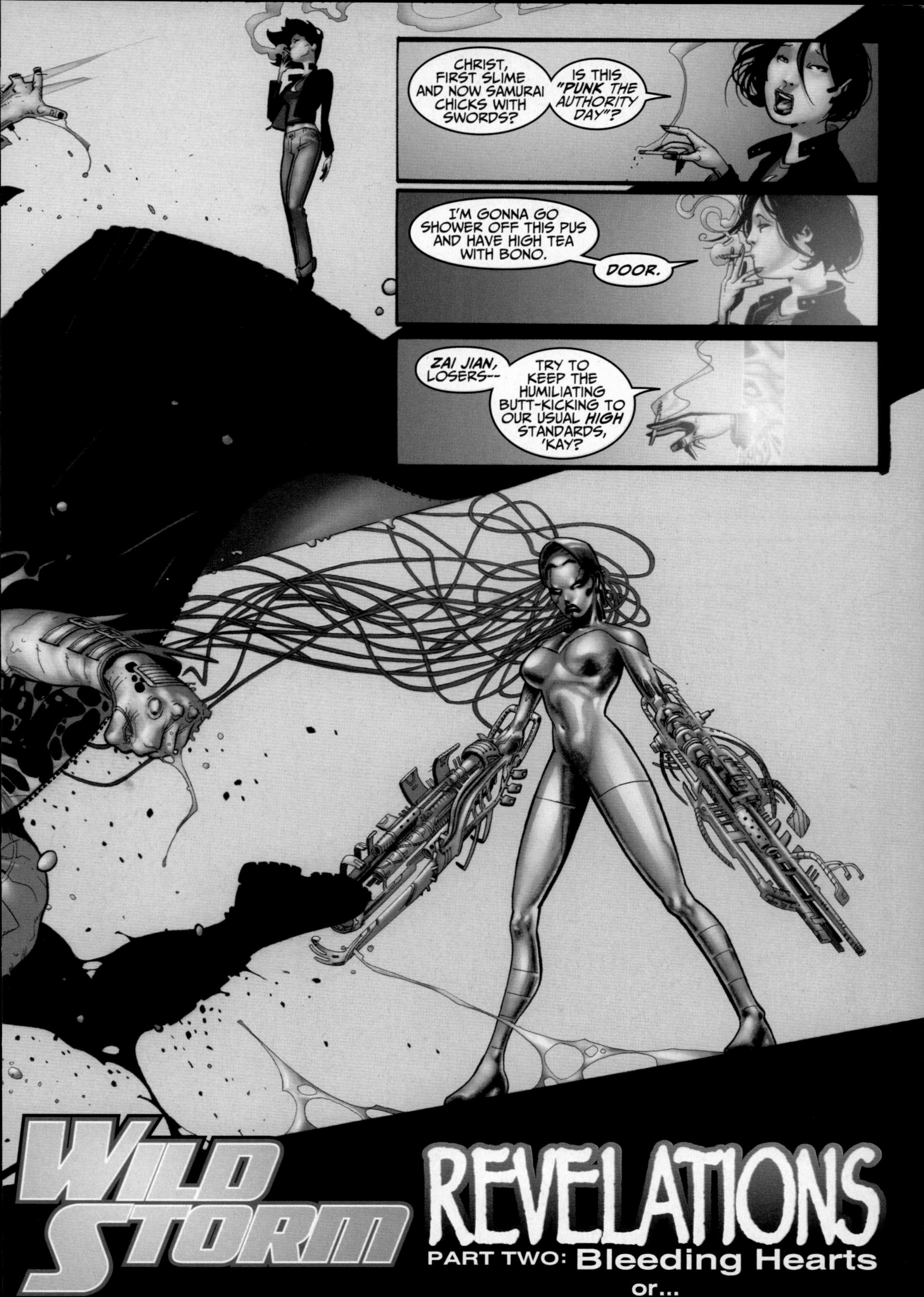
CHRIST, FIRST SLIME AND NOW SAMURAI CHICKS WITH SWORDS?
IS THIS "PUNK THE AUTHORITY DAY"?
I'M GONNA GO SHOWER OFF THIS PUS AND HAVE HIGH TEA WITH BONO.
DOOR.
ZAI JIAN, LOSERS--
TRY TO KEEP THE HUMILIATING BUTT-KICKING TO OUR USUAL HIGH STANDARDS, 'KAY?
WILD STORM
REVELATIONS
PART TWO: Bleeding Hearts
or...

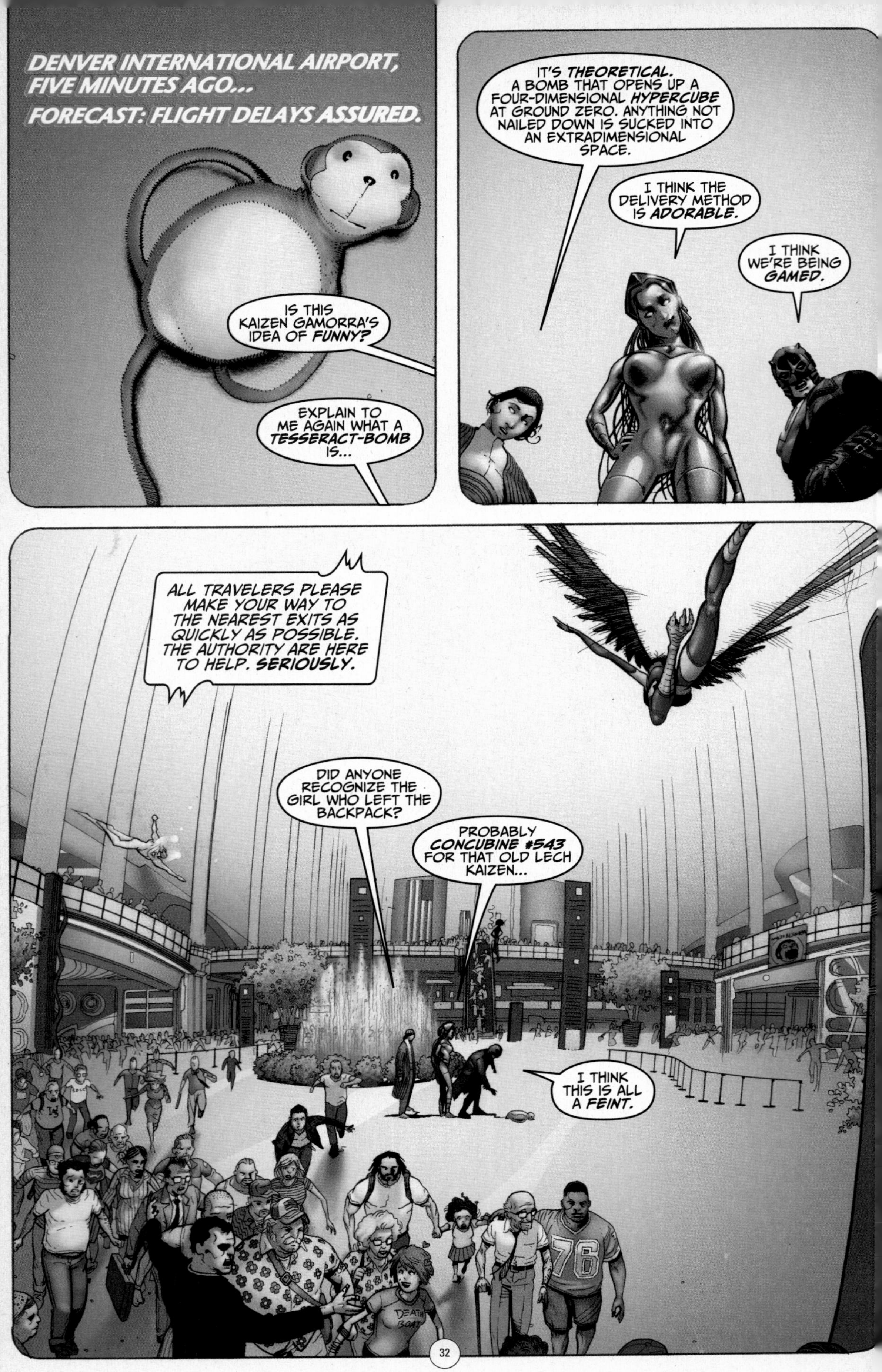
DENVER INTERNATIONAL AIRPORT, FIVE MINUTES AGO...
FORECAST: FLIGHT DELAYS ASSURED.
IS THIS KAIZEN GAMORRA'S IDEA OF FUNNY?
EXPLAIN TO ME AGAIN WHAT A TESSERACT-BOMB IS...
IT'S THEORETICAL. A BOMB THAT OPENS UP A FOUR-DIMENSIONAL HYPERCUBE AT GROUND ZERO. ANYTHING NOT NAILED DOWN IS SUCKED INTO AN EXTRADIMENSIONAL SPACE.
I THINK THE DELIVERY METHOD IS ADORABLE.
I THINK WE'RE BEING GAMED.
ALL TRAVELERS PLEASE MAKE YOUR WAY TO THE NEAREST EXITS AS QUICKLY AS POSSIBLE. THE AUTHORITY ARE HERE TO HELP. SERIOUSLY.
DID ANYONE RECOGNIZE THE GIRL WHO LEFT THE BACKPACK?
PROBABLY CONCUBINE #543 FOR THAT OLD LECH KAIZEN...
I THINK THIS IS ALL A FEINT.
76
DEATH BOAT

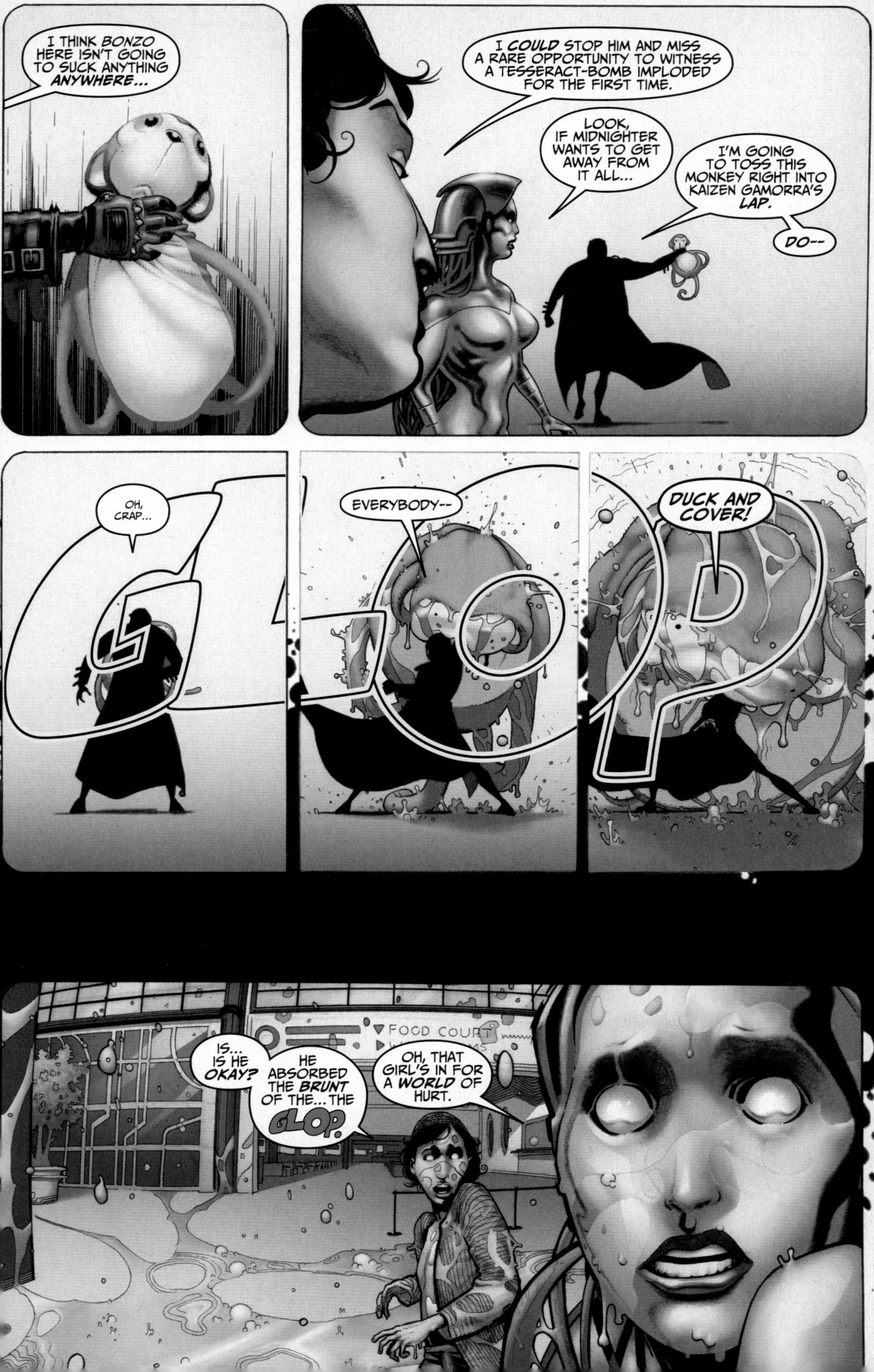

I THINK BONZO HERE ISN'T GOING TO SUCK ANYTHING ANYWHERE...
I COULD STOP HIM AND MISS A RARE OPPORTUNITY TO WITNESS A TESSERACT-BOMB IMPLODED FOR THE FIRST TIME.
LOOK, IF MIDNIGHTER WANTS TO GET AWAY FROM IT ALL...
I'M GOING TO TOSS THIS MONKEY RIGHT INTO KAIZEN GAMORRA'S LAP.
DO--
OH, CRAP...
GLOP
EVERYBODY--
DUCK AND COVER!
FOOD COURT
IS... IS HE OKAY?
HE ABSORBED THE BRUNT OF THE... THE GLOP.
OH, THAT GIRL'S IN FOR A WORLD OF HURT.

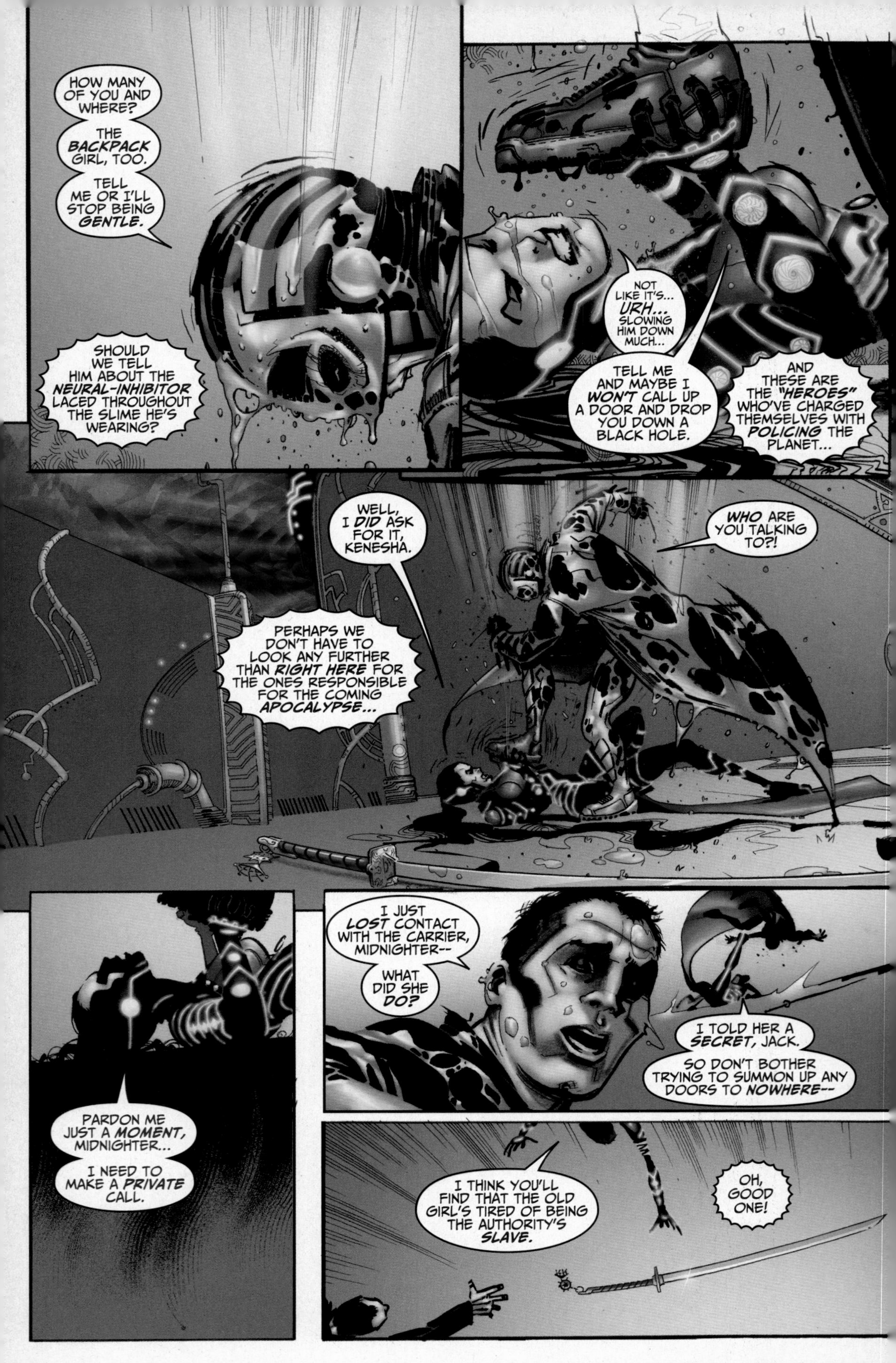
HOW MANY OF YOU AND WHERE?
THE BACKPACK GIRL, TOO.
TELL ME OR I'LL STOP BEING GENTLE.
SHOULD WE TELL HIM ABOUT THE NEURAL-INHIBITOR LACED THROUGHOUT THE SLIME HE'S WEARING?
NOT LIKE IT'S... URH... SLOWING HIM DOWN MUCH...
TELL ME AND MAYBE I WON'T CALL UP A DOOR AND DROP YOU DOWN A BLACK HOLE.
AND THESE ARE THE "HEROES" WHO'VE CHARGED THEMSELVES WITH POLICING THE PLANET...
WELL, I DID ASK FOR IT, KENESHA.
WHO ARE YOU TALKING TO?!
PERHAPS WE DON'T HAVE TO LOOK ANY FURTHER THAN RIGHT HERE FOR THE ONES RESPONSIBLE FOR THE COMING APOCALYPSE...
PARDON ME JUST A MOMENT, MIDNIGHTER...
I NEED TO MAKE A PRIVATE CALL.
I JUST LOST CONTACT WITH THE CARRIER, MIDNIGHTER--
WHAT DID SHE DO?
I TOLD HER A SECRET, JACK.
SO DON'T BOTHER TRYING TO SUMMON UP ANY DOORS TO NOWHERE--
I THINK YOU'LL FIND THAT THE OLD GIRL'S TIRED OF BEING THE AUTHORITY'S SLAVE.
OH, GOOD ONE!

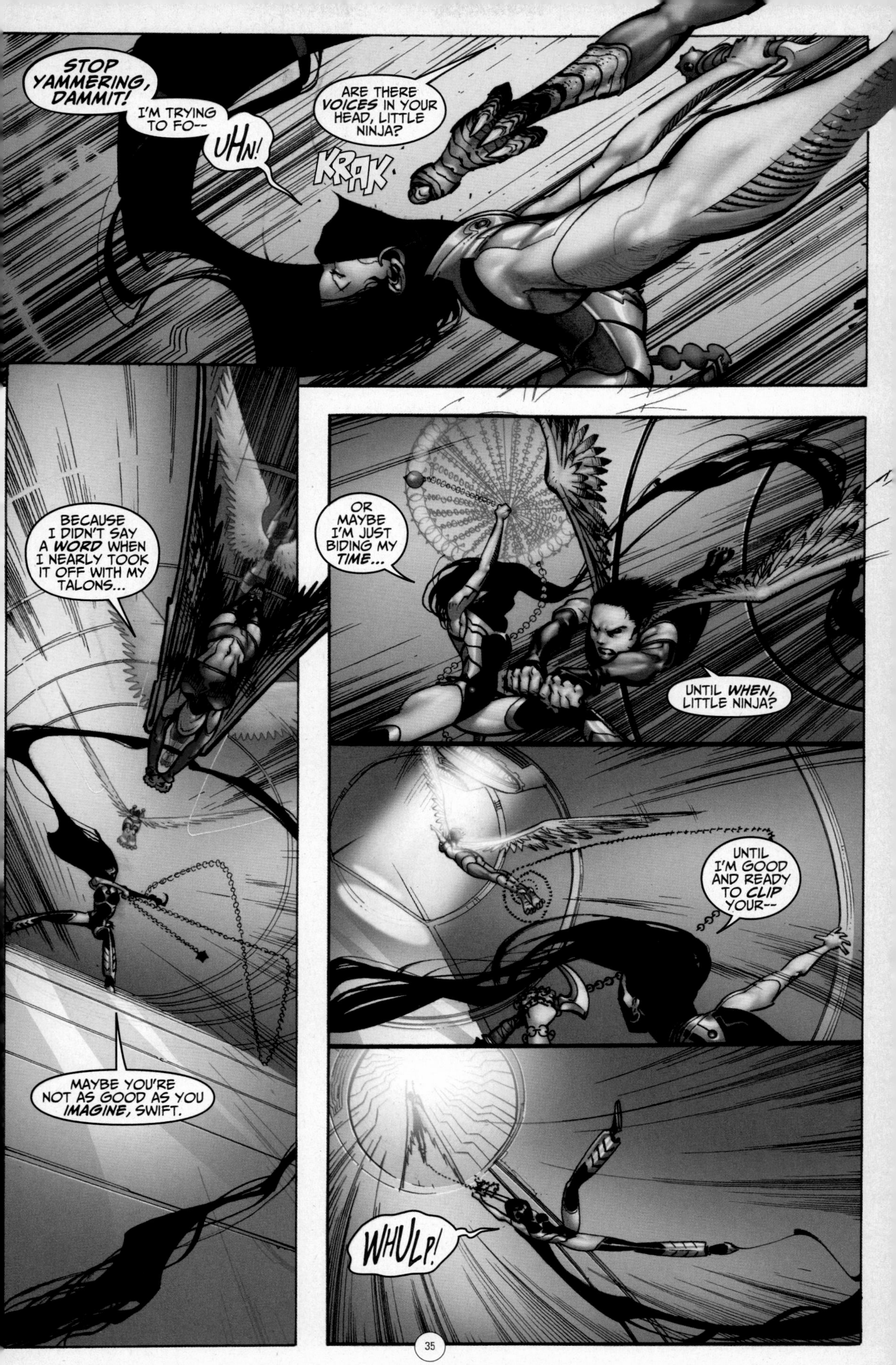
STOP YAMMERING, DAMMIT!
I'M TRYING TO FO--
UHN!
ARE THERE VOICES IN YOUR HEAD, LITTLE NINJA?
KRAK
BECAUSE I DIDN'T SAY A WORD WHEN I NEARLY TOOK IT OFF WITH MY TALONS...
MAYBE YOU'RE NOT AS GOOD AS YOU IMAGINE, SWIFT.
OR MAYBE I'M JUST BIDING MY TIME...
UNTIL WHEN, LITTLE NINJA?
UNTIL I'M GOOD AND READY TO CLIP YOUR--
WHULP!

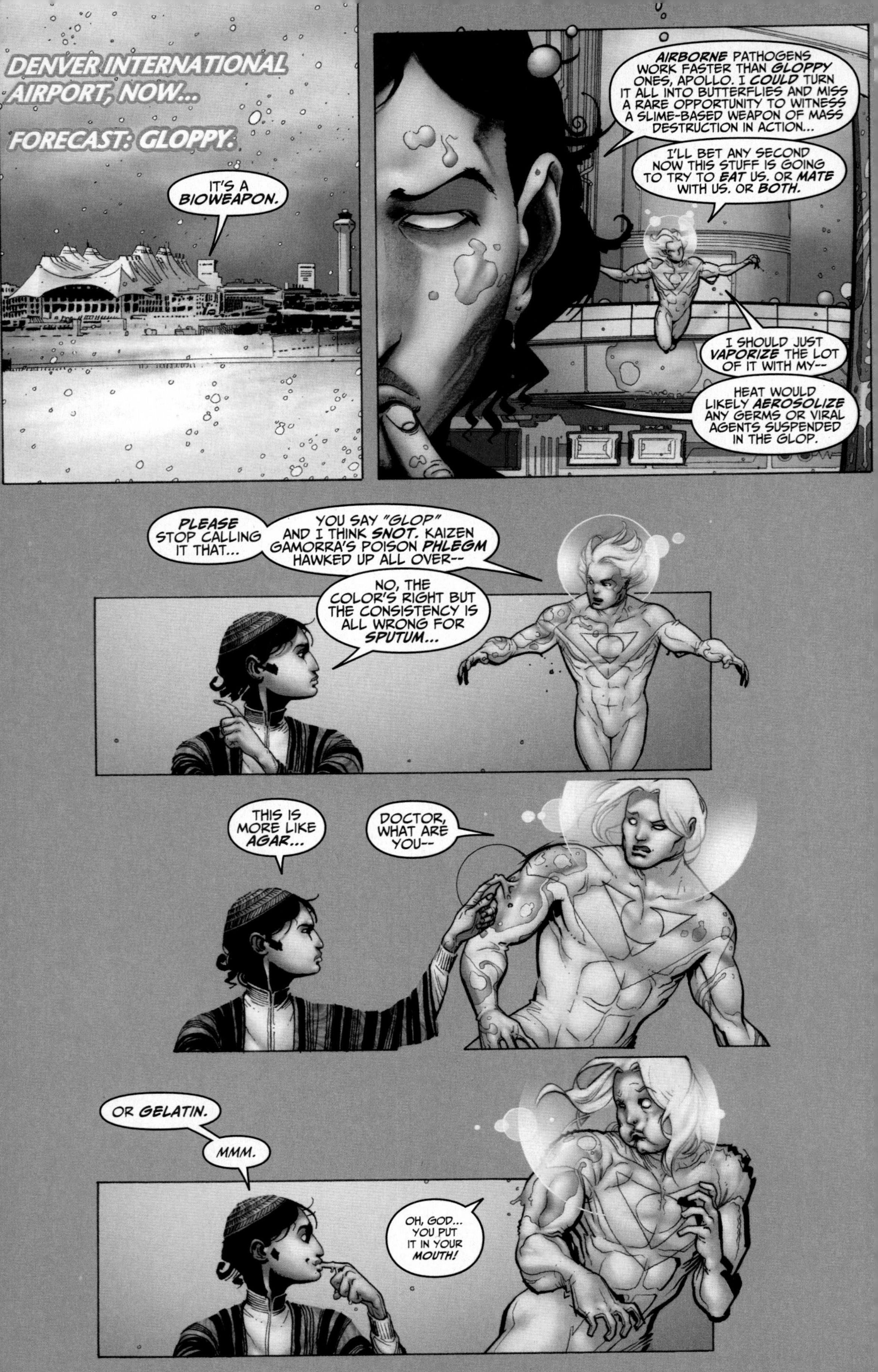
DENVER INTERNATIONAL AIRPORT, NOW...
FORECAST: GLOPPY.
IT'S A BIOWEAPON.
AIRBORNE PATHOGENS WORK FASTER THAN GLOPPY ONES, APOLLO. I COULD TURN IT ALL INTO BUTTERFLIES AND MISS A RARE OPPORTUNITY TO WITNESS A SLIME-BASED WEAPON OF MASS DESTRUCTION IN ACTION...
I'LL BET ANY SECOND NOW THIS STUFF IS GOING TO TRY TO EAT US. OR MATE WITH US. OR BOTH.
I SHOULD JUST VAPORIZE THE LOT OF IT WITH MY--
HEAT WOULD LIKELY AEROSOLIZE ANY GERMS OR VIRAL AGENTS SUSPENDED IN THE GLOP.
PLEASE STOP CALLING IT THAT...
YOU SAY "GLOP" AND I THINK SNOT. KAIZEN GAMORRA'S POISON PHLEGM HAWKED UP ALL OVER--
NO, THE COLOR'S RIGHT BUT THE CONSISTENCY IS ALL WRONG FOR SPUTUM...
THIS IS MORE LIKE AGAR...
DOCTOR, WHAT ARE YOU--
OR GELATIN.
MMM.
OH, GOD... YOU PUT IT IN YOUR MOUTH!

WHO SAYS THE CODA DON'T COOK...

JUST KEEP IT UP GIRLS--

retrieving 78% of data queue...

I'M ALMOST DONE WITH--

DONE WITH WHAT?

OH, SNAP...

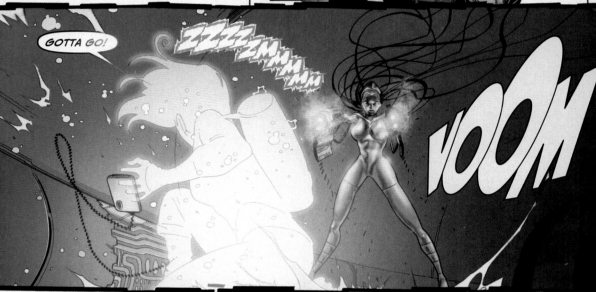

GOTTA GO!

ZZZZZ ZMM MM

VOOM

JACK, I JUST SCARED OFF A LITTLE BLONDE CHICA TRYING TO HACK INTO THE CARRIER'S MEMORY-BUNDLES.

retrieving 95% of data queue...

I'M NOT SURE IF THIS IS SOME SORT OF POST-HUMAN ESPIONAGE OR IF WE'RE BEING SPAM--

ZZZZZ ZMM MM MM

TAG, YOU'RE IT!

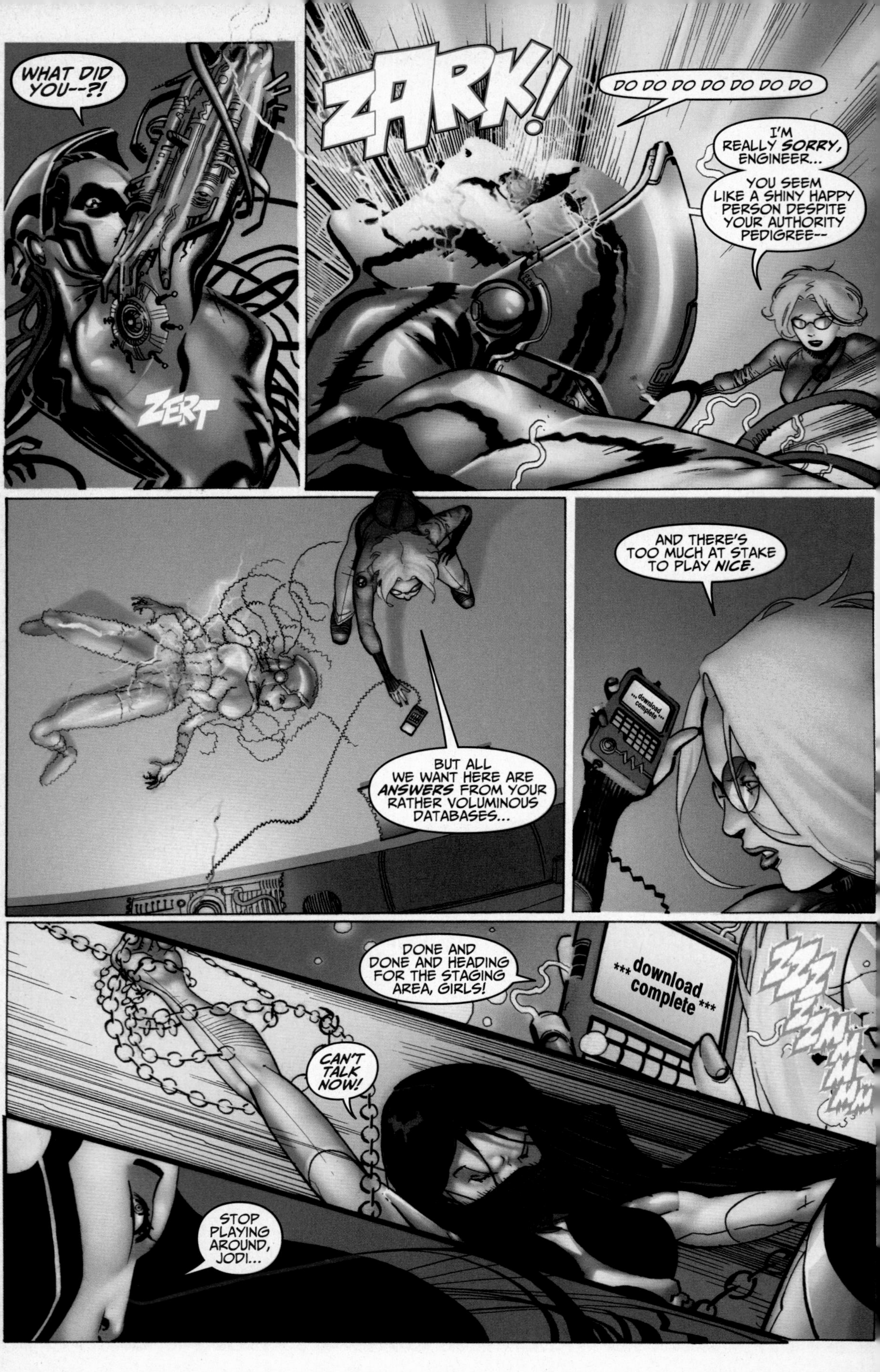
WHAT DID YOU--?!
ZERT
ZARK!
DO DO DO DO DO DO DO DO
I'M REALLY SORRY, ENGINEER...
YOU SEEM LIKE A SHINY HAPPY PERSON DESPITE YOUR AUTHORITY PEDIGREE--
BUT ALL WE WANT HERE ARE ANSWERS FROM YOUR RATHER VOLUMINOUS DATABASES...
AND THERE'S TOO MUCH AT STAKE TO PLAY NICE.
... download complete ...
DONE AND DONE AND HEADING FOR THE STAGING AREA, GIRLS!
*** download complete ***
CAN'T TALK NOW!
STOP PLAYING AROUND, JODI...

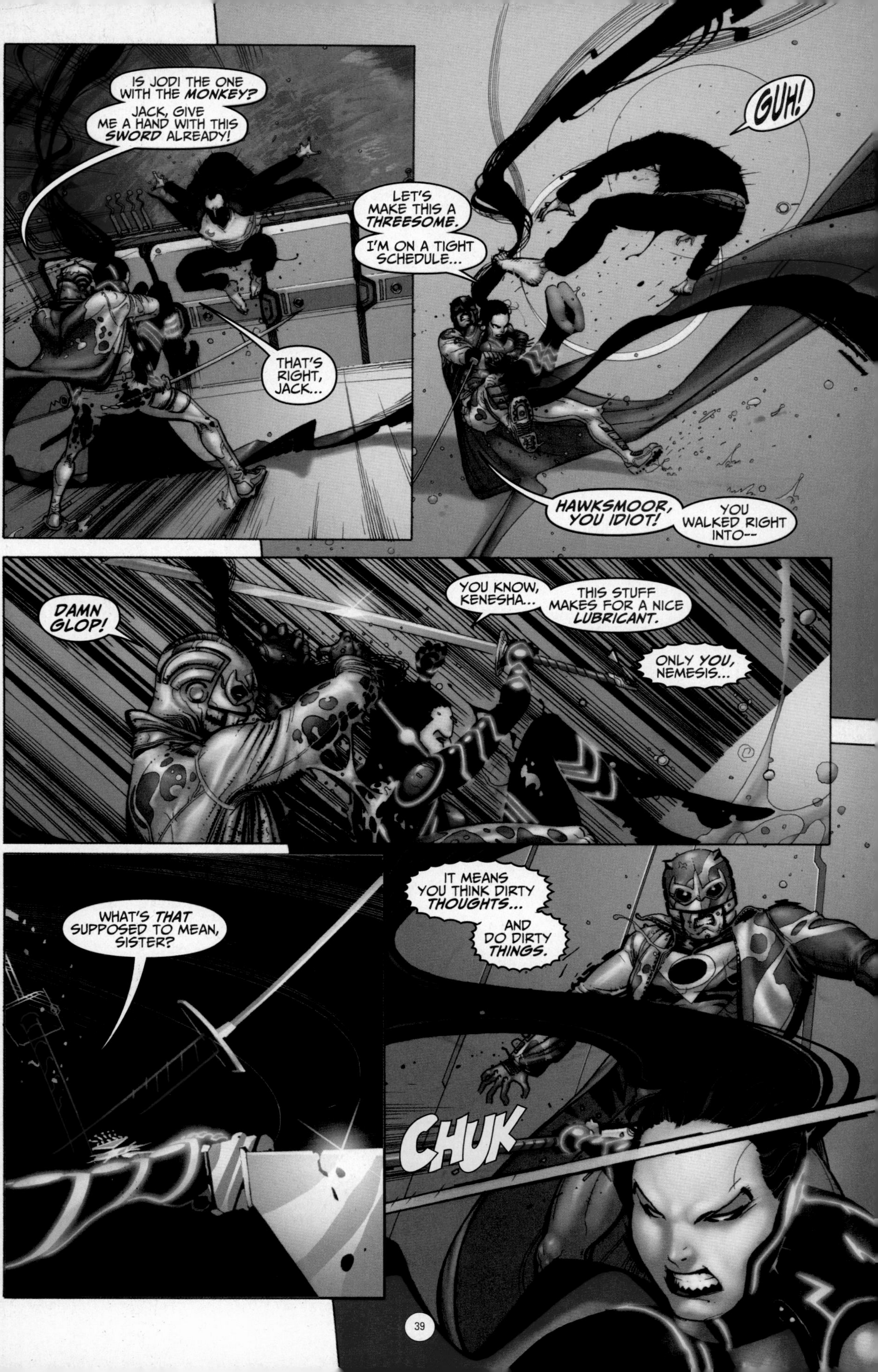
IS JODI THE ONE WITH THE MONKEY?
JACK, GIVE ME A HAND WITH THIS SWORD ALREADY!
THAT'S RIGHT, JACK...
GUH!
LET'S MAKE THIS A THREESOME.
I'M ON A TIGHT SCHEDULE...
HAWKSMOOR, YOU IDIOT!
YOU WALKED RIGHT INTO--
DAMN GLOP!
YOU KNOW, KENESHA...
THIS STUFF MAKES FOR A NICE LUBRICANT.
ONLY YOU, NEMESIS...
WHAT'S THAT SUPPOSED TO MEAN, SISTER?
IT MEANS YOU THINK DIRTY THOUGHTS...
AND DO DIRTY THINGS.
CHUK

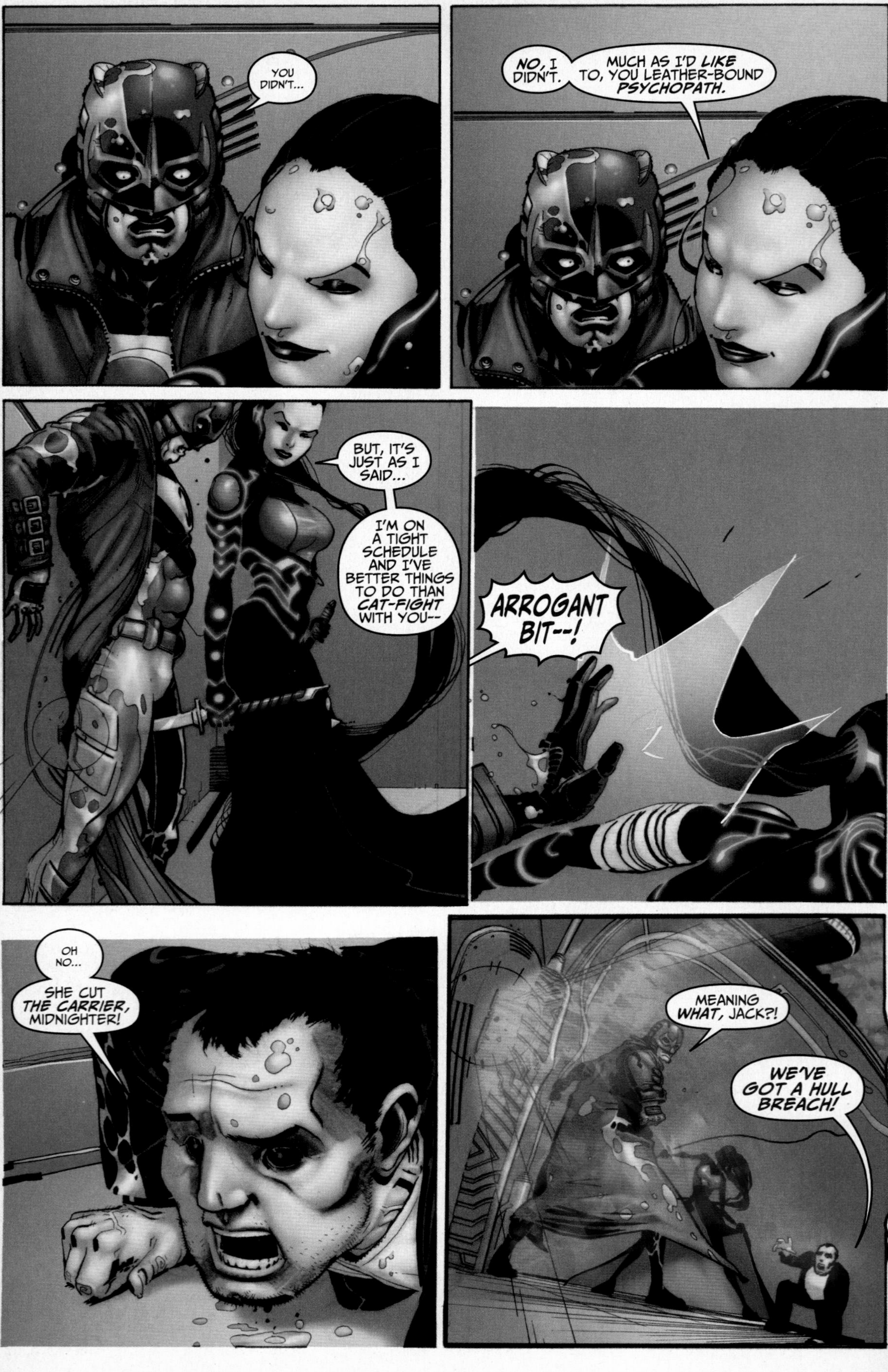

YOU DIDN'T...
NO, I DIDN'T.
MUCH AS I'D LIKE TO, YOU LEATHER-BOUND PSYCHOPATH.
BUT, IT'S JUST AS I SAID...
I'M ON A TIGHT SCHEDULE AND I'VE BETTER THINGS TO DO THAN CAT-FIGHT WITH YOU--
ARROGANT BIT--!
OH NO...
SHE CUT THE CARRIER, MIDNIGHTER!
MEANING WHAT, JACK?!
WE'VE GOT A HULL BREACH!

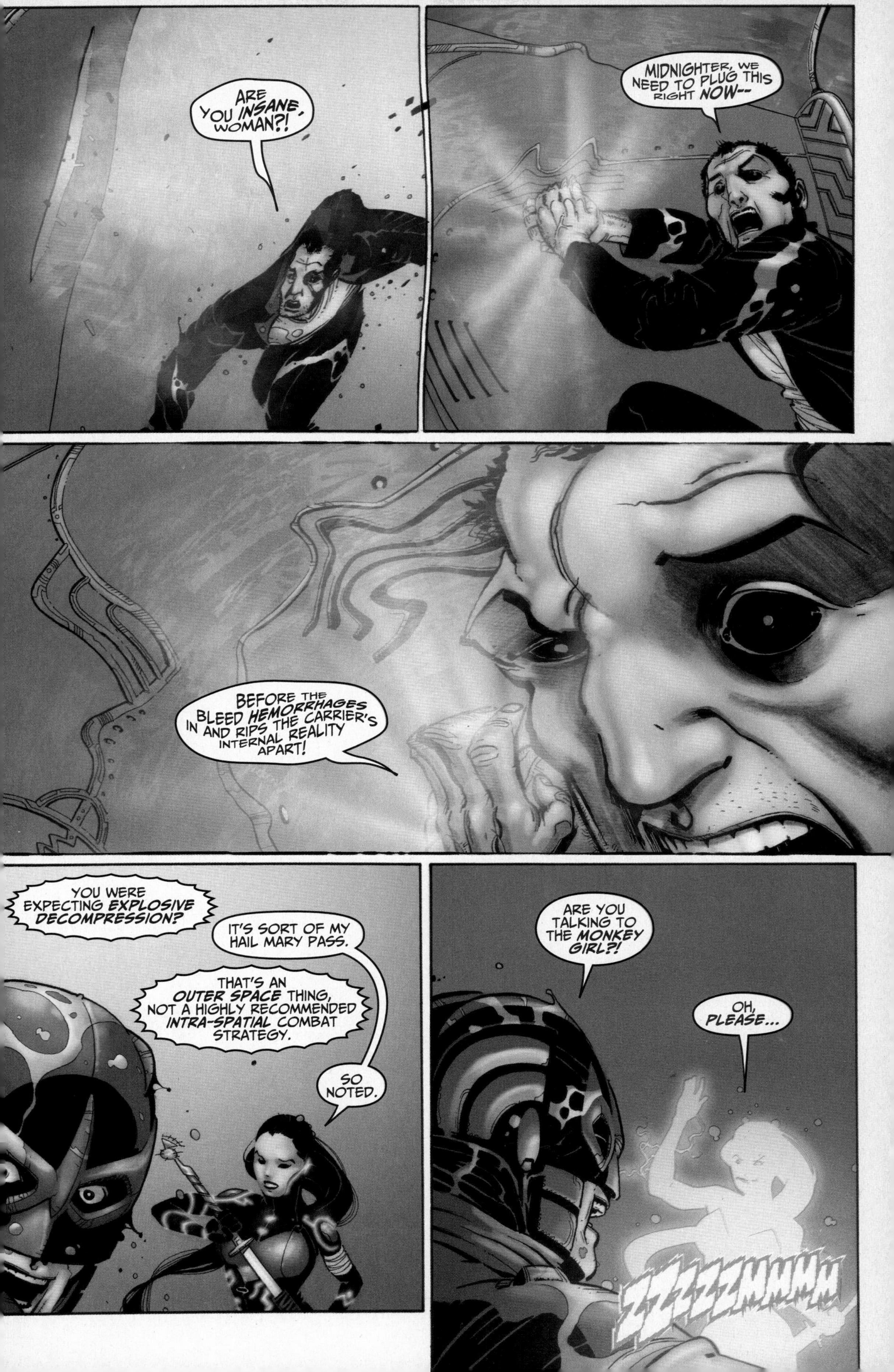
ARE YOU INSANE, WOMAN?!
MIDNIGHTER, WE NEED TO PLUG THIS RIGHT NOW--
BEFORE THE BLEED HEMORRHAGES IN AND RIPS THE CARRIER'S INTERNAL REALITY APART!
YOU WERE EXPECTING EXPLOSIVE DECOMPRESSION?
IT'S SORT OF MY HAIL MARY PASS.
THAT'S AN OUTER SPACE THING, NOT A HIGHLY RECOMMENDED INTRA-SPATIAL COMBAT STRATEGY.
SO NOTED.
ARE YOU TALKING TO THE MONKEY GIRL?!
OH, PLEASE...
ZZZZZMMMMH

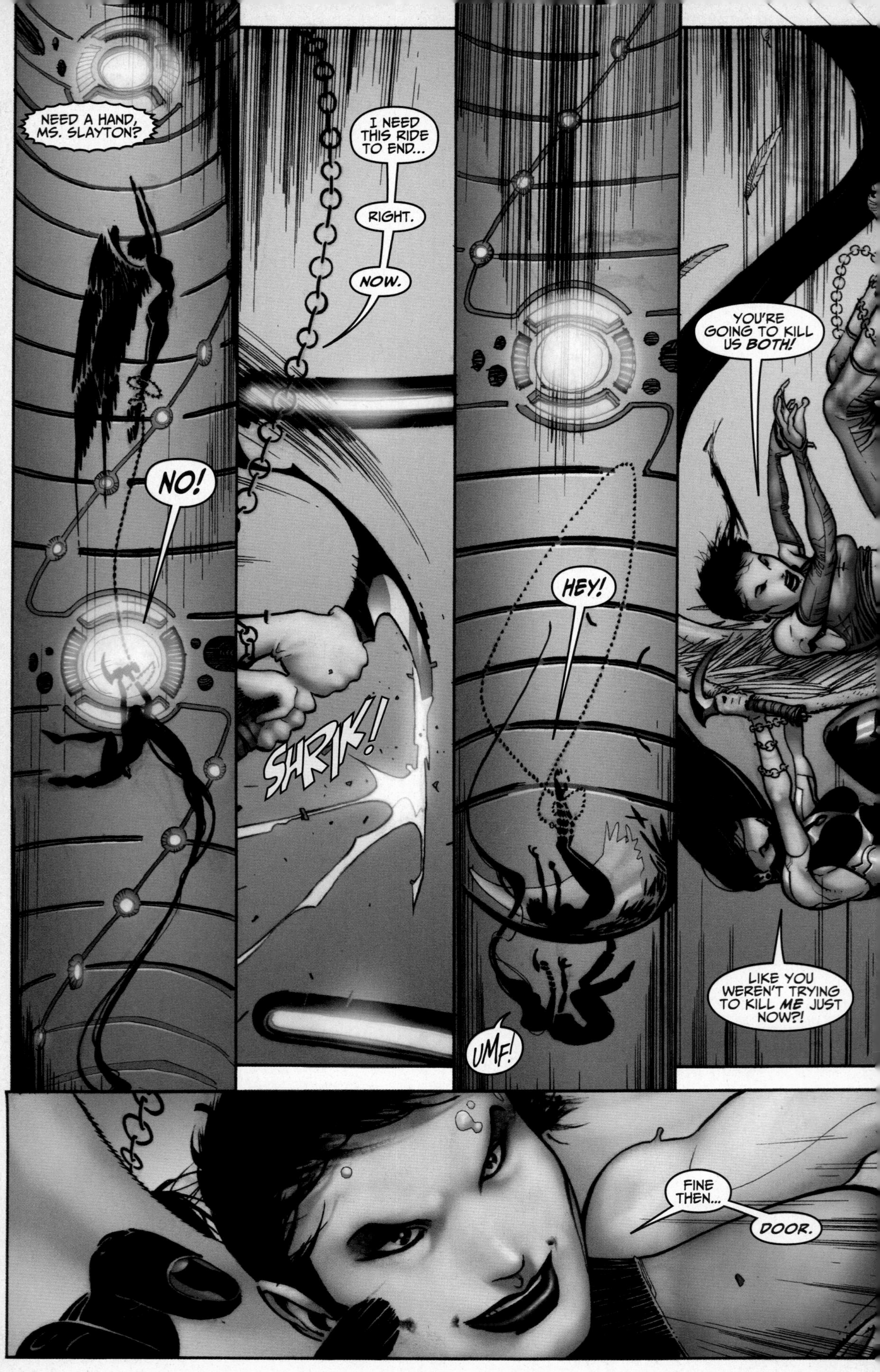
NEED A HAND, MS. SLAYTON?
NO!
I NEED THIS RIDE TO END...
RIGHT.
NOW.
SHRIK!
HEY!
UMF!
YOU'RE GOING TO KILL US BOTH!
LIKE YOU WEREN'T TRYING TO KILL ME JUST NOW?!
FINE THEN...
DOOR.

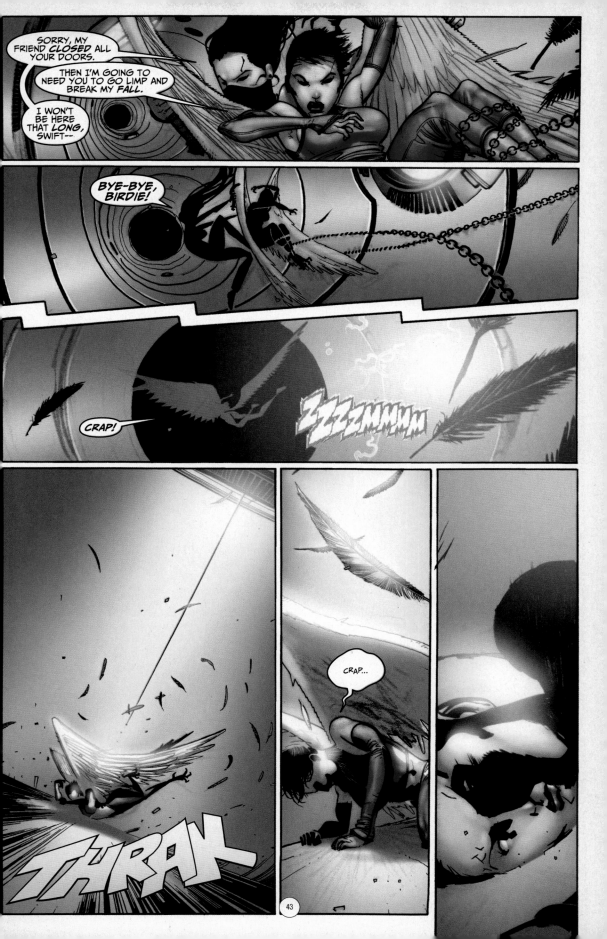

SORRY, MY FRIEND *CLOSED* ALL YOUR DOORS.

THEN I'M GOING TO NEED YOU TO GO LIMP AND BREAK MY *FALL.*

I WON'T BE HERE THAT *LONG,* SWIFT--

BYE-BYE, BIRDIE!

CRAP!

ZZZMMMM

CRAP...

THRAK

THAT'S THE MOST *BEAUTIFUL* THING I'VE EVER SEEN...

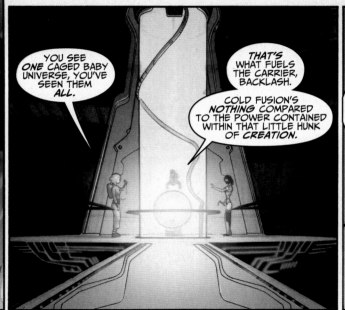

YOU SEE *ONE CAGED BABY UNIVERSE,* YOU'VE SEEN THEM *ALL.*

THAT'S WHAT FUELS THE CARRIER, BACKLASH.

COLD FUSION'S *NOTHING* COMPARED TO THE POWER CONTAINED WITHIN THAT LITTLE HUNK OF *CREATION.*

THEN MAYBE WE SHOULD JUST *DRAIN* THE CARRIER'S BATTERY SO THE AUTHORITY DON'T END UP USING IT TO DESTROY THE WORLD...

THE CARRIER *ISN'T* THE PROBLEM, JODI. LEAVE HER BE.

SHE'S *HELPING* US.

SORRY I STABBED YOU, OLD GIRL...

LOOK, BEFORE WE GET ALL *MAUDLIN*...

WE JUST ADDED THE AUTHORITY TO THE GROWING LIST OF PEOPLE WE'VE RIGHTEOUSLY *PISSED OFF.*

WAIT UNTIL *TOMORROW.*

ZZZZZMMMM

GREAT, THERE GOES WHAT LITTLE FUTURE I HAVE...

NO, REALLY-- IT'S JUST *LIME JELLO.*

WITH A PROTEIN-CHAIN ACCELERANT TO INCREASE ITS MASS *EXPONENTIALLY* UPON OXYGENATION. THE SECRET INGREDIENT IS A TASTY LITTLE NEURAL *PARASITE* SLAVED TO THE--

A *LITTLE HELP?*

WELL, THAT *MIGHT* EXPLAIN WHY THE DOORS AREN'T WORKING.

I HAD TO TELEPORT US BACK BY MY *OWN* POWER...

I *COULD* SEAL THE BREACH--

GETTING HARD TO KEEP *CONCENTRATING,* DOC.

THE BLEED IS PUSHING PAST MY *TELEPATHIC* SHUNT.

THE CARRIER'S BASICALLY A SMALL CITY, BUT THIS ISN'T LIKE PATCHING A *POTHOLE...*

LET ME CAUTERIZE THE WOUND WITH A LITTLE *CONCENTRATED* HEAT OF MY OWN, JACK.

SFFZZZ

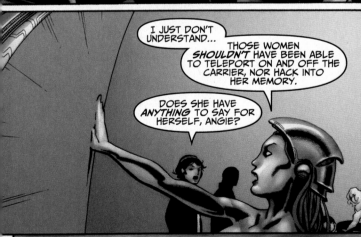

I JUST DON'T UNDERSTAND...

THOSE WOMEN *SHOULDN'T* HAVE BEEN ABLE TO TELEPORT ON AND OFF THE CARRIER, NOR HACK INTO HER MEMORY.

DOES SHE HAVE *ANYTHING* TO SAY FOR HERSELF, ANGIE?

NOT *WORDS,* JUST A CASCADE OF OVERWHELMING EMOTIONS COURSING THROUGH HER SYSTEMS...

SHE'S MOSTLY SAD...

"SO VERY *SAD...*"

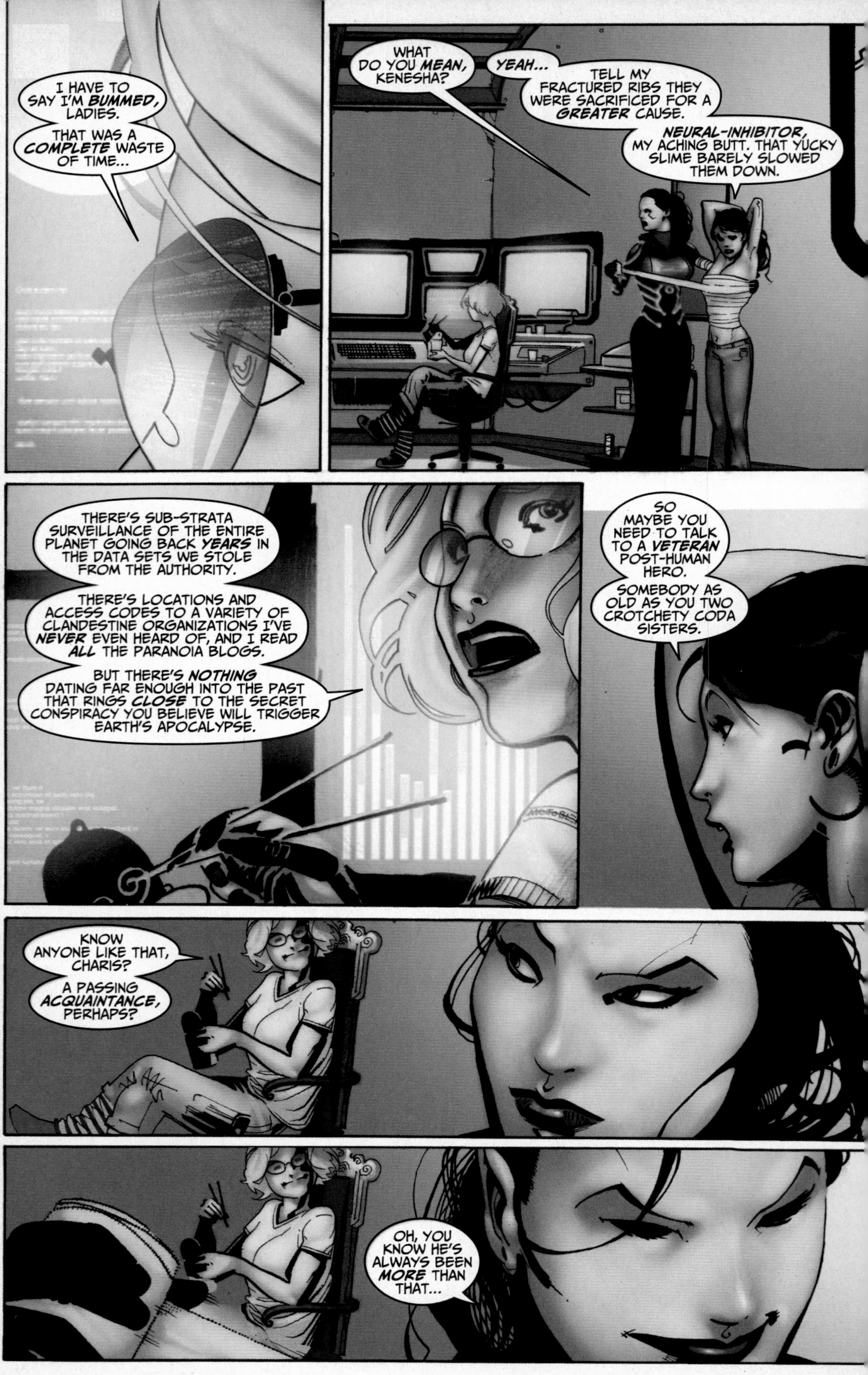
I HAVE TO SAY I'M BUMMED, LADIES.
THAT WAS A COMPLETE WASTE OF TIME...
WHAT DO YOU MEAN, KENESHA?
YEAH... TELL MY FRACTURED RIBS THEY WERE SACRIFICED FOR A GREATER CAUSE.
NEURAL-INHIBITOR, MY ACHING BUTT. THAT YUCKY SLIME BARELY SLOWED THEM DOWN.
THERE'S SUB-STRATA SURVEILLANCE OF THE ENTIRE PLANET GOING BACK YEARS IN THE DATA SETS WE STOLE FROM THE AUTHORITY.
THERE'S LOCATIONS AND ACCESS CODES TO A VARIETY OF CLANDESTINE ORGANIZATIONS I'VE NEVER EVEN HEARD OF, AND I READ ALL THE PARANOIA BLOGS.
BUT THERE'S NOTHING DATING FAR ENOUGH INTO THE PAST THAT RINGS CLOSE TO THE SECRET CONSPIRACY YOU BELIEVE WILL TRIGGER EARTH'S APOCALYPSE.
SO MAYBE YOU NEED TO TALK TO A VETERAN POST-HUMAN HERO.
SOMEBODY AS OLD AS YOU TWO CROTCHETY CODA SISTERS.
KNOW ANYONE LIKE THAT, CHARIS?
A PASSING ACQUAINTANCE, PERHAPS?
OH, YOU KNOW HE'S ALWAYS BEEN MORE THAN THAT...

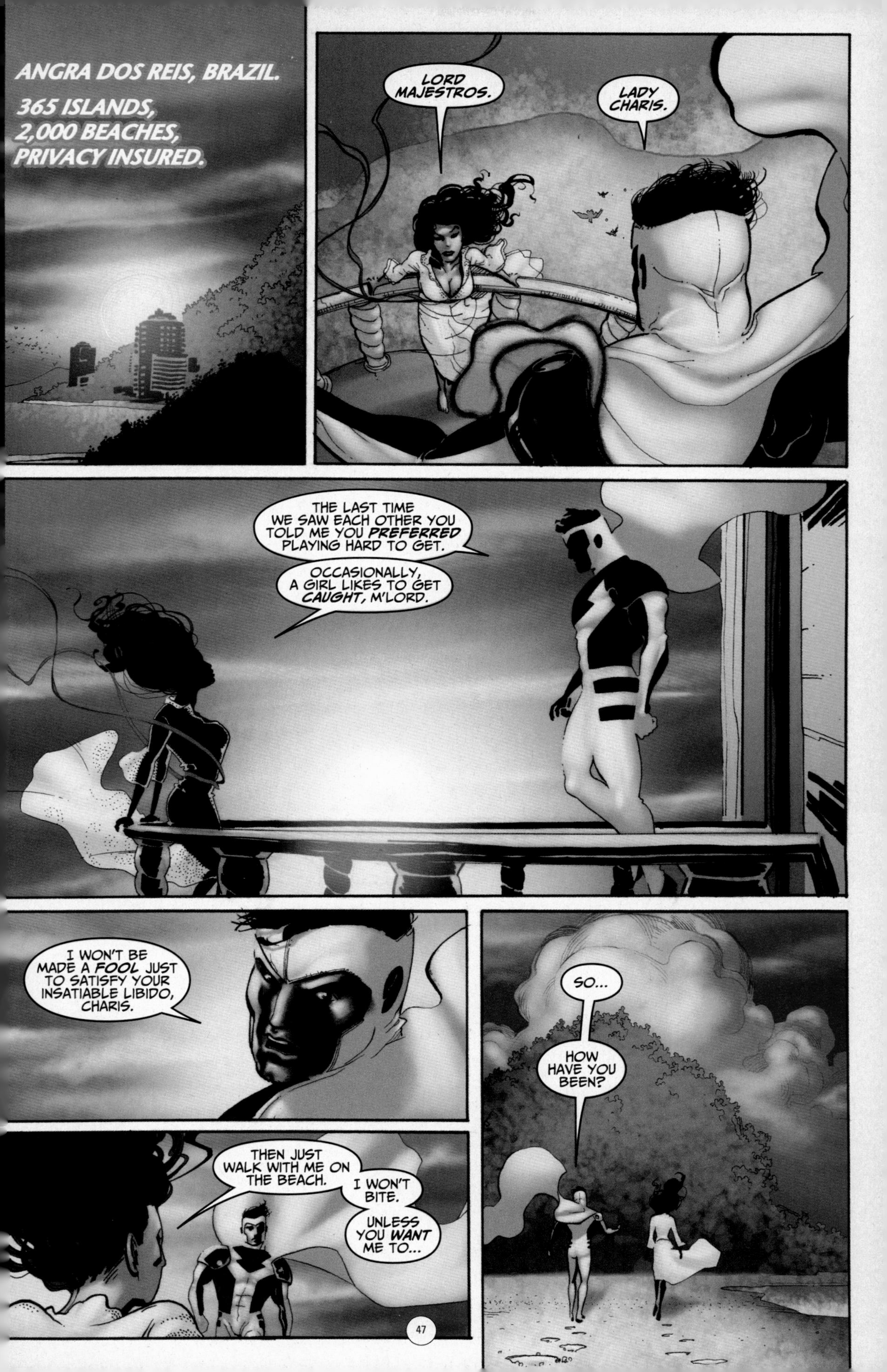
ANGRA DOS REIS, BRAZIL.
365 ISLANDS, 2,000 BEACHES, PRIVACY INSURED.
LORD MAJESTROS.
LADY CHARIS.
THE LAST TIME WE SAW EACH OTHER YOU TOLD ME YOU PREFERRED PLAYING HARD TO GET.
OCCASIONALLY, A GIRL LIKES TO GET CAUGHT, M'LORD.
I WON'T BE MADE A FOOL JUST TO SATISFY YOUR INSATIABLE LIBIDO, CHARIS.
THEN JUST WALK WITH ME ON THE BEACH.
I WON'T BITE.
UNLESS YOU WANT ME TO...
SO...
HOW HAVE YOU BEEN?

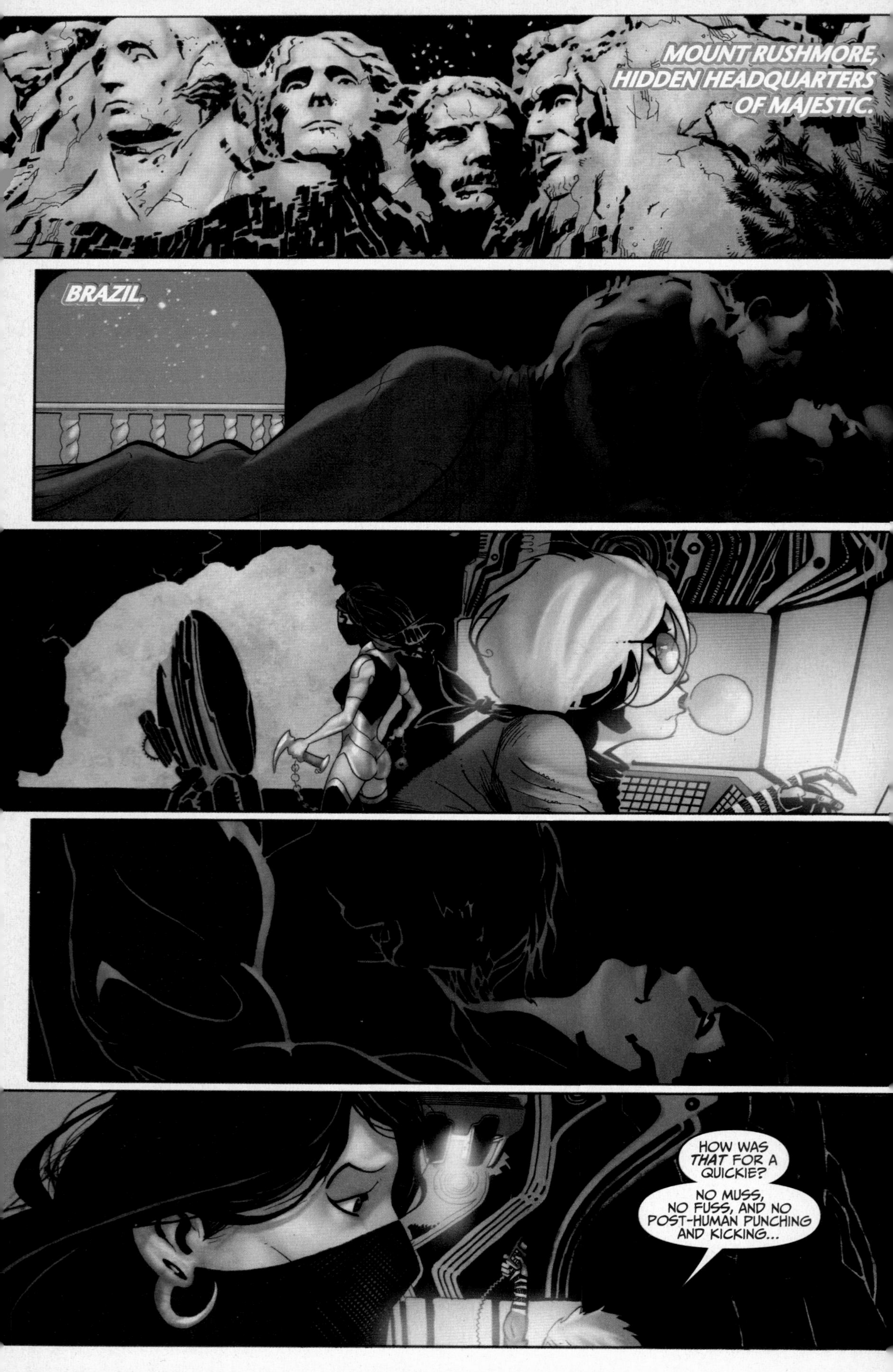
MOUNT RUSHMORE, HIDDEN HEADQUARTERS OF MAJESTIC.
BRAZIL.
HOW WAS THAT FOR A QUICKIE?
NO MUSS, NO FUSS, AND NO POST-HUMAN PUNCHING AND KICKING...

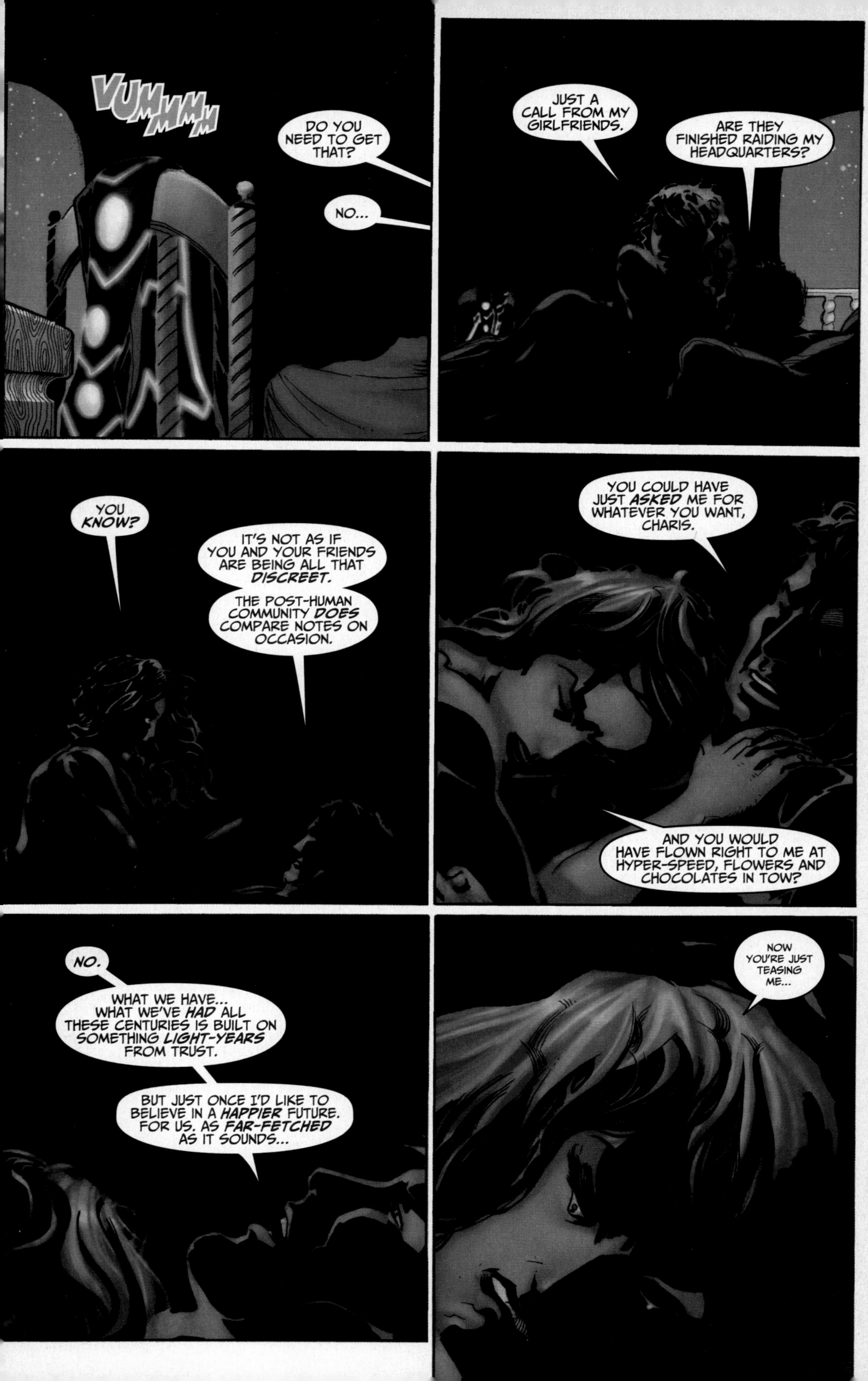
VUMMMMM
DO YOU NEED TO GET THAT?
NO...
JUST A CALL FROM MY GIRLFRIENDS.
ARE THEY FINISHED RAIDING MY HEADQUARTERS?
YOU KNOW?
IT'S NOT AS IF YOU AND YOUR FRIENDS ARE BEING ALL THAT DISCREET.
THE POST-HUMAN COMMUNITY DOES COMPARE NOTES ON OCCASION.
YOU COULD HAVE JUST ASKED ME FOR WHATEVER YOU WANT, CHARIS.
AND YOU WOULD HAVE FLOWN RIGHT TO ME AT HYPER-SPEED, FLOWERS AND CHOCOLATES IN TOW?
NO.
WHAT WE HAVE... WHAT WE'VE HAD ALL THESE CENTURIES IS BUILT ON SOMETHING LIGHT-YEARS FROM TRUST.
BUT JUST ONCE I'D LIKE TO BELIEVE IN A HAPPIER FUTURE. FOR US. AS FAR-FETCHED AS IT SOUNDS...
NOW YOU'RE JUST TEASING ME...

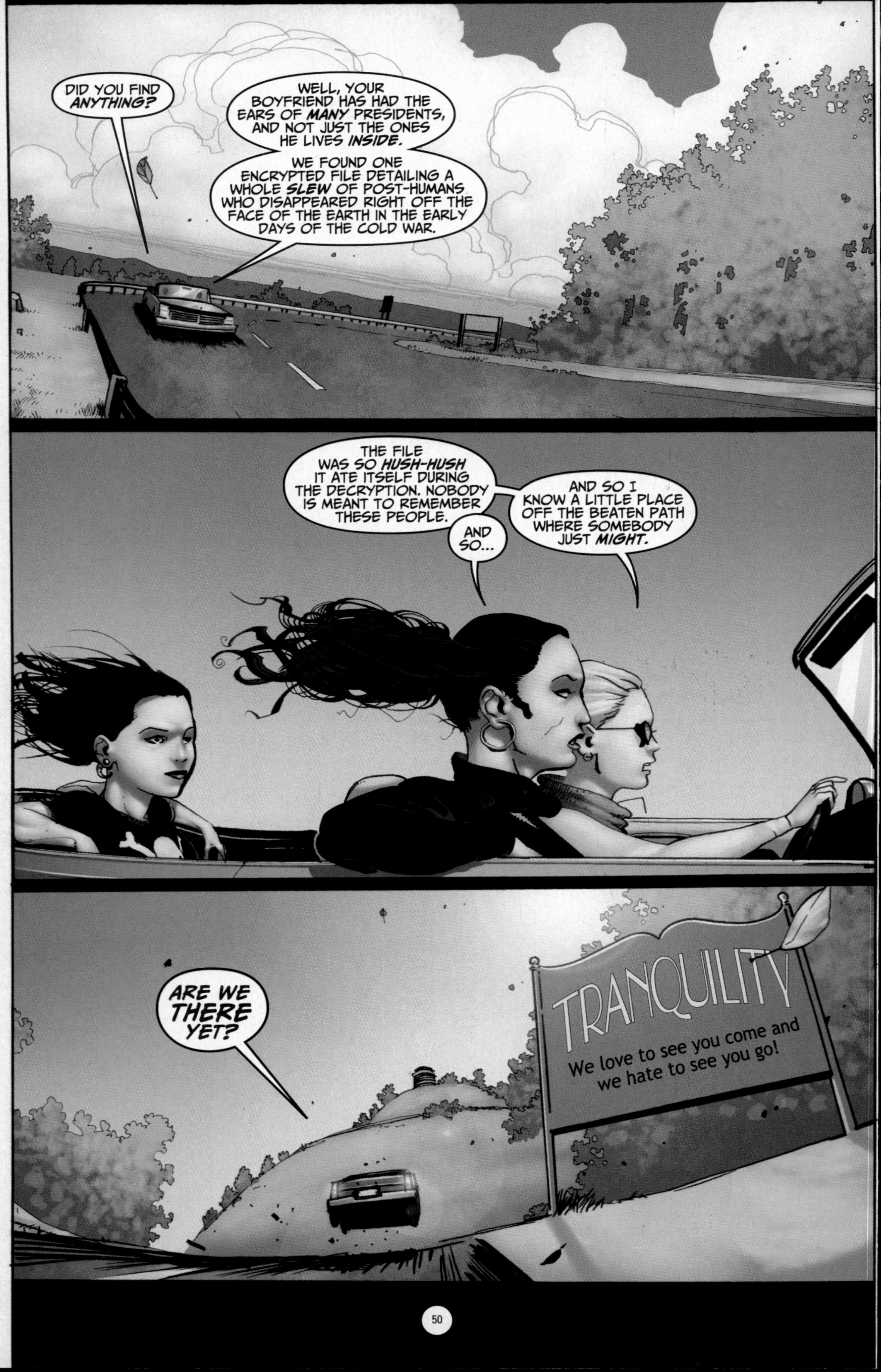
DID YOU FIND ANYTHING?
WELL, YOUR BOYFRIEND HAS HAD THE EARS OF MANY PRESIDENTS, AND NOT JUST THE ONES HE LIVES INSIDE.
WE FOUND ONE ENCRYPTED FILE DETAILING A WHOLE SLEW OF POST-HUMANS WHO DISAPPEARED RIGHT OFF THE FACE OF THE EARTH IN THE EARLY DAYS OF THE COLD WAR.
THE FILE WAS SO HUSH-HUSH IT ATE ITSELF DURING THE DECRYPTION. NOBODY IS MEANT TO REMEMBER THESE PEOPLE.
AND SO...
AND SO I KNOW A LITTLE PLACE OFF THE BEATEN PATH WHERE SOMEBODY JUST MIGHT.
ARE WE THERE YET?
TRANQUILITY
We love to see you come and we hate to see you go!

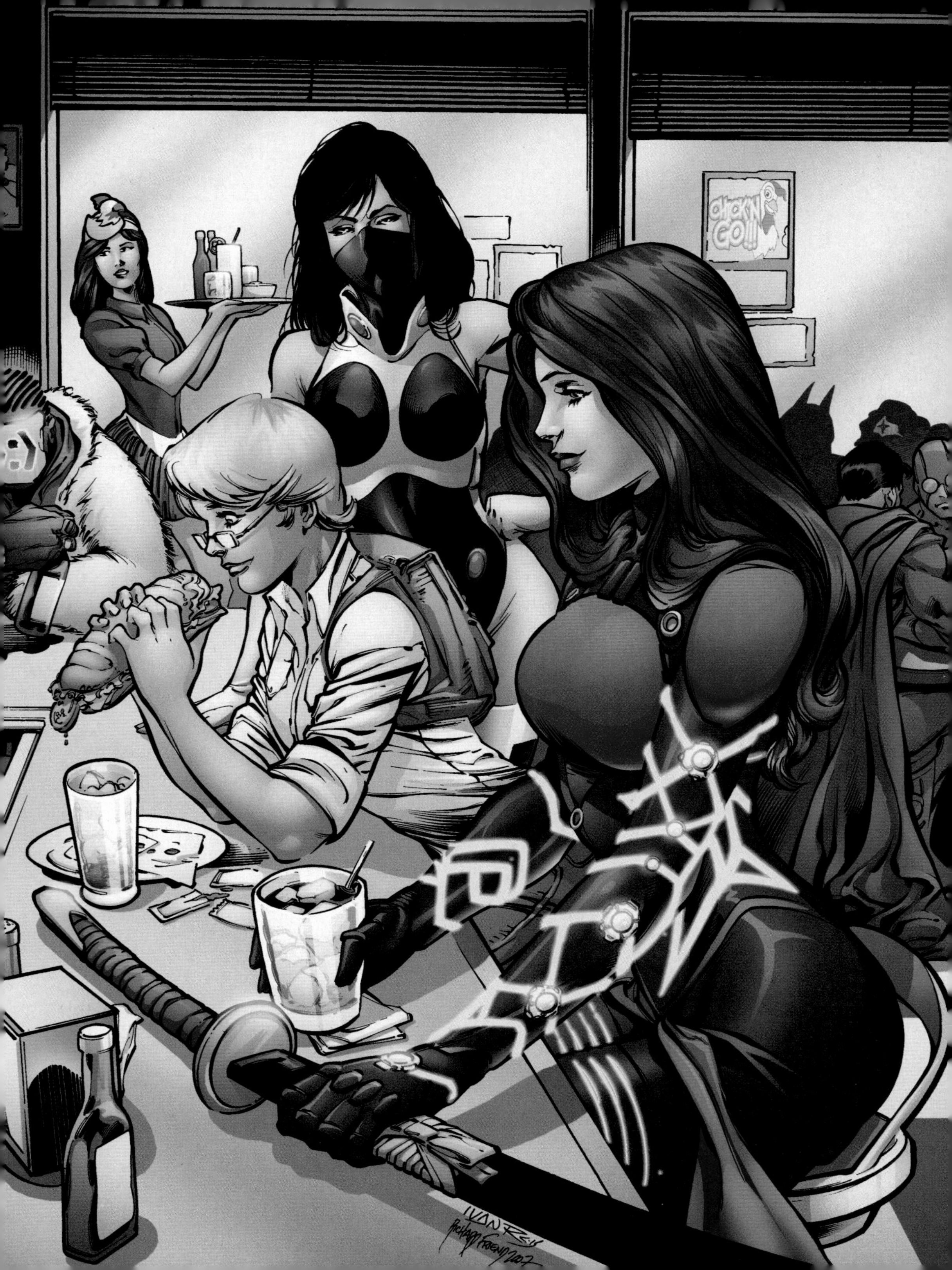
CHICK'N GO!!

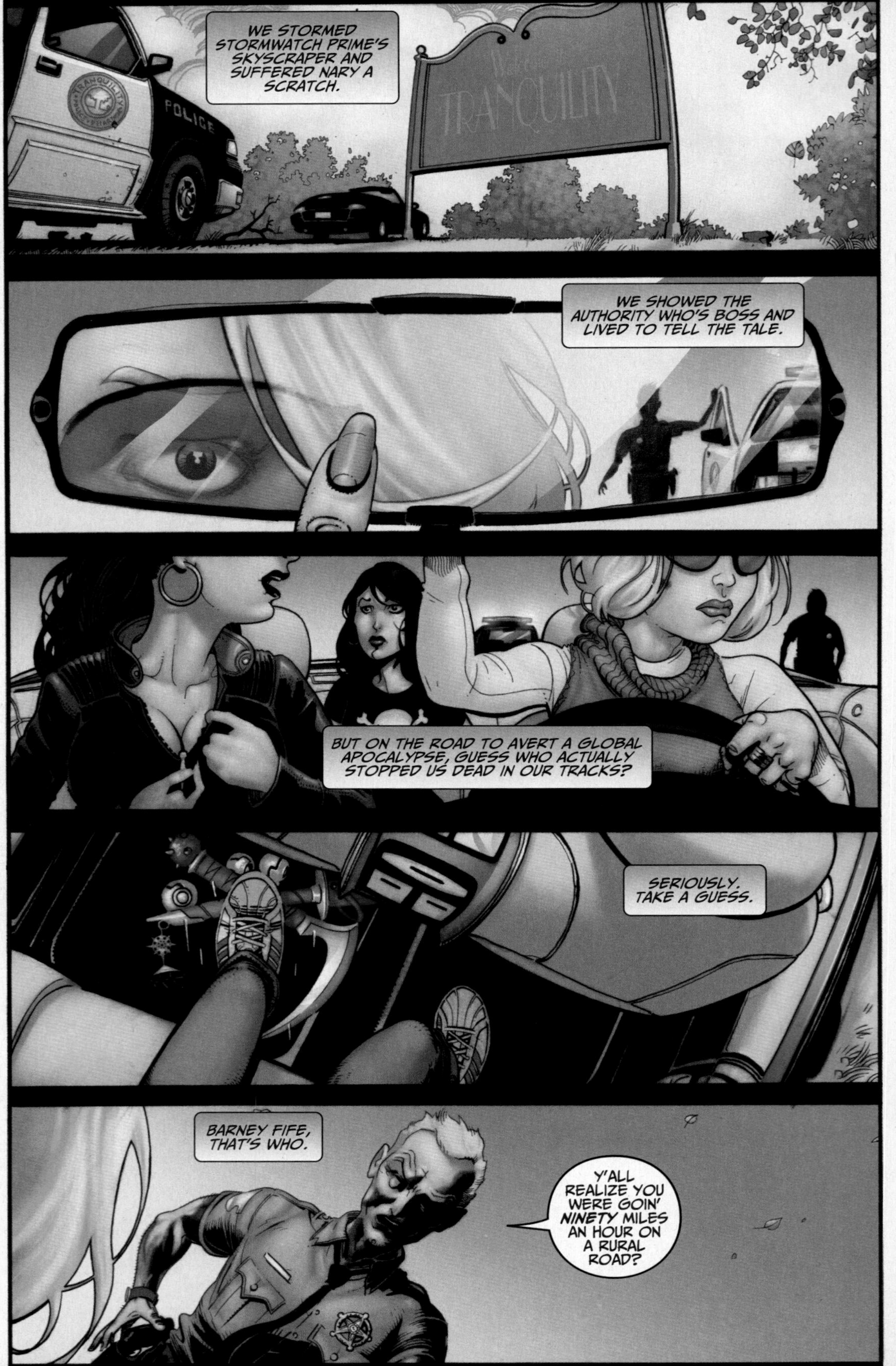

WE STORMED STORMWATCH PRIME'S SKYSCRAPER AND SUFFERED NARY A SCRATCH.
TRANQUILITY
POLICE
WE SHOWED THE AUTHORITY WHO'S BOSS AND LIVED TO TELL THE TALE.
BUT ON THE ROAD TO AVERT A GLOBAL APOCALYPSE, GUESS WHO ACTUALLY STOPPED US DEAD IN OUR TRACKS?
SERIOUSLY. TAKE A GUESS.
BARNEY FIFE, THAT'S WHO.
Y'ALL REALIZE YOU WERE GOIN' NINETY MILES AN HOUR ON A RURAL ROAD?

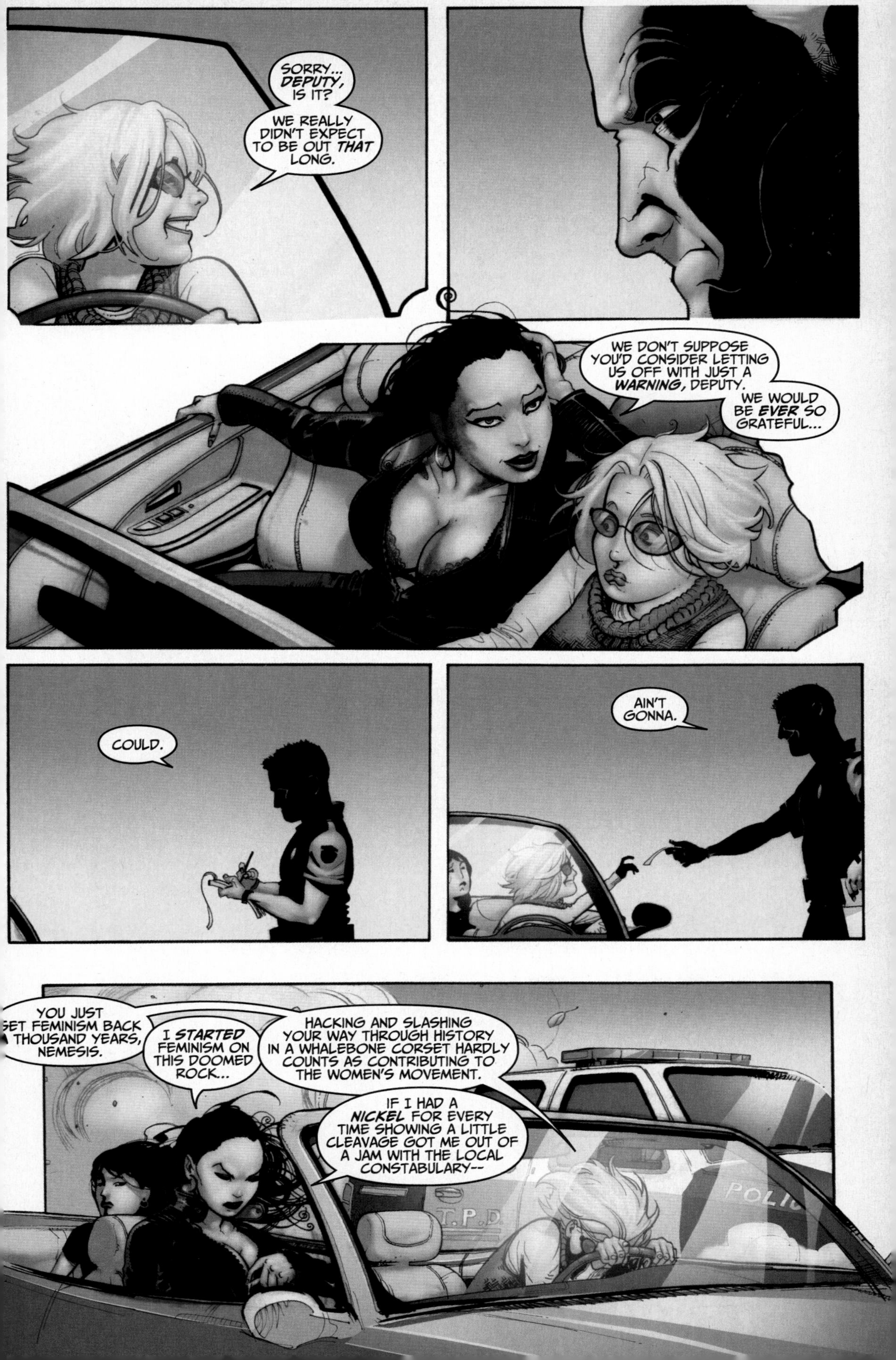
SORRY... DEPUTY, IS IT?
WE REALLY DIDN'T EXPECT TO BE OUT THAT LONG.
WE DON'T SUPPOSE YOU'D CONSIDER LETTING US OFF WITH JUST A WARNING, DEPUTY.
WE WOULD BE EVER SO GRATEFUL...
COULD.
AIN'T GONNA.
YOU JUST SET FEMINISM BACK A THOUSAND YEARS, NEMESIS.
I STARTED FEMINISM ON THIS DOOMED ROCK...
HACKING AND SLASHING YOUR WAY THROUGH HISTORY IN A WHALEBONE CORSET HARDLY COUNTS AS CONTRIBUTING TO THE WOMEN'S MOVEMENT.
IF I HAD A NICKEL FOR EVERY TIME SHOWING A LITTLE CLEAVAGE GOT ME OUT OF A JAM WITH THE LOCAL CONSTABULARY--
T.P.D.
POLIC

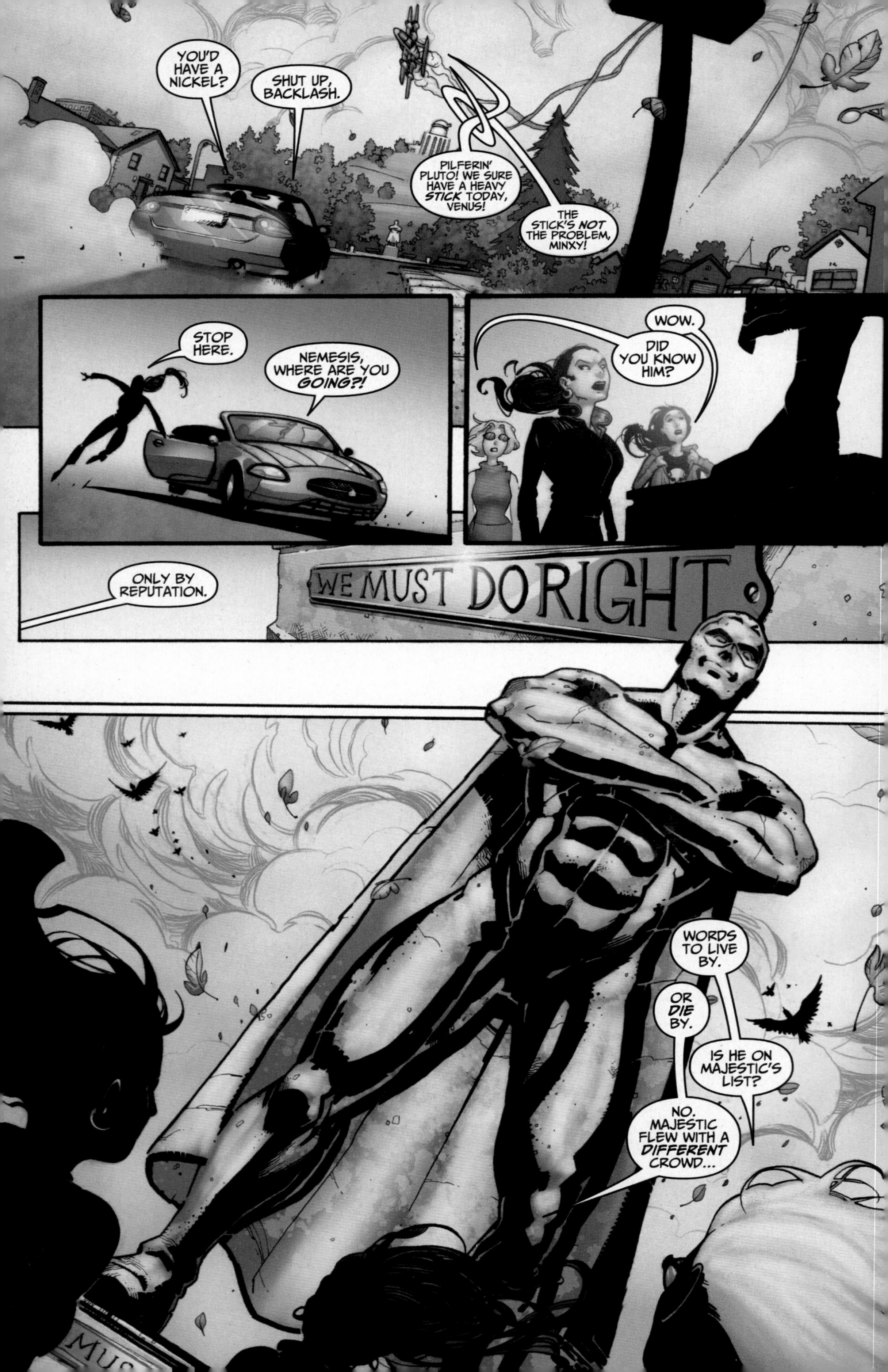
YOU'D HAVE A NICKEL?
SHUT UP, BACKLASH.
PILFERIN' PLUTO! WE SURE HAVE A HEAVY STICK TODAY, VENUS!
THE STICK'S NOT THE PROBLEM, MINXY!
STOP HERE.
NEMESIS, WHERE ARE YOU GOING?!
WOW.
DID YOU KNOW HIM?
ONLY BY REPUTATION.
WE MUST DO RIGHT
WORDS TO LIVE BY.
OR DIE BY.
IS HE ON MAJESTIC'S LIST?
NO. MAJESTIC FLEW WITH A DIFFERENT CROWD...

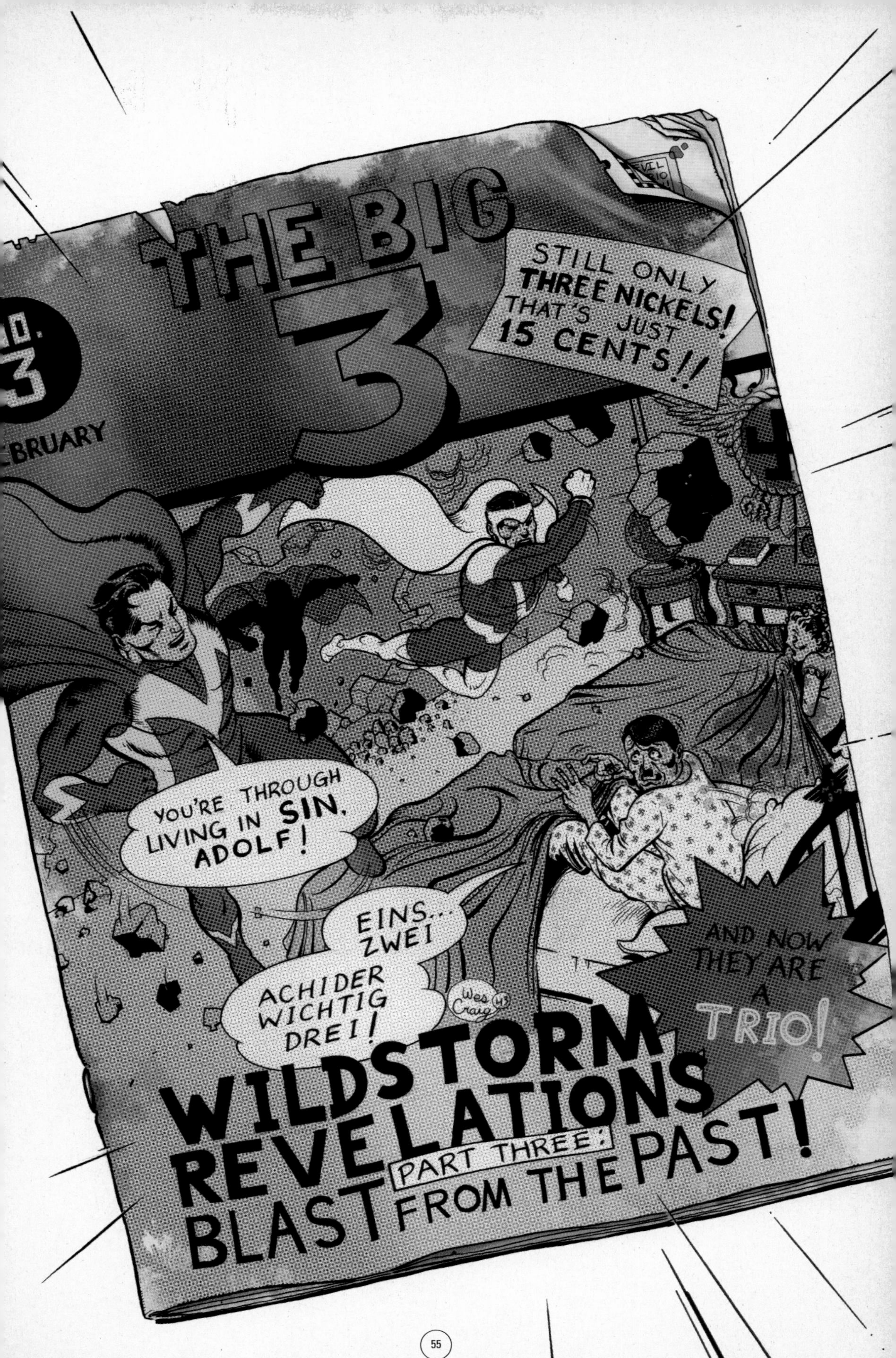
THE BIG 3
NO. 3
FEBRUARY
STILL ONLY THREE NICKELS! THAT'S JUST 15 CENTS!!
YOU'RE THROUGH LIVING IN SIN, ADOLF!
EINS... ZWEI
ACHIDER WICHTIG DREI!
Wes Craig '43
AND NOW THEY ARE A TRIO!
WILDSTORM REVELATIONS
PART THREE:
BLAST FROM THE PAST!

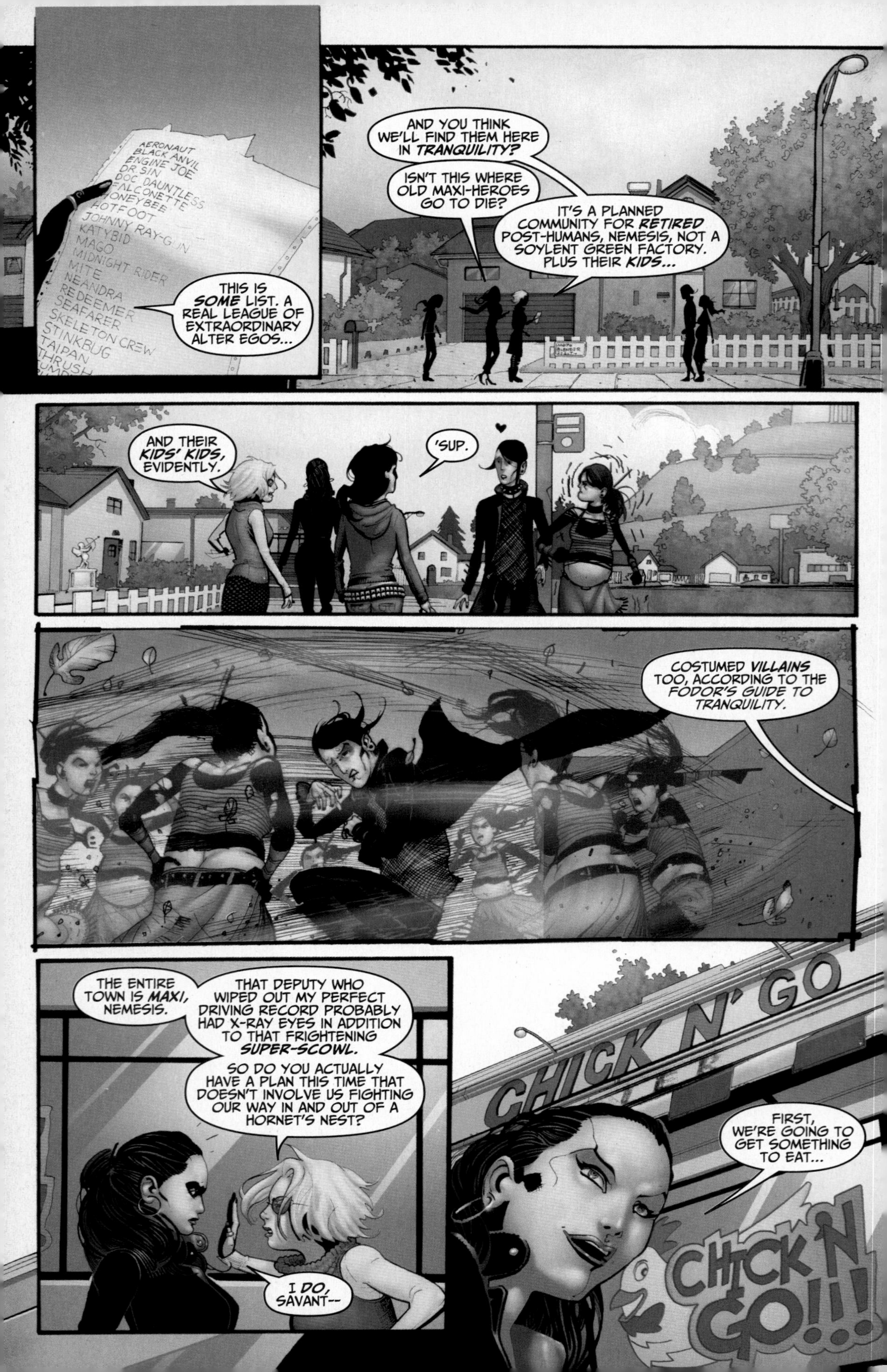
AERONAUT
BLACK ANVIL
ENGINE JOE
DR. SIN
DOC DAUNTLESS
FALCONETTE
HONEYBEE
HOTFOOT
JOHNNY RAY-GUN
KATYBID
MAGO
MIDNIGHT RIDER
MITE
NEANDRA
REDEEMER
SEAFARER
SKELETON CREW
STINKBUG
TAIPAN
THRUSH
THIS IS SOME LIST. A REAL LEAGUE OF EXTRAORDINARY ALTER EGOS...
AND YOU THINK WE'LL FIND THEM HERE IN TRANQUILITY?
ISN'T THIS WHERE OLD MAXI-HEROES GO TO DIE?
IT'S A PLANNED COMMUNITY FOR RETIRED POST-HUMANS, NEMESIS, NOT A SOYLENT GREEN FACTORY. PLUS THEIR KIDS...
AND THEIR KIDS' KIDS, EVIDENTLY.
'SUP.
COSTUMED VILLAINS TOO, ACCORDING TO THE FODOR'S GUIDE TO TRANQUILITY.
THE ENTIRE TOWN IS MAXI, NEMESIS.
THAT DEPUTY WHO WIPED OUT MY PERFECT DRIVING RECORD PROBABLY HAD X-RAY EYES IN ADDITION TO THAT FRIGHTENING SUPER-SCOWL.
SO DO YOU ACTUALLY HAVE A PLAN THIS TIME THAT DOESN'T INVOLVE US FIGHTING OUR WAY IN AND OUT OF A HORNET'S NEST?
I DO, SAVANT--
CHICK N' GO
FIRST, WE'RE GOING TO GET SOMETHING TO EAT...
CHICK 'N GO!!!

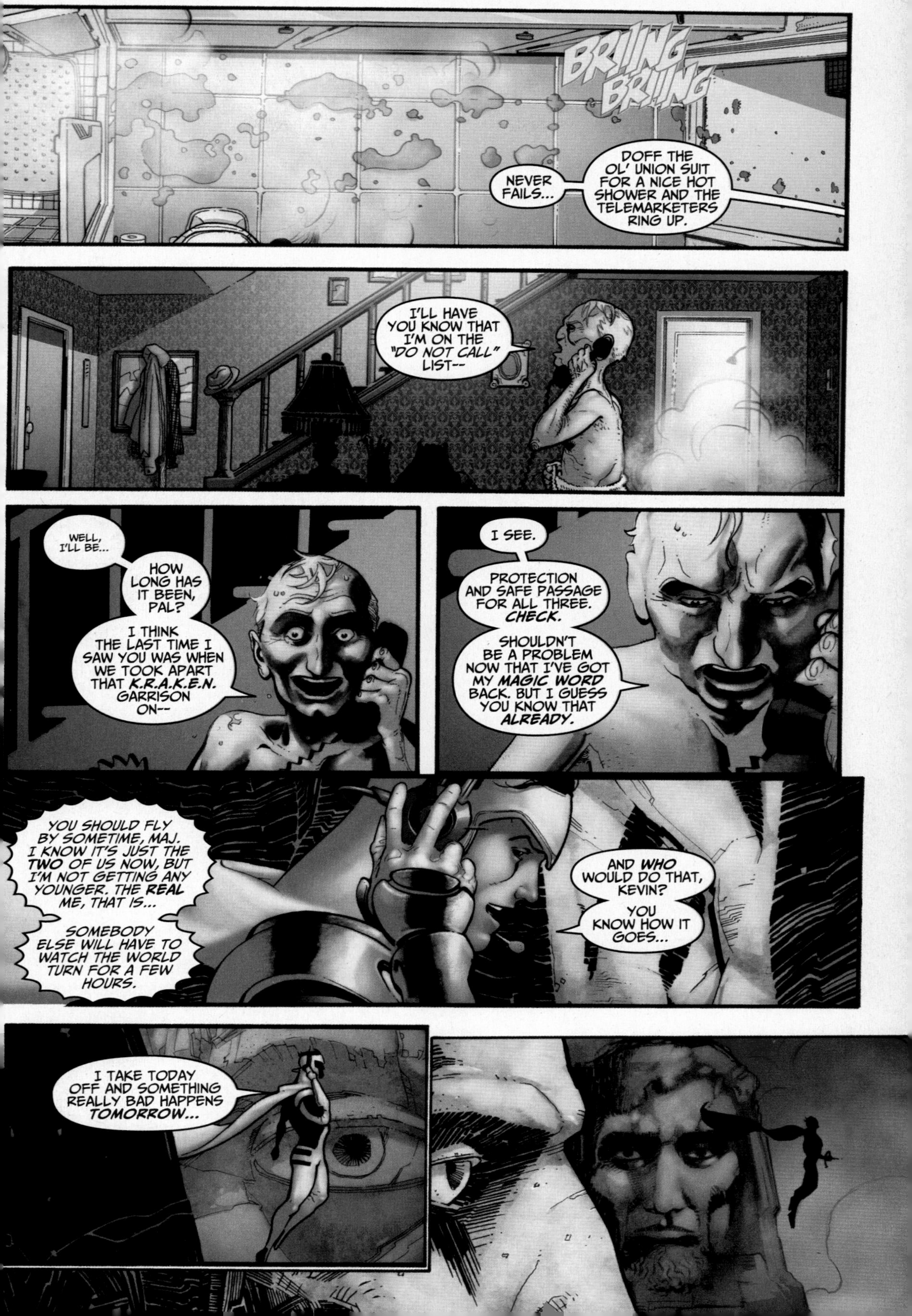
BRIING BRIING
NEVER FAILS...
DOFF THE OL' UNION SUIT FOR A NICE HOT SHOWER AND THE TELEMARKETERS RING UP.
I'LL HAVE YOU KNOW THAT I'M ON THE "DO NOT CALL" LIST--
WELL, I'LL BE...
HOW LONG HAS IT BEEN, PAL?
I THINK THE LAST TIME I SAW YOU WAS WHEN WE TOOK APART THAT K.R.A.K.E.N. GARRISON ON--
I SEE.
PROTECTION AND SAFE PASSAGE FOR ALL THREE. CHECK.
SHOULDN'T BE A PROBLEM NOW THAT I'VE GOT MY MAGIC WORD BACK. BUT I GUESS YOU KNOW THAT ALREADY.
YOU SHOULD FLY BY SOMETIME, MAJ. I KNOW IT'S JUST THE TWO OF US NOW, BUT I'M NOT GETTING ANY YOUNGER. THE REAL ME, THAT IS...
SOMEBODY ELSE WILL HAVE TO WATCH THE WORLD TURN FOR A FEW HOURS.
AND WHO WOULD DO THAT, KEVIN?
YOU KNOW HOW IT GOES...
I TAKE TODAY OFF AND SOMETHING REALLY BAD HAPPENS TOMORROW...

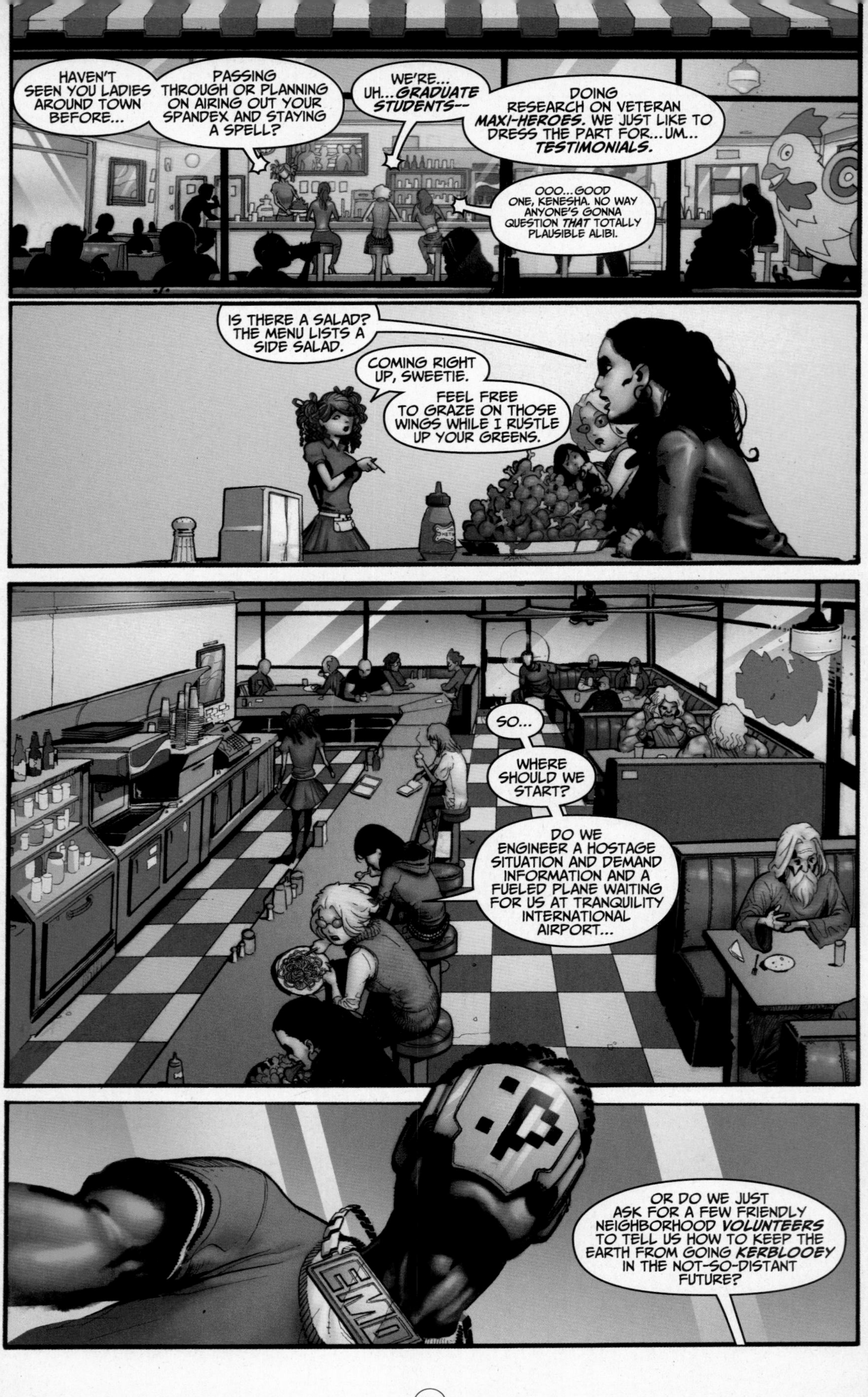
HAVEN'T SEEN YOU LADIES AROUND TOWN BEFORE...
PASSING THROUGH OR PLANNING ON AIRING OUT YOUR SPANDEX AND STAYING A SPELL?
WE'RE... UH...GRADUATE STUDENTS--
DOING RESEARCH ON VETERAN MAXI-HEROES. WE JUST LIKE TO DRESS THE PART FOR...UM... TESTIMONIALS.
OOO...GOOD ONE, KENESHA. NO WAY ANYONE'S GONNA QUESTION THAT TOTALLY PLAUSIBLE ALIBI.
IS THERE A SALAD? THE MENU LISTS A SIDE SALAD.
COMING RIGHT UP, SWEETIE.
FEEL FREE TO GRAZE ON THOSE WINGS WHILE I RUSTLE UP YOUR GREENS.
SO...
WHERE SHOULD WE START?
DO WE ENGINEER A HOSTAGE SITUATION AND DEMAND INFORMATION AND A FUELED PLANE WAITING FOR US AT TRANQUILITY INTERNATIONAL AIRPORT...
OR DO WE JUST ASK FOR A FEW FRIENDLY NEIGHBORHOOD VOLUNTEERS TO TELL US HOW TO KEEP THE EARTH FROM GOING KERBLOOEY IN THE NOT-SO-DISTANT FUTURE?

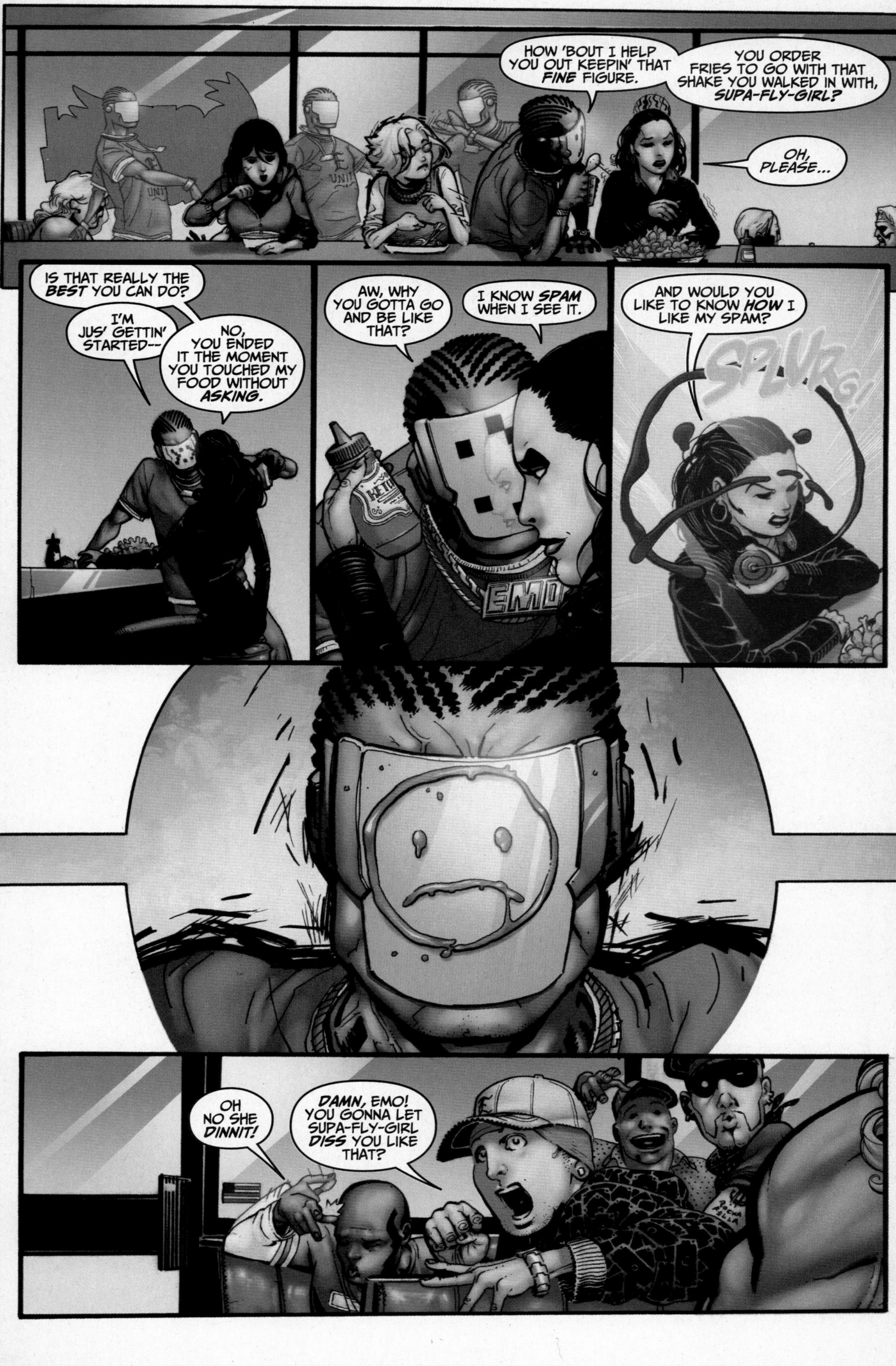
HOW 'BOUT I HELP YOU OUT KEEPIN' THAT FINE FIGURE.
YOU ORDER FRIES TO GO WITH THAT SHAKE YOU WALKED IN WITH, SUPA-FLY-GIRL?
OH, PLEASE...
IS THAT REALLY THE BEST YOU CAN DO?
I'M JUS' GETTIN' STARTED--
NO, YOU ENDED IT THE MOMENT YOU TOUCHED MY FOOD WITHOUT ASKING.
AW, WHY YOU GOTTA GO AND BE LIKE THAT?
I KNOW SPAM WHEN I SEE IT.
AND WOULD YOU LIKE TO KNOW HOW I LIKE MY SPAM?
SPLURG!
OH NO SHE DINNIT!
DAMN, EMO! YOU GONNA LET SUPA-FLY-GIRL DISS YOU LIKE THAT?

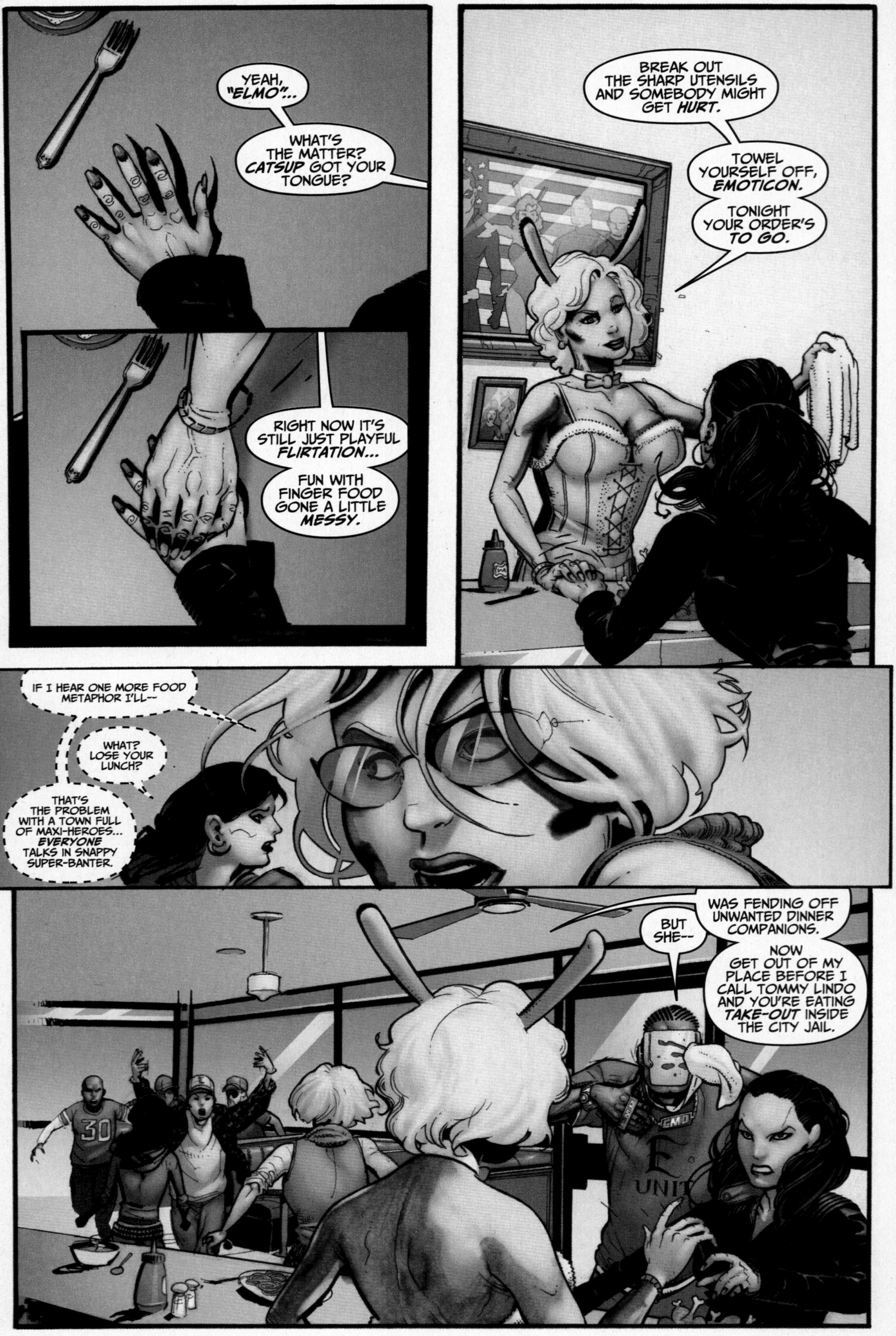
YEAH, "ELMO"...
WHAT'S THE MATTER? CATSUP GOT YOUR TONGUE?
RIGHT NOW IT'S STILL JUST PLAYFUL FLIRTATION...
FUN WITH FINGER FOOD GONE A LITTLE MESSY.
BREAK OUT THE SHARP UTENSILS AND SOMEBODY MIGHT GET HURT.
TOWEL YOURSELF OFF, EMOTICON.
TONIGHT YOUR ORDER'S TO GO.
IF I HEAR ONE MORE FOOD METAPHOR I'LL--
WHAT? LOSE YOUR LUNCH?
THAT'S THE PROBLEM WITH A TOWN FULL OF MAXI-HEROES... EVERYONE TALKS IN SNAPPY SUPER-BANTER.
BUT SHE--
WAS FENDING OFF UNWANTED DINNER COMPANIONS.
NOW GET OUT OF MY PLACE BEFORE I CALL TOMMY LINDO AND YOU'RE EATING TAKE-OUT INSIDE THE CITY JAIL.

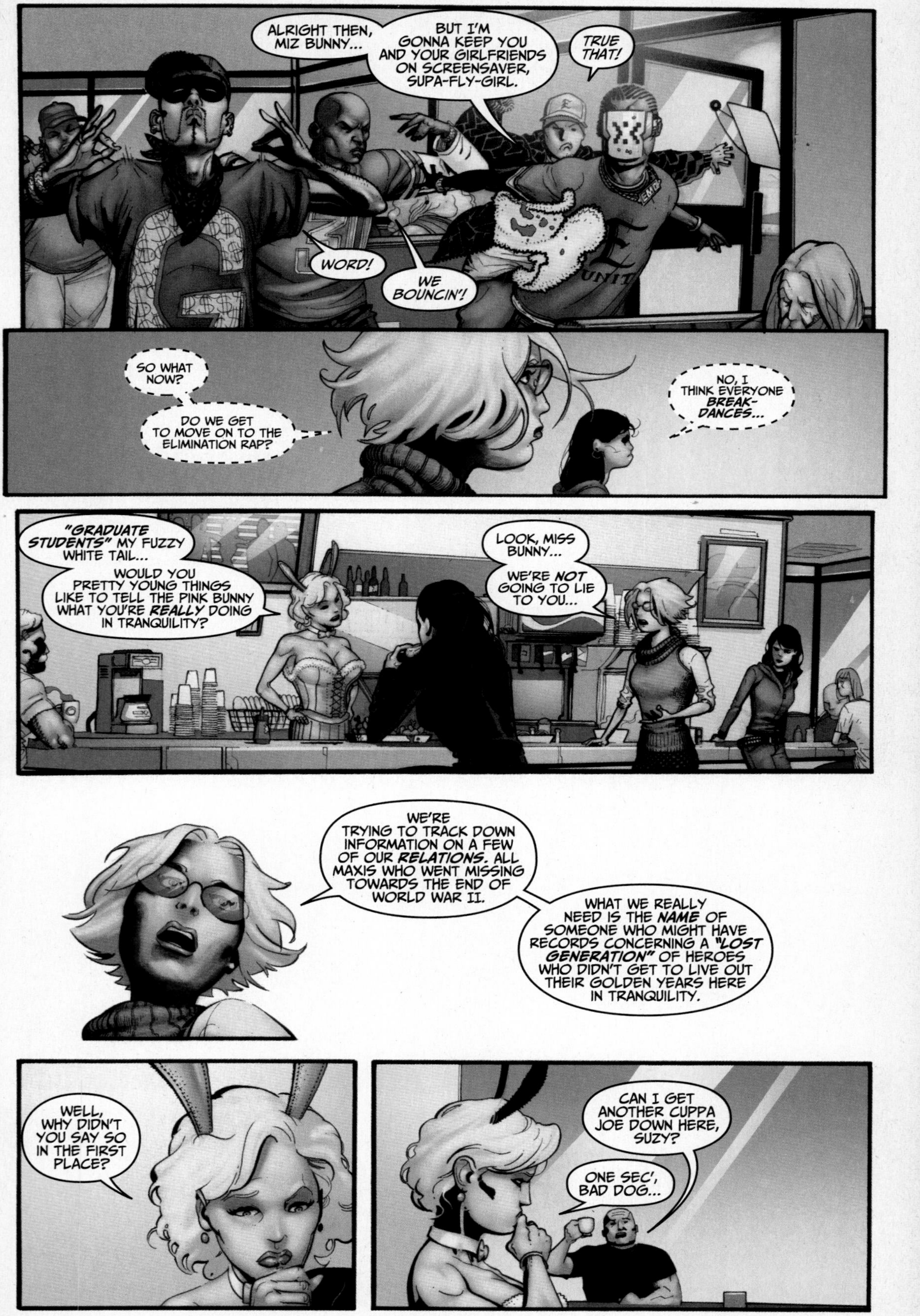
ALRIGHT THEN, MIZ BUNNY...
BUT I'M GONNA KEEP YOU AND YOUR GIRLFRIENDS ON SCREENSAVER, SUPA-FLY-GIRL.
TRUE THAT!
WORD!
WE BOUNCIN'!
SO WHAT NOW?
DO WE GET TO MOVE ON TO THE ELIMINATION RAP?
NO, I THINK EVERYONE BREAK-DANCES...
"GRADUATE STUDENTS" MY FUZZY WHITE TAIL...
WOULD YOU PRETTY YOUNG THINGS LIKE TO TELL THE PINK BUNNY WHAT YOU'RE REALLY DOING IN TRANQUILITY?
LOOK, MISS BUNNY...
WE'RE NOT GOING TO LIE TO YOU...
WE'RE TRYING TO TRACK DOWN INFORMATION ON A FEW OF OUR RELATIONS. ALL MAXIS WHO WENT MISSING TOWARDS THE END OF WORLD WAR II.
WHAT WE REALLY NEED IS THE NAME OF SOMEONE WHO MIGHT HAVE RECORDS CONCERNING A "LOST GENERATION" OF HEROES WHO DIDN'T GET TO LIVE OUT THEIR GOLDEN YEARS HERE IN TRANQUILITY.
WELL, WHY DIDN'T YOU SAY SO IN THE FIRST PLACE?
CAN I GET ANOTHER CUPPA JOE DOWN HERE, SUZY?
ONE SEC', BAD DOG...

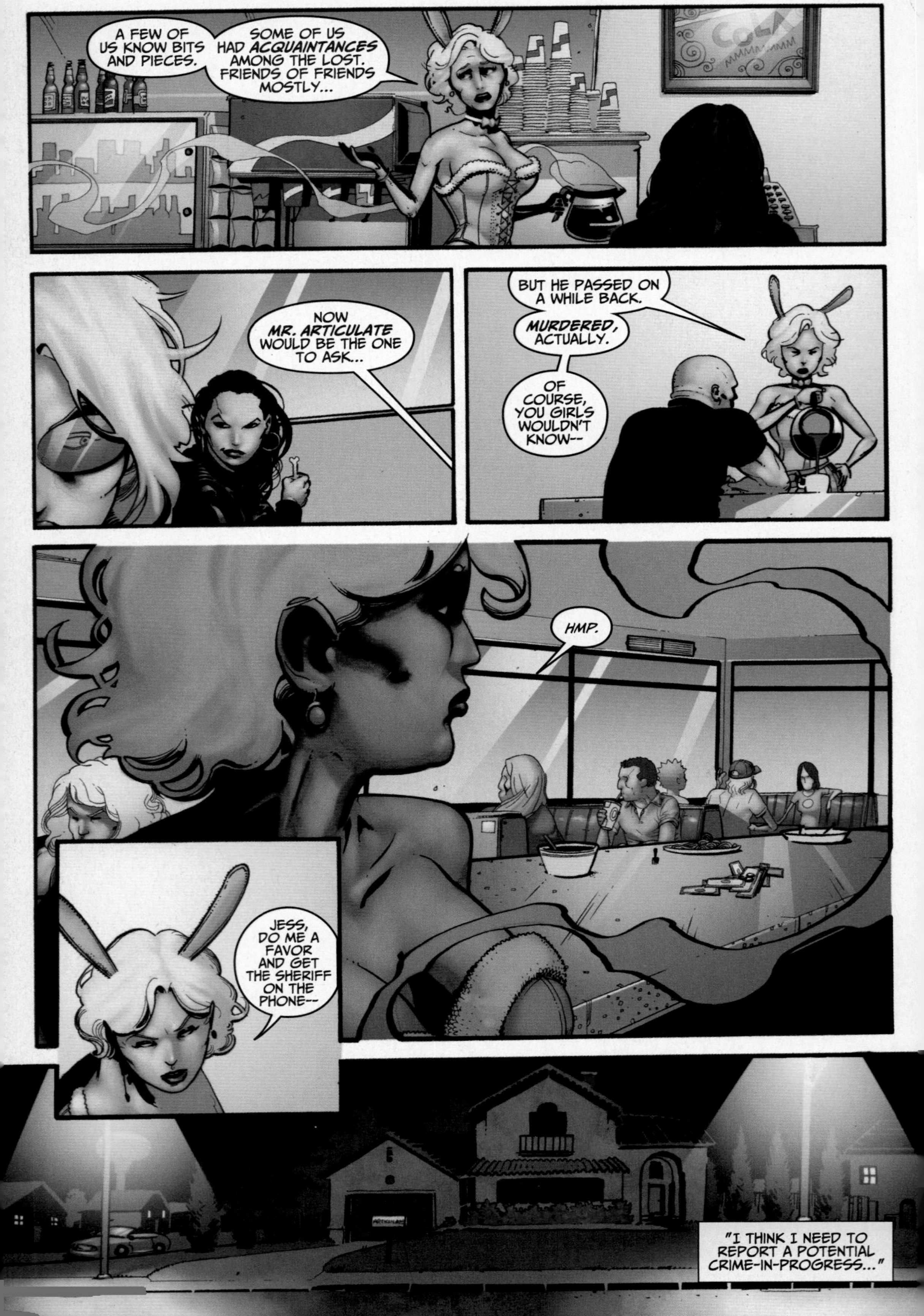
A FEW OF US KNOW BITS AND PIECES.
SOME OF US HAD *ACQUAINTANCES* AMONG THE LOST. FRIENDS OF FRIENDS MOSTLY...
NOW *MR. ARTICULATE* WOULD BE THE ONE TO ASK...
BUT HE PASSED ON A WHILE BACK.
MURDERED, ACTUALLY.
OF COURSE, YOU GIRLS WOULDN'T KNOW--
HMP.
JESS, DO ME A FAVOR AND GET THE SHERIFF ON THE PHONE--
"I THINK I NEED TO REPORT A POTENTIAL CRIME-IN-PROGRESS..."

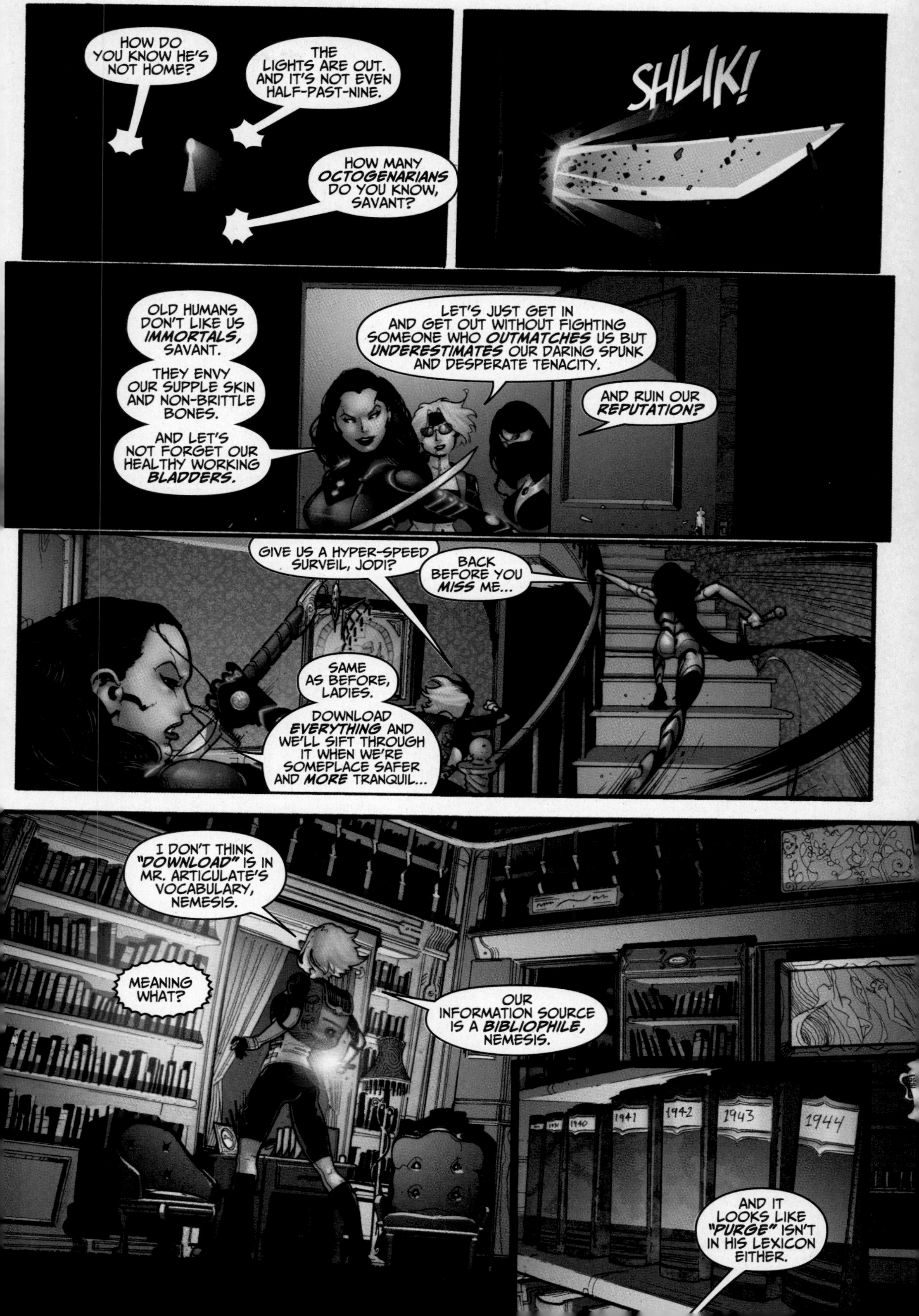
HOW DO YOU KNOW HE'S NOT HOME?
THE LIGHTS ARE OUT. AND IT'S NOT EVEN HALF-PAST-NINE.
HOW MANY OCTOGENARIANS DO YOU KNOW, SAVANT?
SHLIK!
OLD HUMANS DON'T LIKE US IMMORTALS, SAVANT.
THEY ENVY OUR SUPPLE SKIN AND NON-BRITTLE BONES.
AND LET'S NOT FORGET OUR HEALTHY WORKING BLADDERS.
LET'S JUST GET IN AND GET OUT WITHOUT FIGHTING SOMEONE WHO OUTMATCHES US BUT UNDERESTIMATES OUR DARING SPUNK AND DESPERATE TENACITY.
AND RUIN OUR REPUTATION?
GIVE US A HYPER-SPEED SURVEIL, JODI?
BACK BEFORE YOU MISS ME...
SAME AS BEFORE, LADIES.
DOWNLOAD EVERYTHING AND WE'LL SIFT THROUGH IT WHEN WE'RE SOMEPLACE SAFER AND MORE TRANQUIL...
I DON'T THINK "DOWNLOAD" IS IN MR. ARTICULATE'S VOCABULARY, NEMESIS.
MEANING WHAT?
OUR INFORMATION SOURCE IS A BIBLIOPHILE, NEMESIS.
1940
1941
1942
1943
1944
AND IT LOOKS LIKE "PURGE" ISN'T IN HIS LEXICON EITHER.

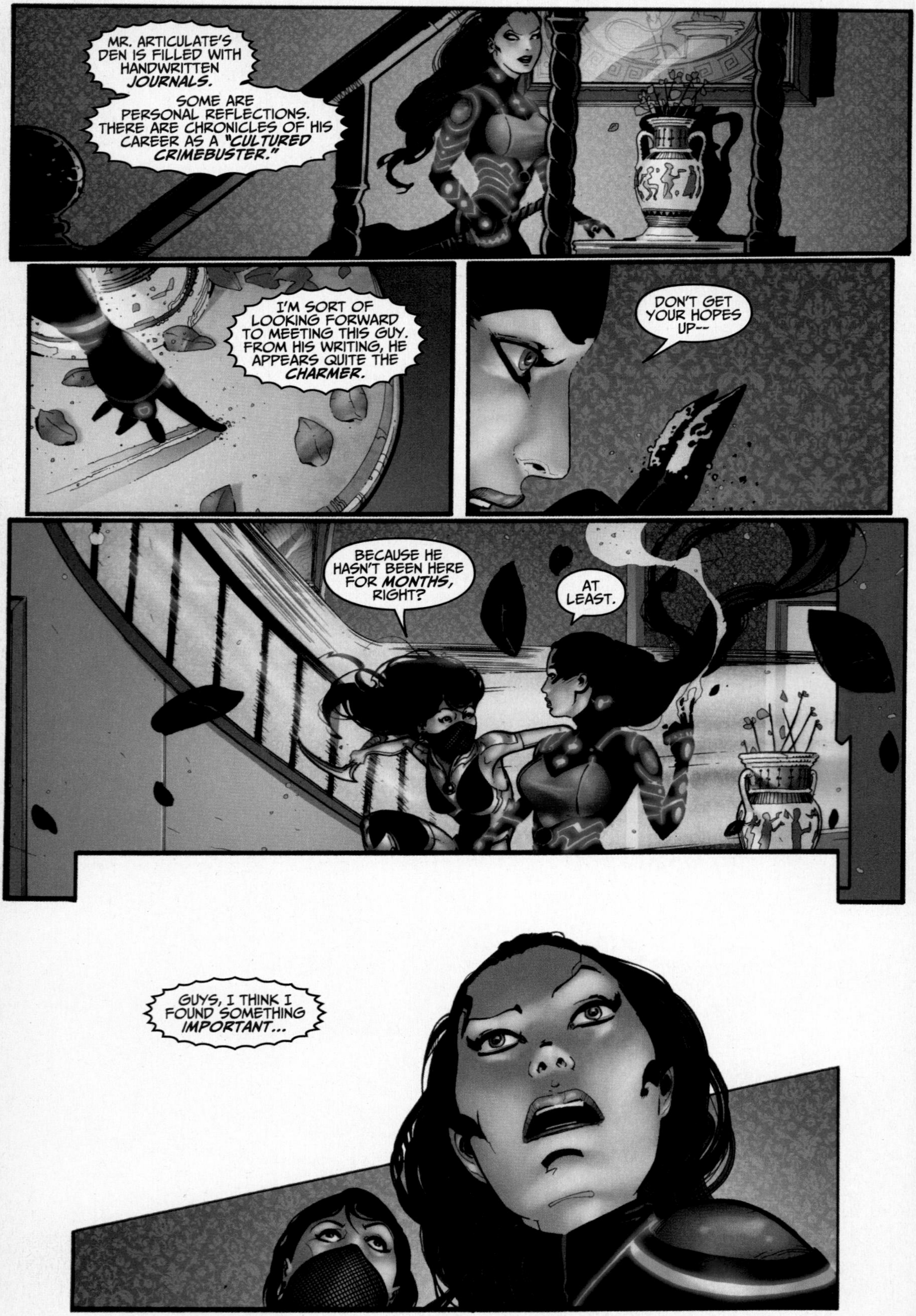
MR. ARTICULATE'S DEN IS FILLED WITH HANDWRITTEN JOURNALS.
SOME ARE PERSONAL REFLECTIONS. THERE ARE CHRONICLES OF HIS CAREER AS A "CULTURED CRIMEBUSTER."
I'M SORT OF LOOKING FORWARD TO MEETING THIS GUY. FROM HIS WRITING, HE APPEARS QUITE THE CHARMER.
DON'T GET YOUR HOPES UP--
BECAUSE HE HASN'T BEEN HERE FOR MONTHS, RIGHT?
AT LEAST.
GUYS, I THINK I FOUND SOMETHING IMPORTANT...

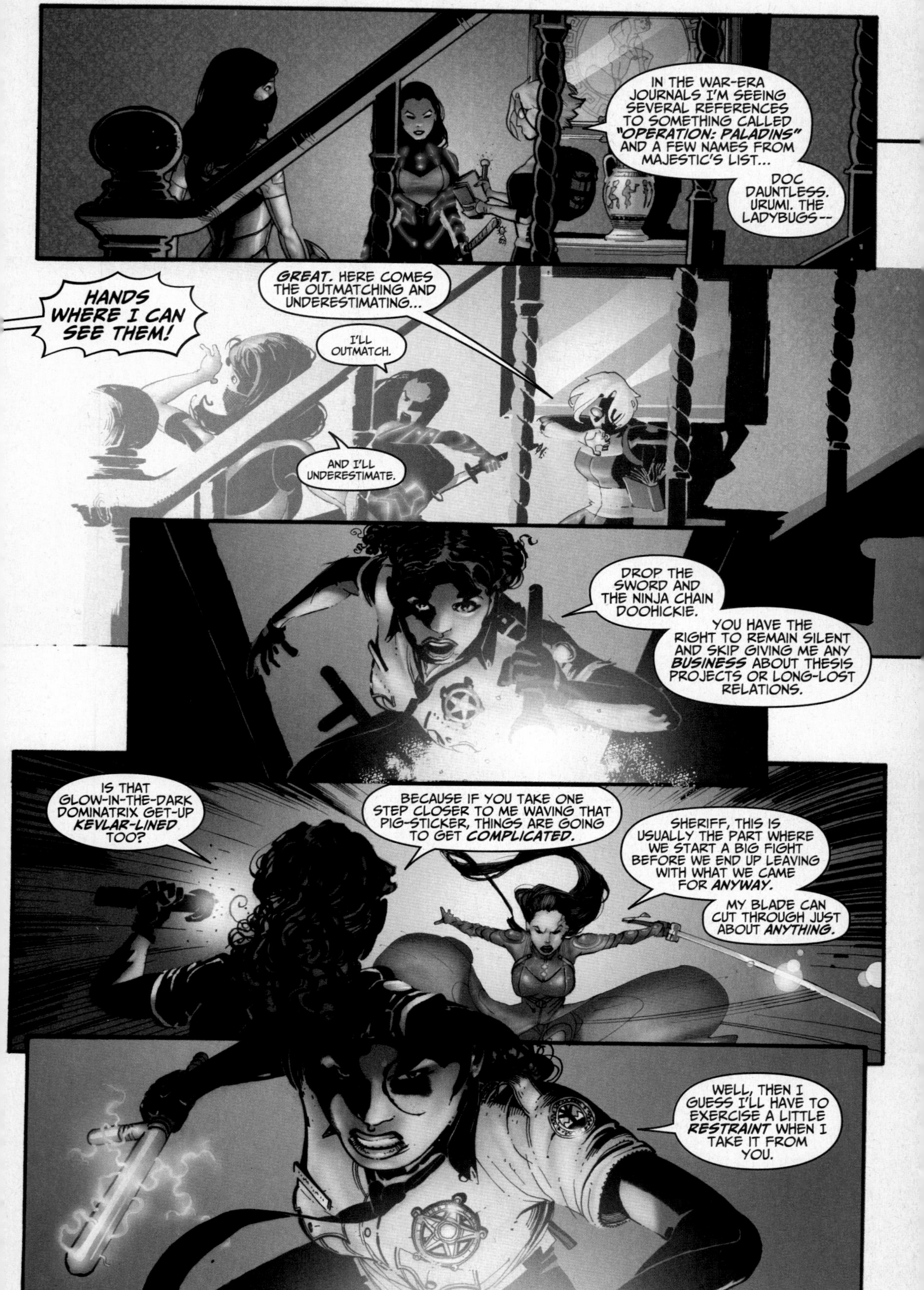
IN THE WAR-ERA JOURNALS I'M SEEING SEVERAL REFERENCES TO SOMETHING CALLED "OPERATION: PALADINS" AND A FEW NAMES FROM MAJESTIC'S LIST...
DOC DAUNTLESS. URUMI. THE LADYBUGS--
HANDS WHERE I CAN SEE THEM!
GREAT. HERE COMES THE OUTMATCHING AND UNDERESTIMATING...
I'LL OUTMATCH.
AND I'LL UNDERESTIMATE.
DROP THE SWORD AND THE NINJA CHAIN DOOHICKIE.
YOU HAVE THE RIGHT TO REMAIN SILENT AND SKIP GIVING ME ANY BUSINESS ABOUT THESIS PROJECTS OR LONG-LOST RELATIONS.
IS THAT GLOW-IN-THE-DARK DOMINATRIX GET-UP KEVLAR-LINED TOO?
BECAUSE IF YOU TAKE ONE STEP CLOSER TO ME WAVING THAT PIG-STICKER, THINGS ARE GOING TO GET COMPLICATED.
SHERIFF, THIS IS USUALLY THE PART WHERE WE START A BIG FIGHT BEFORE WE END UP LEAVING WITH WHAT WE CAME FOR ANYWAY.
MY BLADE CAN CUT THROUGH JUST ABOUT ANYTHING.
WELL, THEN I GUESS I'LL HAVE TO EXERCISE A LITTLE RESTRAINT WHEN I TAKE IT FROM YOU.

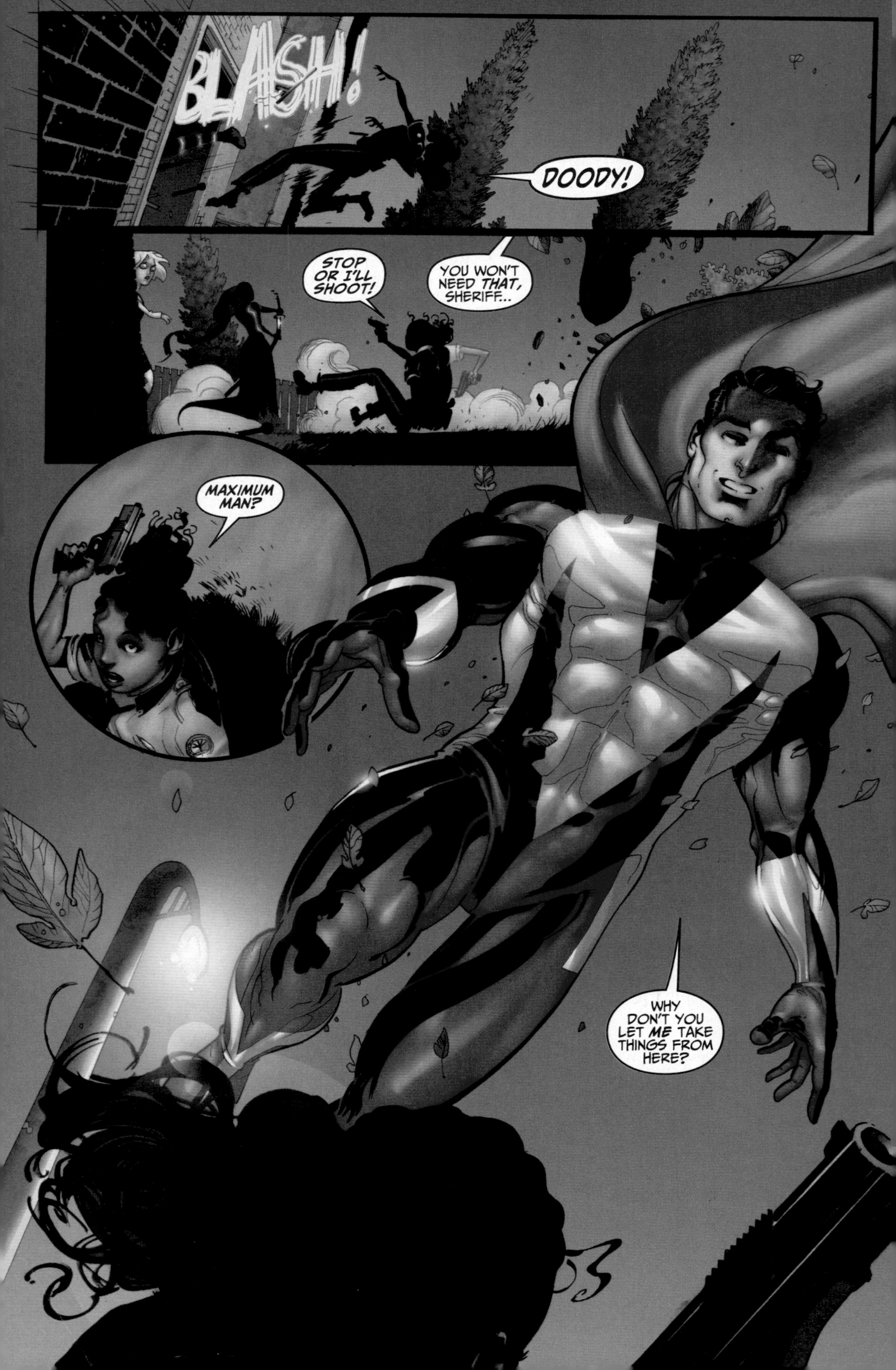
BLASH!
DOODY!
STOP OR I'LL SHOOT!
YOU WON'T NEED THAT, SHERIFF...
MAXIMUM MAN?
WHY DON'T YOU LET ME TAKE THINGS FROM HERE?

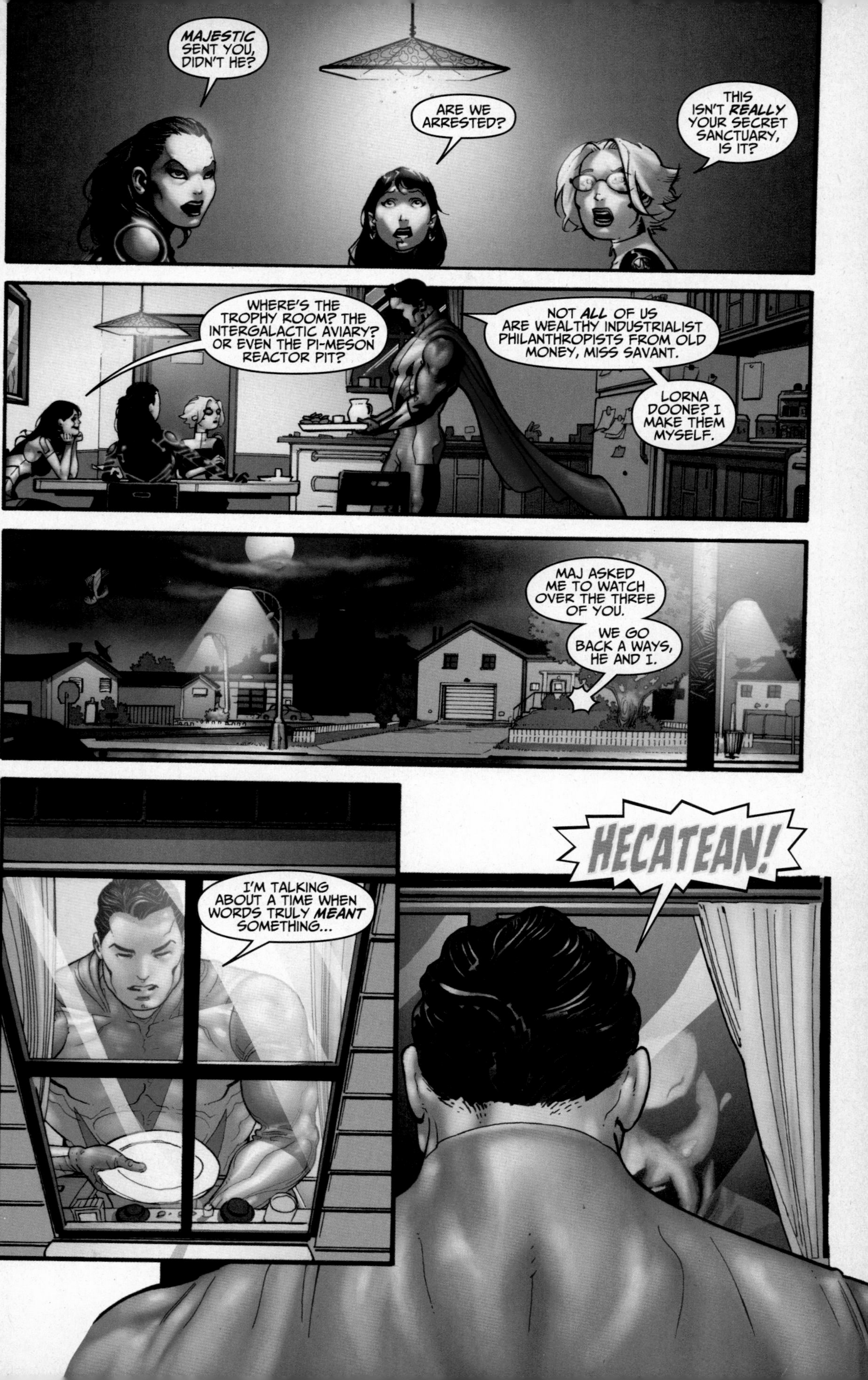
MAJESTIC SENT YOU, DIDN'T HE?
ARE WE ARRESTED?
THIS ISN'T REALLY YOUR SECRET SANCTUARY, IS IT?
WHERE'S THE TROPHY ROOM? THE INTERGALACTIC AVIARY? OR EVEN THE PI-MESON REACTOR PIT?
NOT ALL OF US ARE WEALTHY INDUSTRIALIST PHILANTHROPISTS FROM OLD MONEY, MISS SAVANT.
LORNA DOONE? I MAKE THEM MYSELF.
MAJ ASKED ME TO WATCH OVER THE THREE OF YOU.
WE GO BACK A WAYS, HE AND I.
I'M TALKING ABOUT A TIME WHEN WORDS TRULY MEANT SOMETHING...
HECATEAN!

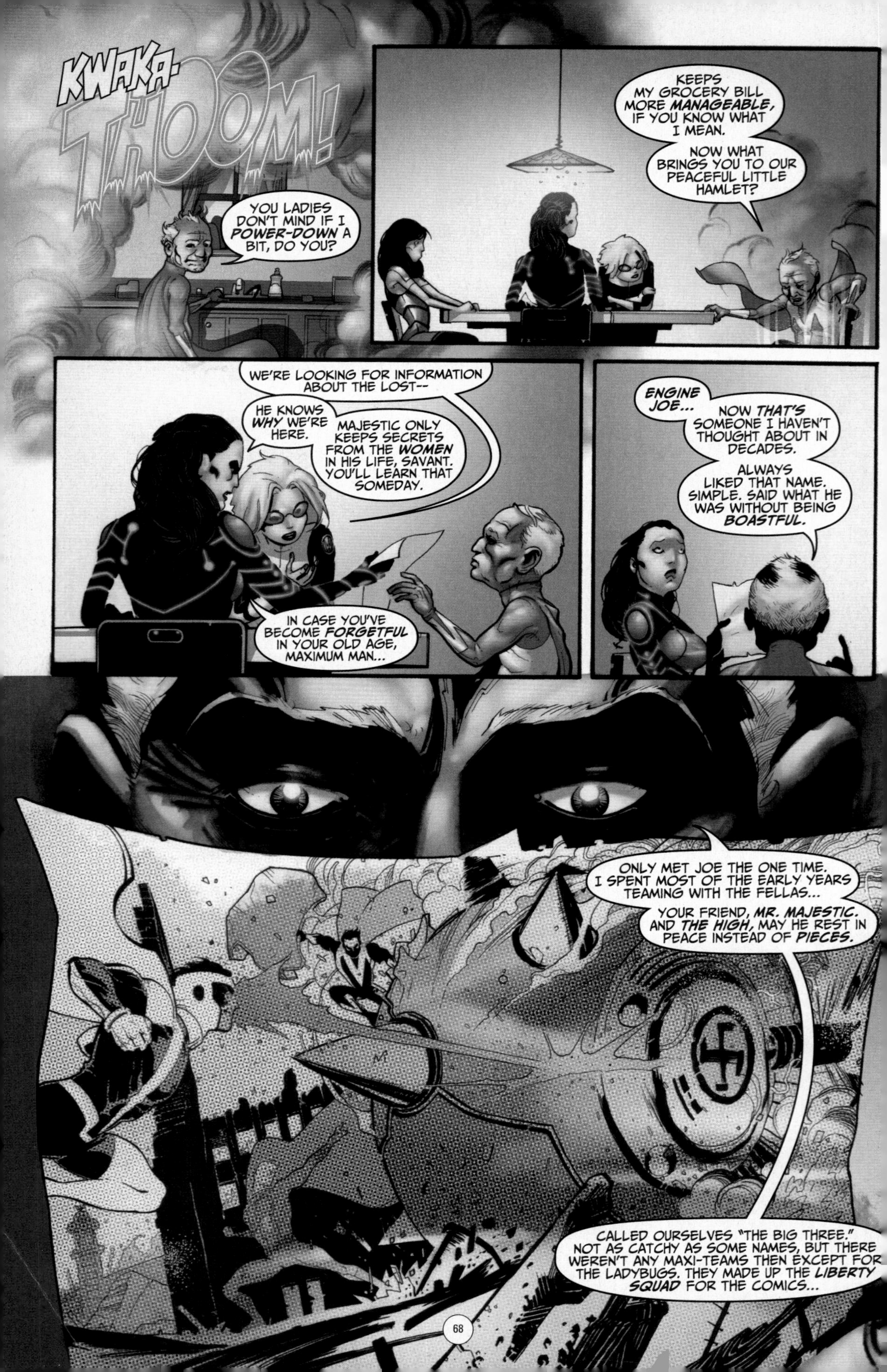

KWAKA-THOOM!
YOU LADIES DON'T MIND IF I POWER-DOWN A BIT, DO YOU?
KEEPS MY GROCERY BILL MORE MANAGEABLE, IF YOU KNOW WHAT I MEAN.
NOW WHAT BRINGS YOU TO OUR PEACEFUL LITTLE HAMLET?
WE'RE LOOKING FOR INFORMATION ABOUT THE LOST--
HE KNOWS WHY WE'RE HERE.
MAJESTIC ONLY KEEPS SECRETS FROM THE WOMEN IN HIS LIFE, SAVANT. YOU'LL LEARN THAT SOMEDAY.
IN CASE YOU'VE BECOME FORGETFUL IN YOUR OLD AGE, MAXIMUM MAN...
ENGINE JOE...
NOW THAT'S SOMEONE I HAVEN'T THOUGHT ABOUT IN DECADES.
ALWAYS LIKED THAT NAME. SIMPLE. SAID WHAT HE WAS WITHOUT BEING BOASTFUL.
ONLY MET JOE THE ONE TIME. I SPENT MOST OF THE EARLY YEARS TEAMING WITH THE FELLAS...
YOUR FRIEND, MR. MAJESTIC. AND THE HIGH, MAY HE REST IN PEACE INSTEAD OF PIECES.
CALLED OURSELVES "THE BIG THREE." NOT AS CATCHY AS SOME NAMES, BUT THERE WEREN'T ANY MAXI-TEAMS THEN EXCEPT FOR THE LADYBUGS. THEY MADE UP THE LIBERTY SQUAD FOR THE COMICS...

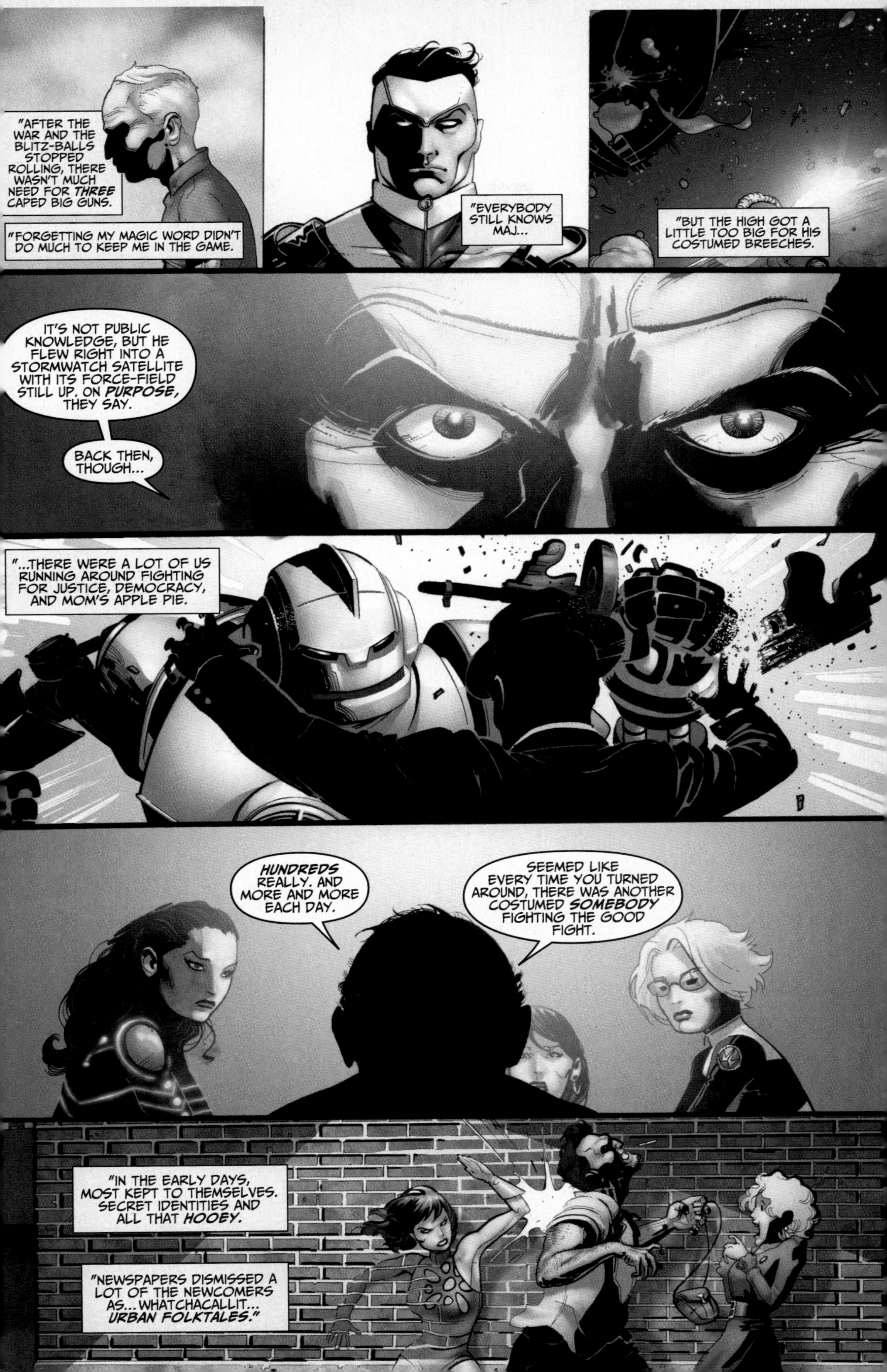

"AFTER THE WAR AND THE BLITZ-BALLS STOPPED ROLLING, THERE WASN'T MUCH NEED FOR THREE CAPED BIG GUNS.
"FORGETTING MY MAGIC WORD DIDN'T DO MUCH TO KEEP ME IN THE GAME.
"EVERYBODY STILL KNOWS MAJ...
"BUT THE HIGH GOT A LITTLE TOO BIG FOR HIS COSTUMED BREECHES.
IT'S NOT PUBLIC KNOWLEDGE, BUT HE FLEW RIGHT INTO A STORMWATCH SATELLITE WITH ITS FORCE-FIELD STILL UP. ON PURPOSE, THEY SAY.
BACK THEN, THOUGH...
"...THERE WERE A LOT OF US RUNNING AROUND FIGHTING FOR JUSTICE, DEMOCRACY, AND MOM'S APPLE PIE.
HUNDREDS REALLY. AND MORE AND MORE EACH DAY.
SEEMED LIKE EVERY TIME YOU TURNED AROUND, THERE WAS ANOTHER COSTUMED SOMEBODY FIGHTING THE GOOD FIGHT.
"IN THE EARLY DAYS, MOST KEPT TO THEMSELVES. SECRET IDENTITIES AND ALL THAT HOOEY.
"NEWSPAPERS DISMISSED A LOT OF THE NEWCOMERS AS...WHATCHACALLIT... URBAN FOLKTALES."

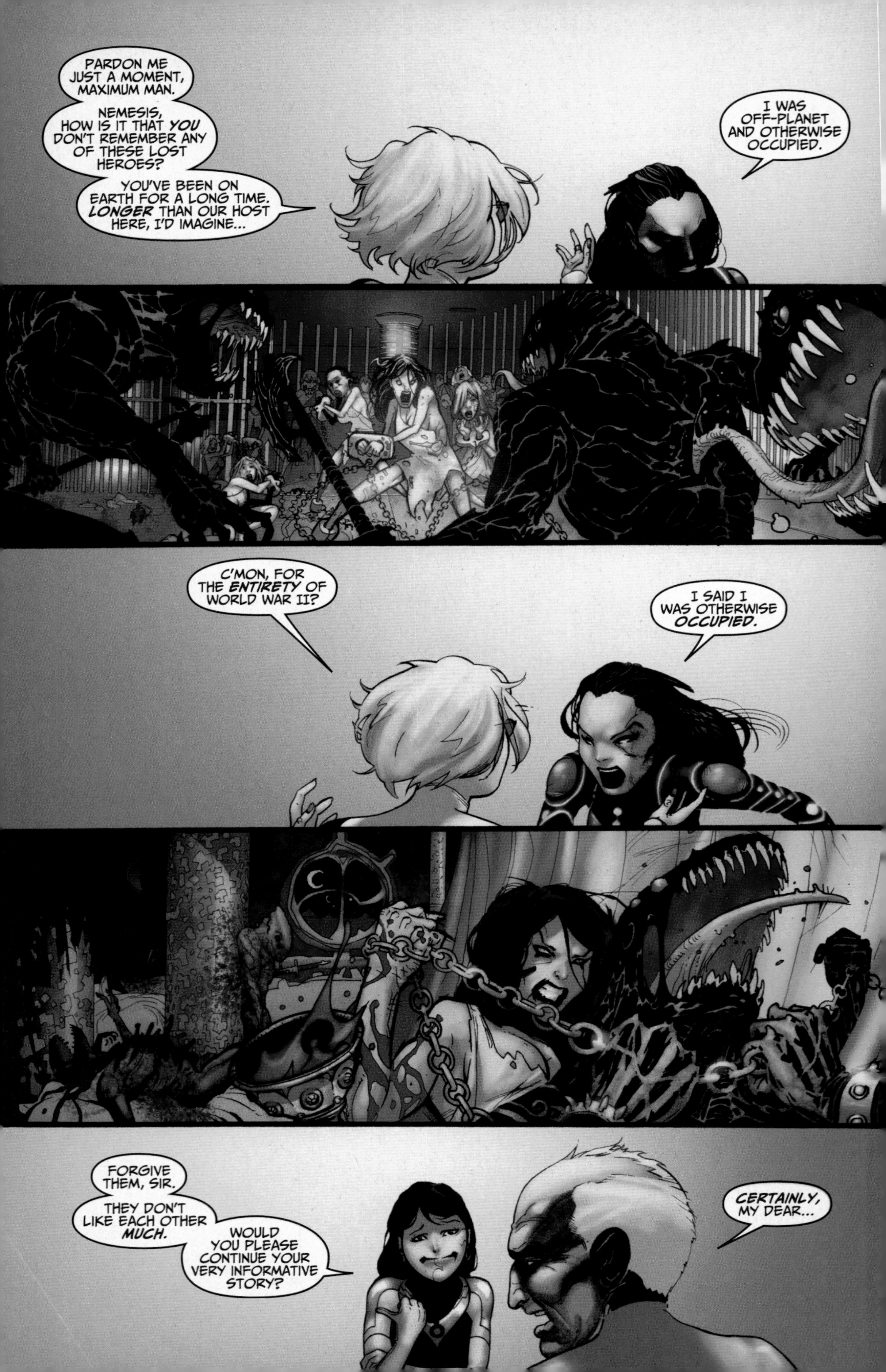
PARDON ME JUST A MOMENT, MAXIMUM MAN.
NEMESIS, HOW IS IT THAT *YOU* DON'T REMEMBER ANY OF THESE LOST HEROES?
YOU'VE BEEN ON EARTH FOR A LONG TIME. *LONGER* THAN OUR HOST HERE, I'D IMAGINE...
I WAS OFF-PLANET AND OTHERWISE OCCUPIED.
C'MON, FOR THE *ENTIRETY* OF WORLD WAR II?
I SAID I WAS OTHERWISE *OCCUPIED.*
FORGIVE THEM, SIR.
THEY DON'T LIKE EACH OTHER *MUCH.*
WOULD YOU PLEASE CONTINUE YOUR VERY INFORMATIVE STORY?
CERTAINLY, MY DEAR...

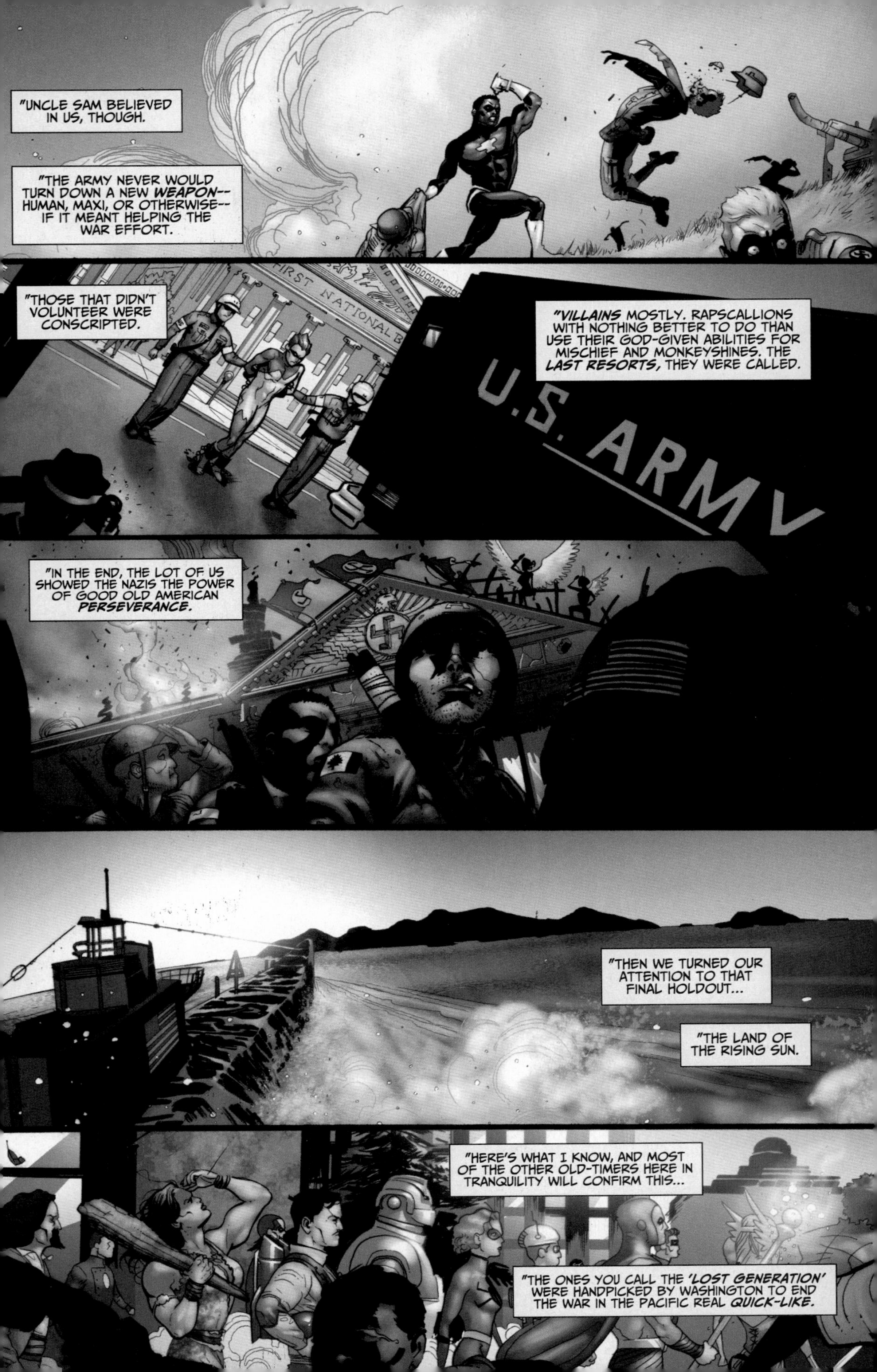
"UNCLE SAM BELIEVED IN US, THOUGH.
"THE ARMY NEVER WOULD TURN DOWN A NEW WEAPON-- HUMAN, MAXI, OR OTHERWISE-- IF IT MEANT HELPING THE WAR EFFORT.
FIRST NATIONAL B
"THOSE THAT DIDN'T VOLUNTEER WERE CONSCRIPTED.
"VILLAINS MOSTLY. RAPSCALLIONS WITH NOTHING BETTER TO DO THAN USE THEIR GOD-GIVEN ABILITIES FOR MISCHIEF AND MONKEYSHINES. THE LAST RESORTS, THEY WERE CALLED.
U.S. ARMY
"IN THE END, THE LOT OF US SHOWED THE NAZIS THE POWER OF GOOD OLD AMERICAN PERSEVERANCE.
"THEN WE TURNED OUR ATTENTION TO THAT FINAL HOLDOUT...
"THE LAND OF THE RISING SUN.
"HERE'S WHAT I KNOW, AND MOST OF THE OTHER OLD-TIMERS HERE IN TRANQUILITY WILL CONFIRM THIS...
"THE ONES YOU CALL THE 'LOST GENERATION' WERE HANDPICKED BY WASHINGTON TO END THE WAR IN THE PACIFIC REAL QUICK-LIKE.

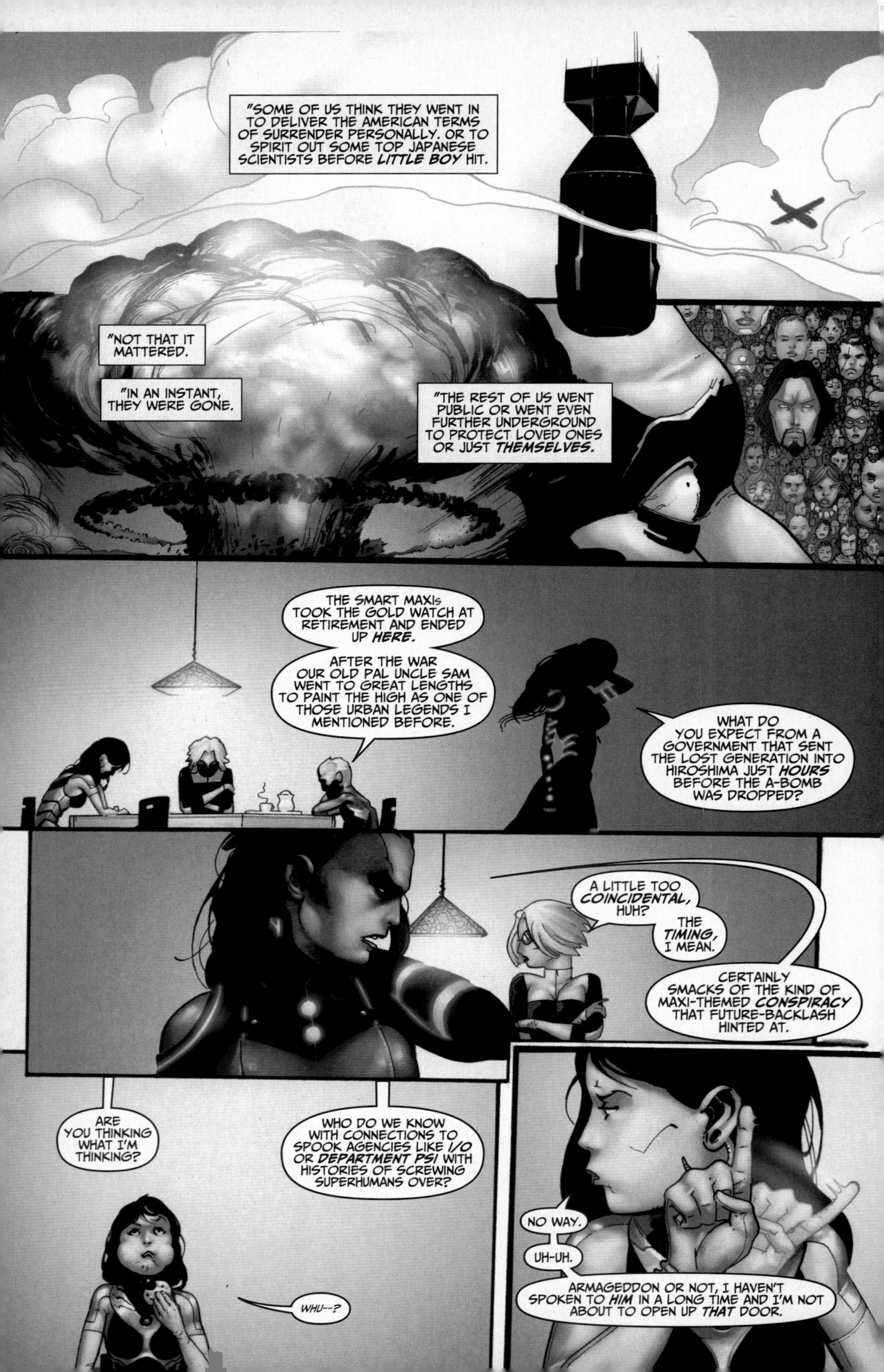
"SOME OF US THINK THEY WENT IN TO DELIVER THE AMERICAN TERMS OF SURRENDER PERSONALLY. OR TO SPIRIT OUT SOME TOP JAPANESE SCIENTISTS BEFORE LITTLE BOY HIT.
"NOT THAT IT MATTERED.
"IN AN INSTANT, THEY WERE GONE.
"THE REST OF US WENT PUBLIC OR WENT EVEN FURTHER UNDERGROUND TO PROTECT LOVED ONES OR JUST THEMSELVES.
THE SMART MAXIs TOOK THE GOLD WATCH AT RETIREMENT AND ENDED UP HERE.
AFTER THE WAR OUR OLD PAL UNCLE SAM WENT TO GREAT LENGTHS TO PAINT THE HIGH AS ONE OF THOSE URBAN LEGENDS I MENTIONED BEFORE.
WHAT DO YOU EXPECT FROM A GOVERNMENT THAT SENT THE LOST GENERATION INTO HIROSHIMA JUST HOURS BEFORE THE A-BOMB WAS DROPPED?
A LITTLE TOO COINCIDENTAL, HUH?
THE TIMING, I MEAN.
CERTAINLY SMACKS OF THE KIND OF MAXI-THEMED CONSPIRACY THAT FUTURE-BACKLASH HINTED AT.
ARE YOU THINKING WHAT I'M THINKING?
WHO DO WE KNOW WITH CONNECTIONS TO SPOOK AGENCIES LIKE I/O OR DEPARTMENT PSI WITH HISTORIES OF SCREWING SUPERHUMANS OVER?
WHU--?
NO WAY.
UH-UH.
ARMAGEDDON OR NOT, I HAVEN'T SPOKEN TO HIM IN A LONG TIME AND I'M NOT ABOUT TO OPEN UP THAT DOOR.

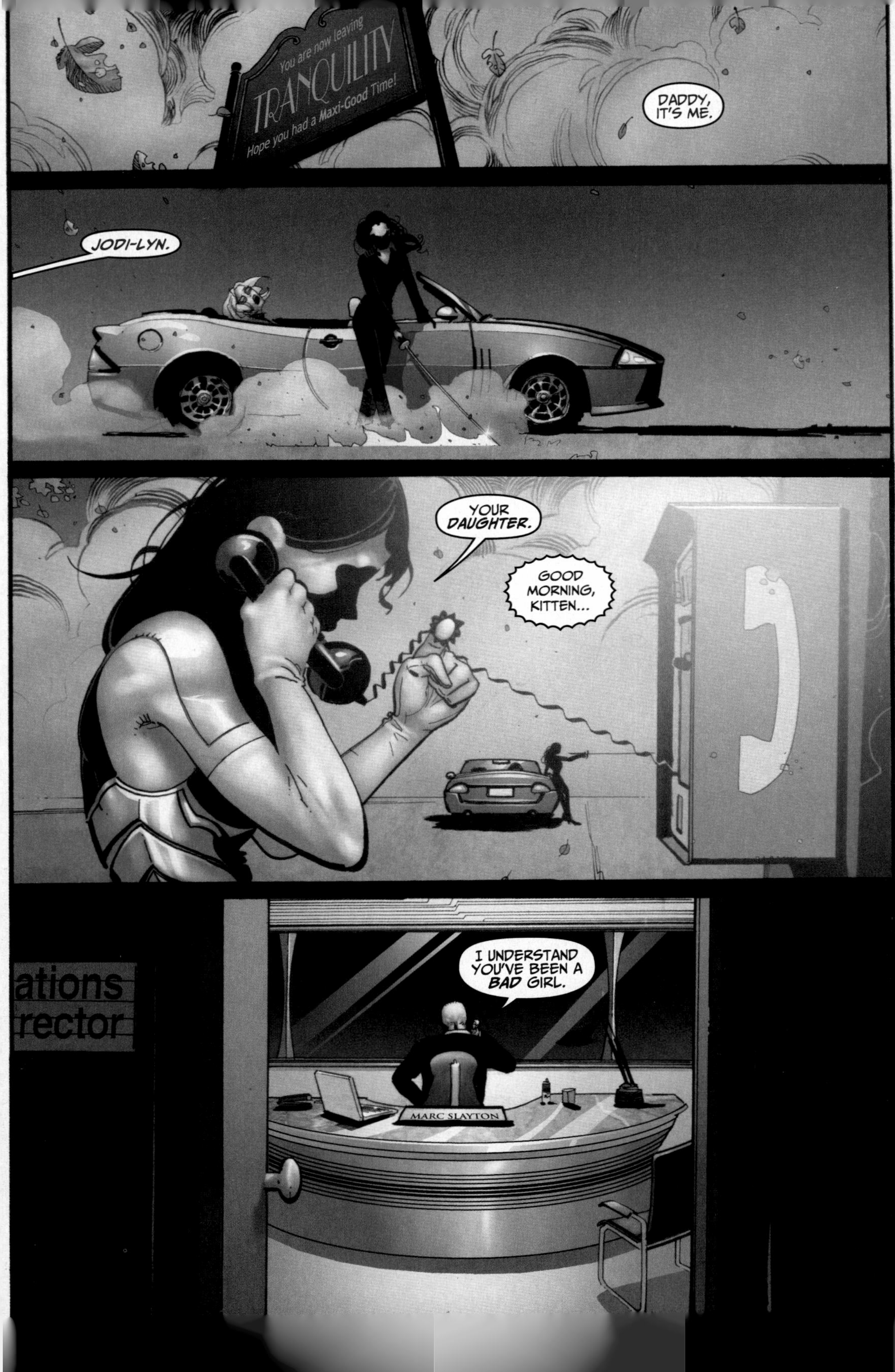
You are now leaving
TRANQUILITY
Hope you had a Maxi-Good Time!
DADDY, IT'S ME.
JODI-LYN.
YOUR DAUGHTER.
GOOD MORNING, KITTEN...
ations
rector
I UNDERSTAND YOU'VE BEEN A BAD GIRL.
MARC SLAYTON

Chapter 4

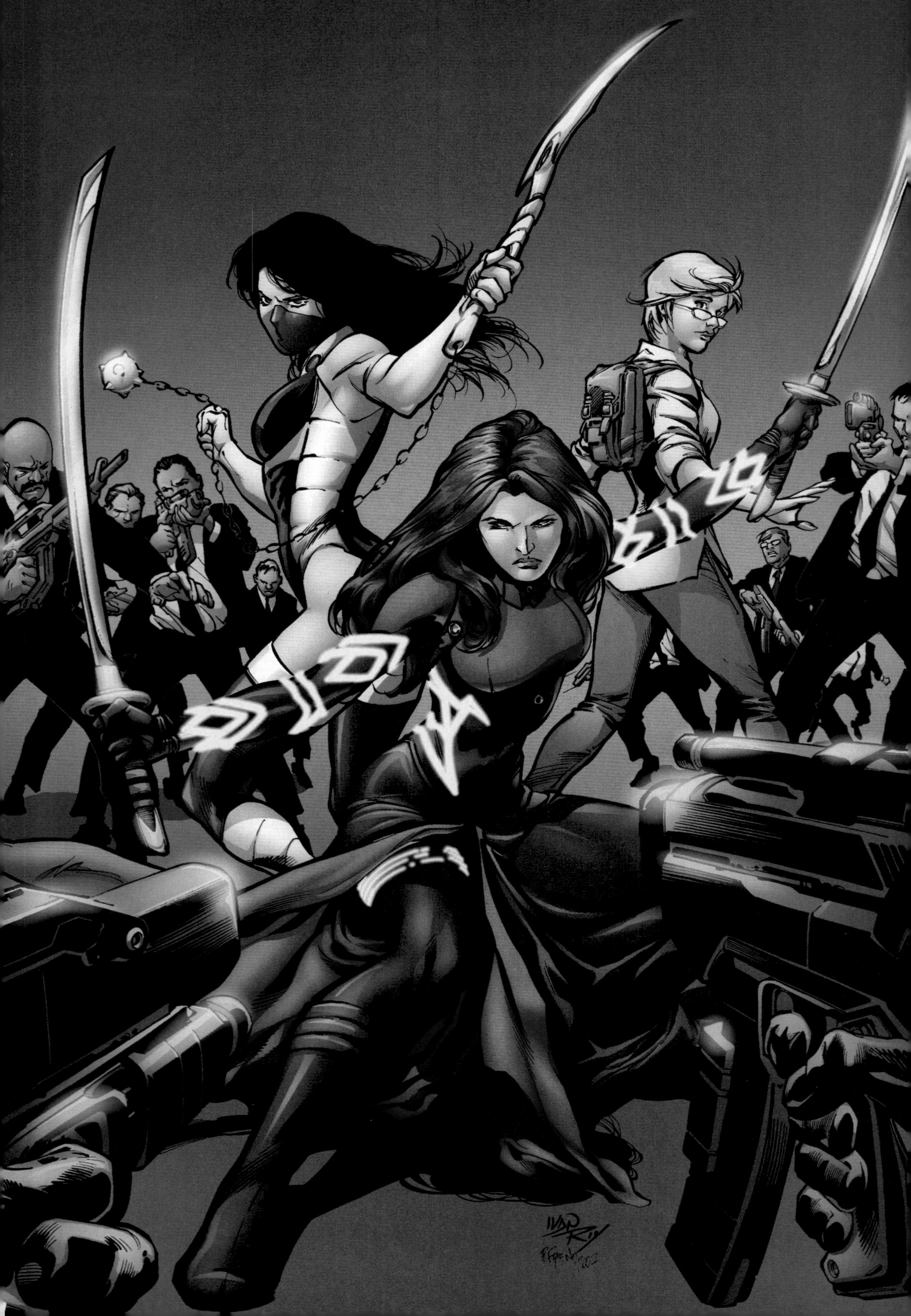

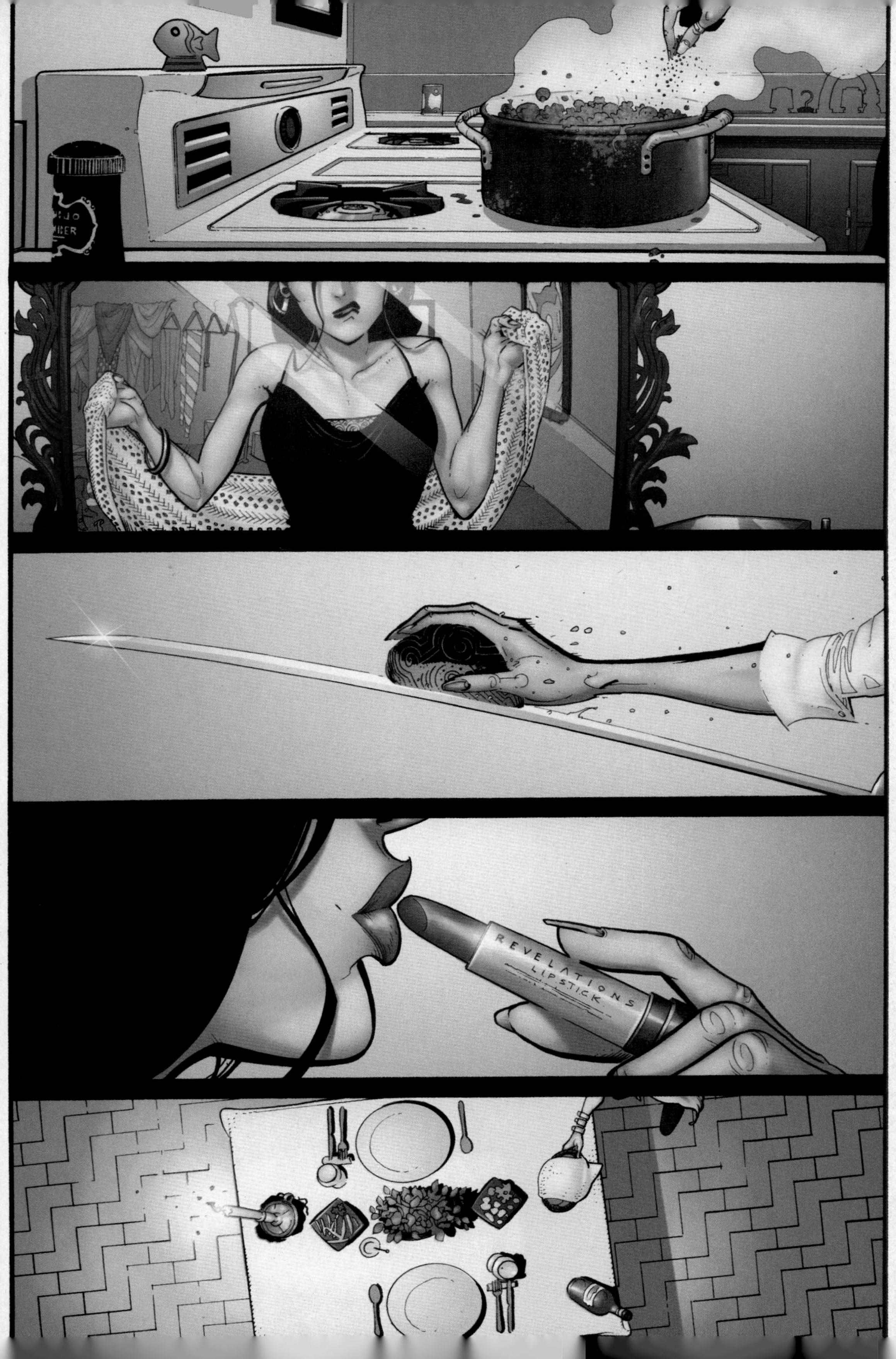
REVELATIONS
LIPSTICK

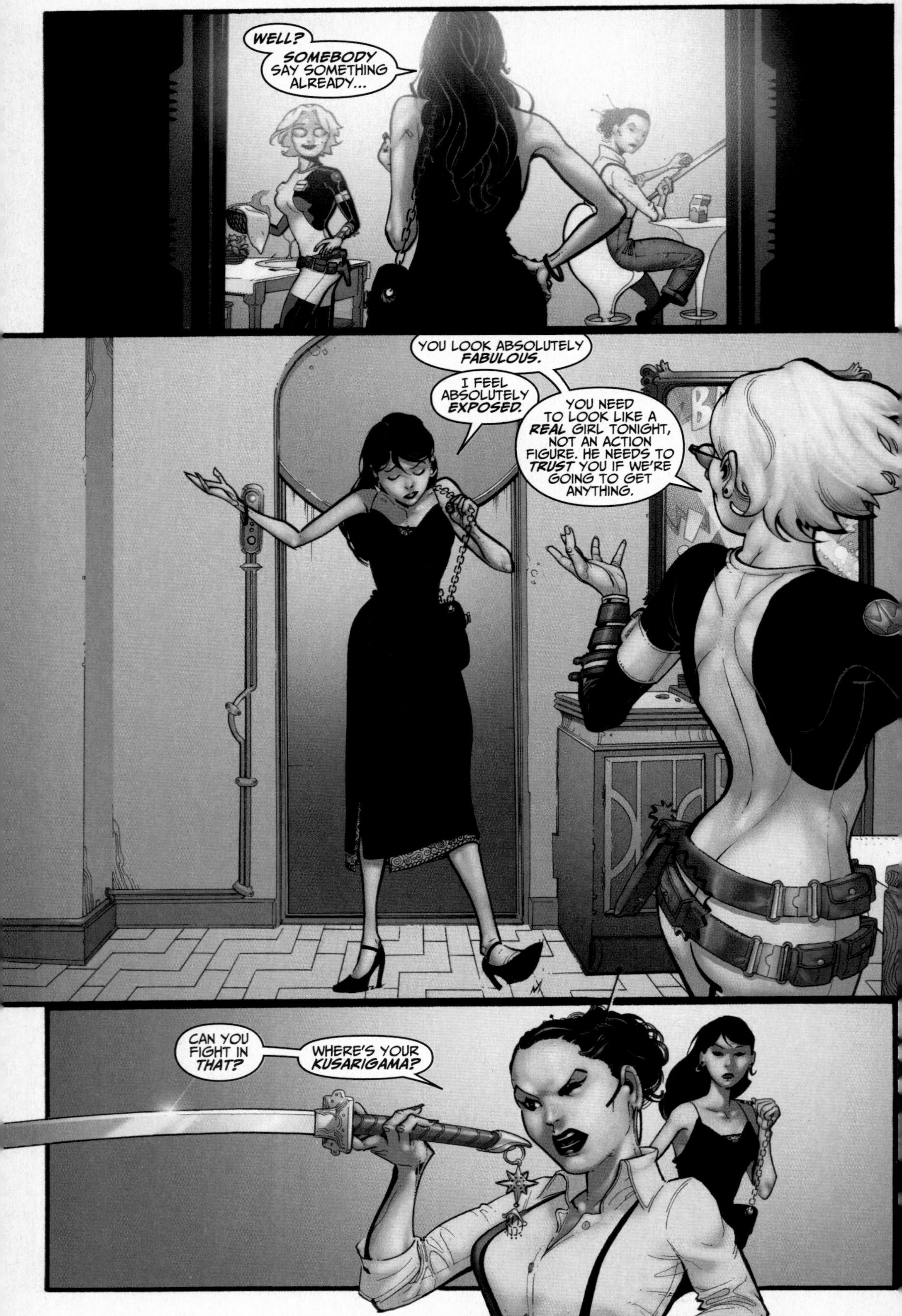
WELL? SOMEBODY SAY SOMETHING ALREADY...
YOU LOOK ABSOLUTELY FABULOUS.
I FEEL ABSOLUTELY EXPOSED.
YOU NEED TO LOOK LIKE A REAL GIRL TONIGHT, NOT AN ACTION FIGURE. HE NEEDS TO TRUST YOU IF WE'RE GOING TO GET ANYTHING.
CAN YOU FIGHT IN THAT?
WHERE'S YOUR KUSARIGAMA?

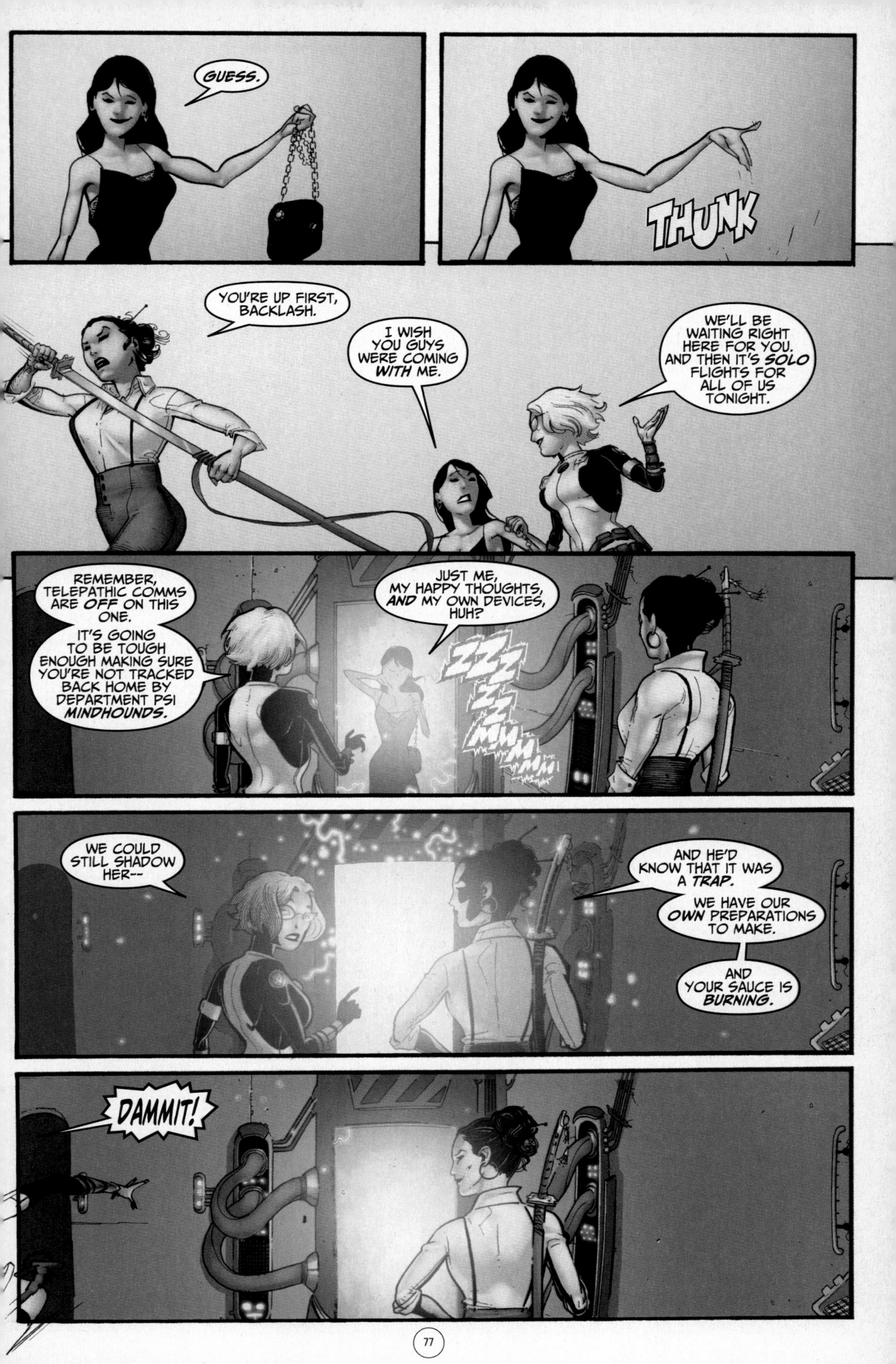
GUESS.
THUNK
YOU'RE UP FIRST, BACKLASH.
I WISH YOU GUYS WERE COMING WITH ME.
WE'LL BE WAITING RIGHT HERE FOR YOU. AND THEN IT'S SOLO FLIGHTS FOR ALL OF US TONIGHT.
REMEMBER, TELEPATHIC COMMS ARE OFF ON THIS ONE.
IT'S GOING TO BE TOUGH ENOUGH MAKING SURE YOU'RE NOT TRACKED BACK HOME BY DEPARTMENT PSI MINDHOUNDS.
JUST ME, MY HAPPY THOUGHTS, AND MY OWN DEVICES, HUH?
ZZZZZZMMMMMM
WE COULD STILL SHADOW HER--
AND HE'D KNOW THAT IT WAS A TRAP.
WE HAVE OUR OWN PREPARATIONS TO MAKE.
AND YOUR SAUCE IS BURNING.
DAMMIT!

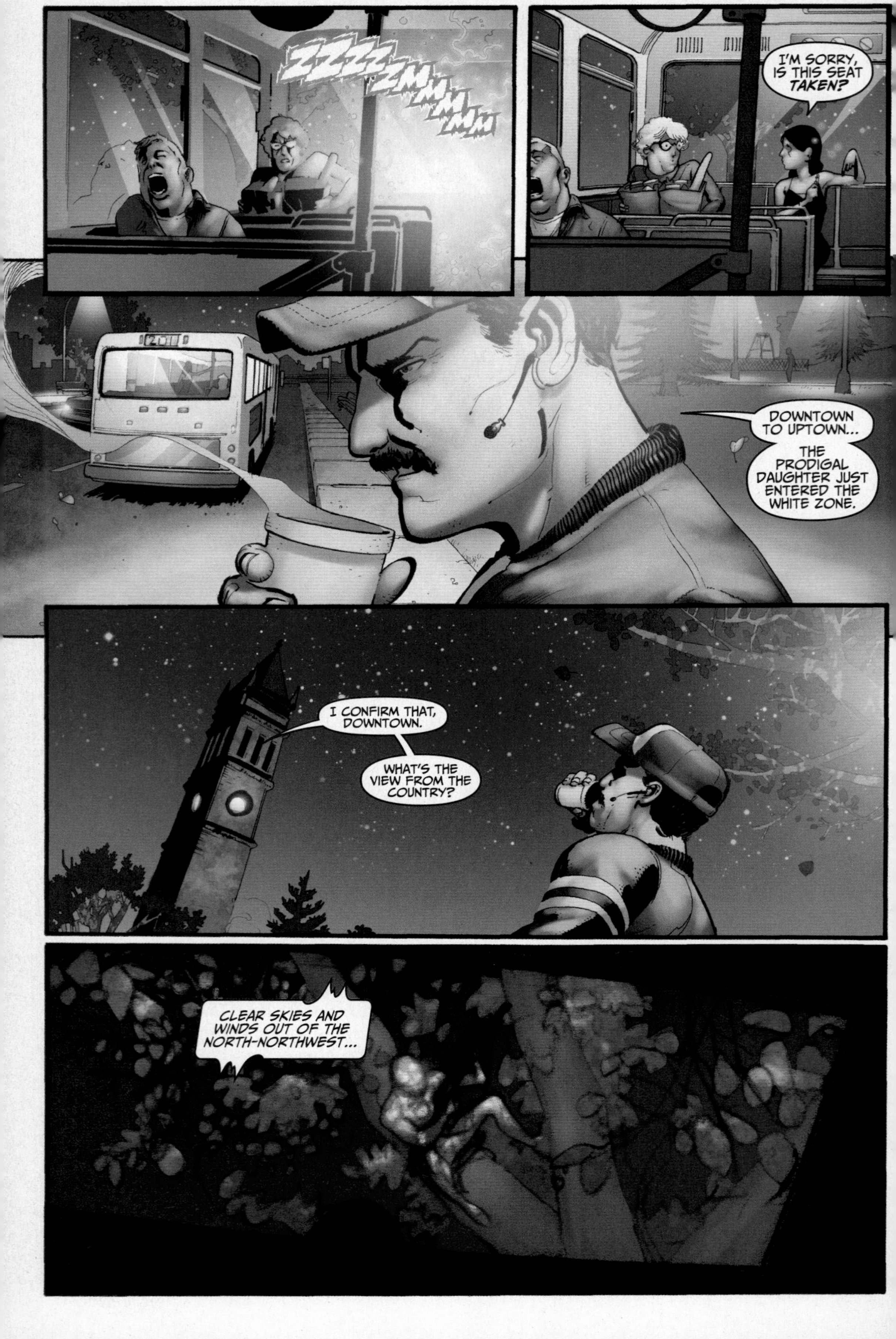
ZZZZZMMMMMMM
I'M SORRY, IS THIS SEAT TAKEN?
DOWNTOWN TO UPTOWN...
THE PRODIGAL DAUGHTER JUST ENTERED THE WHITE ZONE.
I CONFIRM THAT, DOWNTOWN.
WHAT'S THE VIEW FROM THE COUNTRY?
CLEAR SKIES AND WINDS OUT OF THE NORTH-NORTHWEST...

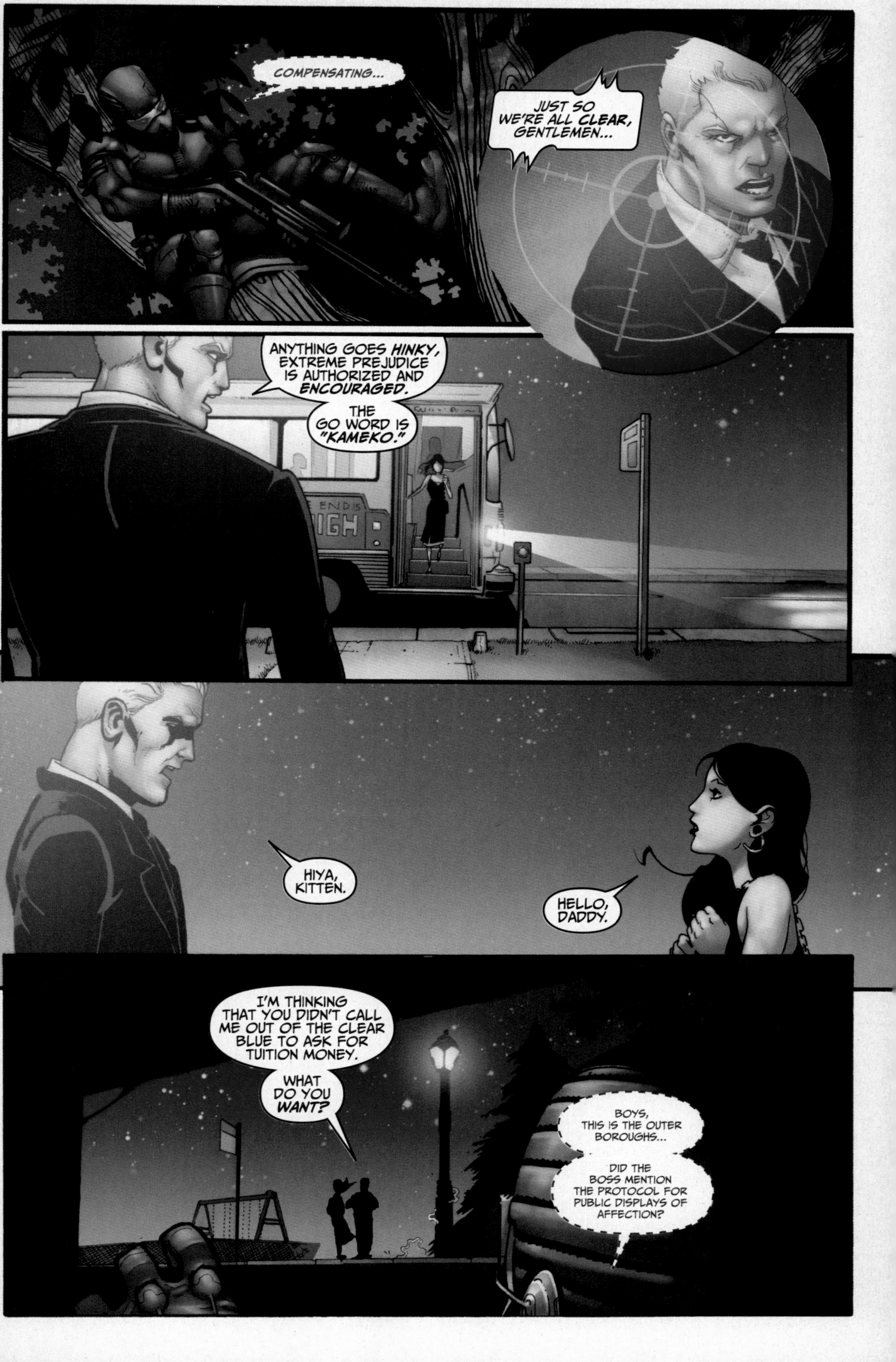
COMPENSATING...
JUST SO WE'RE ALL CLEAR, GENTLEMEN...
ANYTHING GOES HINKY, EXTREME PREJUDICE IS AUTHORIZED AND ENCOURAGED.
THE GO WORD IS "KAMEKO."
HIYA, KITTEN.
HELLO, DADDY.
I'M THINKING THAT YOU DIDN'T CALL ME OUT OF THE CLEAR BLUE TO ASK FOR TUITION MONEY.
WHAT DO YOU WANT?
BOYS, THIS IS THE OUTER BOROUGHS...
DID THE BOSS MENTION THE PROTOCOL FOR PUBLIC DISPLAYS OF AFFECTION?

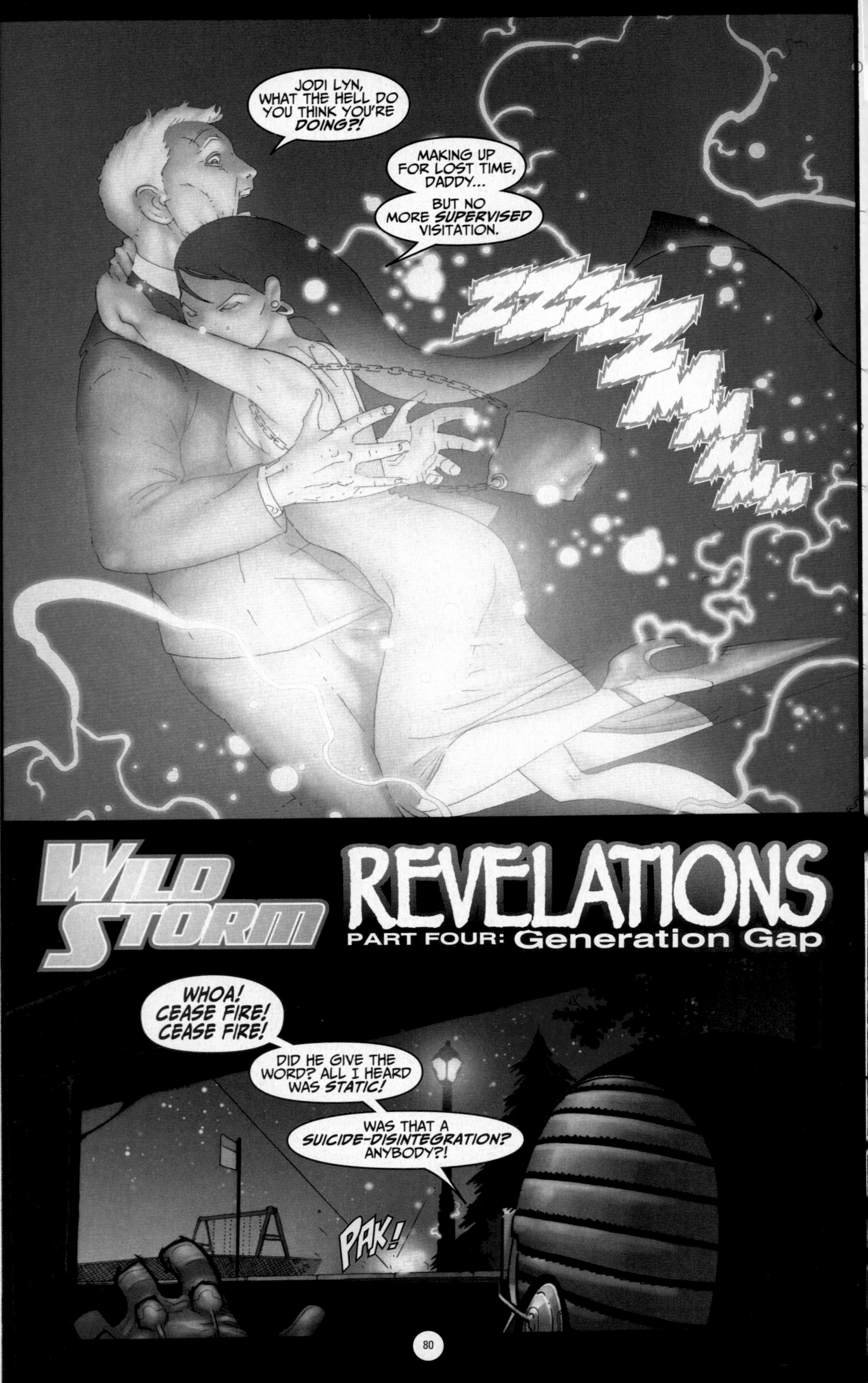
JODI LYN, WHAT THE HELL DO YOU THINK YOU'RE DOING?!
MAKING UP FOR LOST TIME, DADDY...
BUT NO MORE SUPERVISED VISITATION.
ZZZZMMMMMN
WILD STORM
REVELATIONS
PART FOUR: Generation Gap
WHOA! CEASE FIRE! CEASE FIRE!
DID HE GIVE THE WORD? ALL I HEARD WAS STATIC!
WAS THAT A SUICIDE-DISINTEGRATION? ANYBODY?!
PAK!

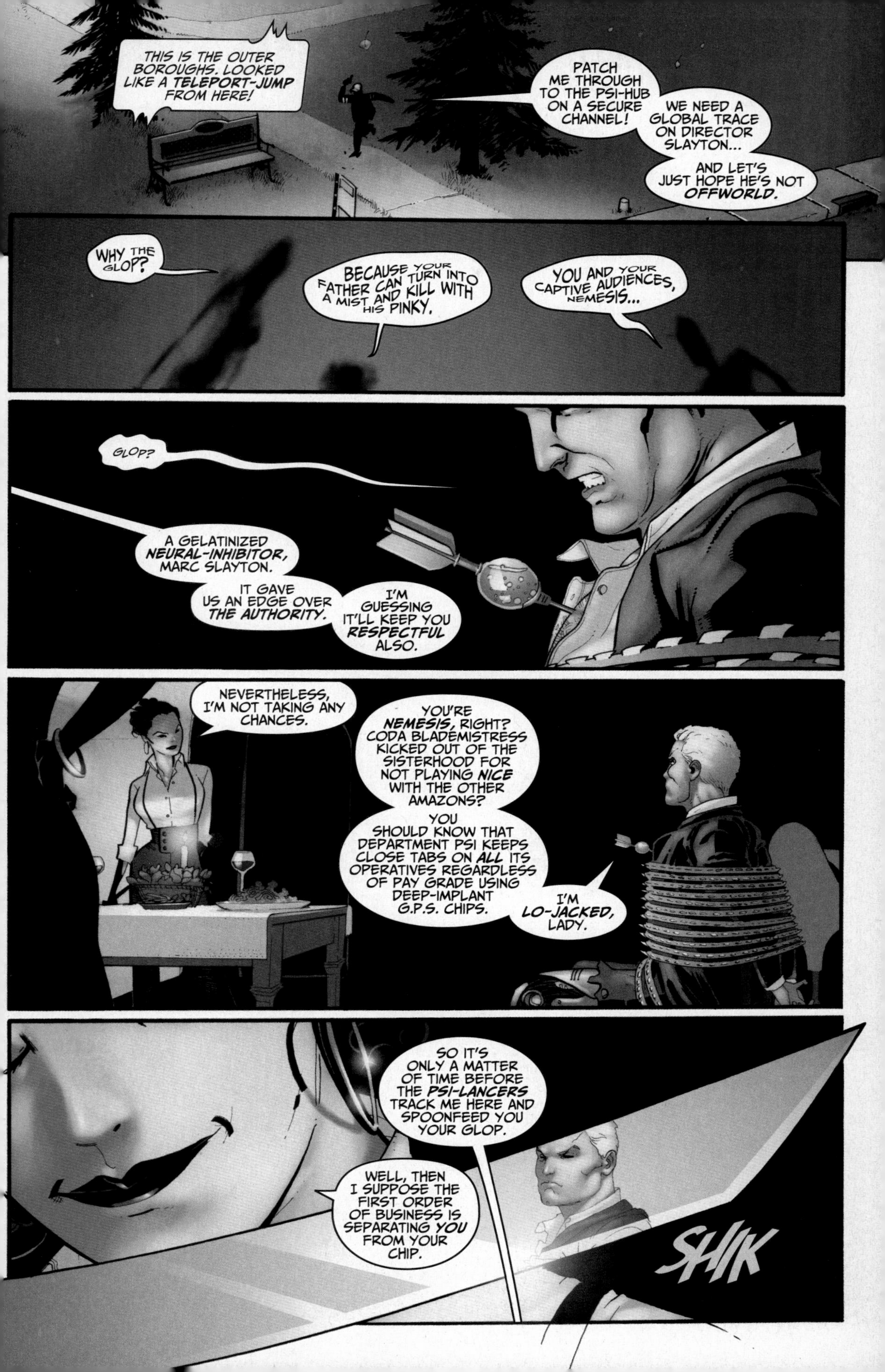
THIS IS THE OUTER BOROUGHS. LOOKED LIKE A TELEPORT-JUMP FROM HERE!
PATCH ME THROUGH TO THE PSI-HUB ON A SECURE CHANNEL!
WE NEED A GLOBAL TRACE ON DIRECTOR SLAYTON...
AND LET'S JUST HOPE HE'S NOT OFFWORLD.
WHY THE GLOP?
BECAUSE YOUR FATHER CAN TURN INTO A MIST AND KILL WITH HIS PINKY.
YOU AND YOUR CAPTIVE AUDIENCES, NEMESIS...
GLOP?
A GELATINIZED NEURAL-INHIBITOR, MARC SLAYTON.
IT GAVE US AN EDGE OVER THE AUTHORITY.
I'M GUESSING IT'LL KEEP YOU RESPECTFUL ALSO.
NEVERTHELESS, I'M NOT TAKING ANY CHANCES.
YOU'RE NEMESIS, RIGHT? CODA BLADEMISTRESS KICKED OUT OF THE SISTERHOOD FOR NOT PLAYING NICE WITH THE OTHER AMAZONS?
YOU SHOULD KNOW THAT DEPARTMENT PSI KEEPS CLOSE TABS ON ALL ITS OPERATIVES REGARDLESS OF PAY GRADE USING DEEP-IMPLANT G.P.S. CHIPS.
I'M LO-JACKED, LADY.
SO IT'S ONLY A MATTER OF TIME BEFORE THE PSI-LANCERS TRACK ME HERE AND SPOONFEED YOU YOUR GLOP.
WELL, THEN I SUPPOSE THE FIRST ORDER OF BUSINESS IS SEPARATING YOU FROM YOUR CHIP.
SHIK

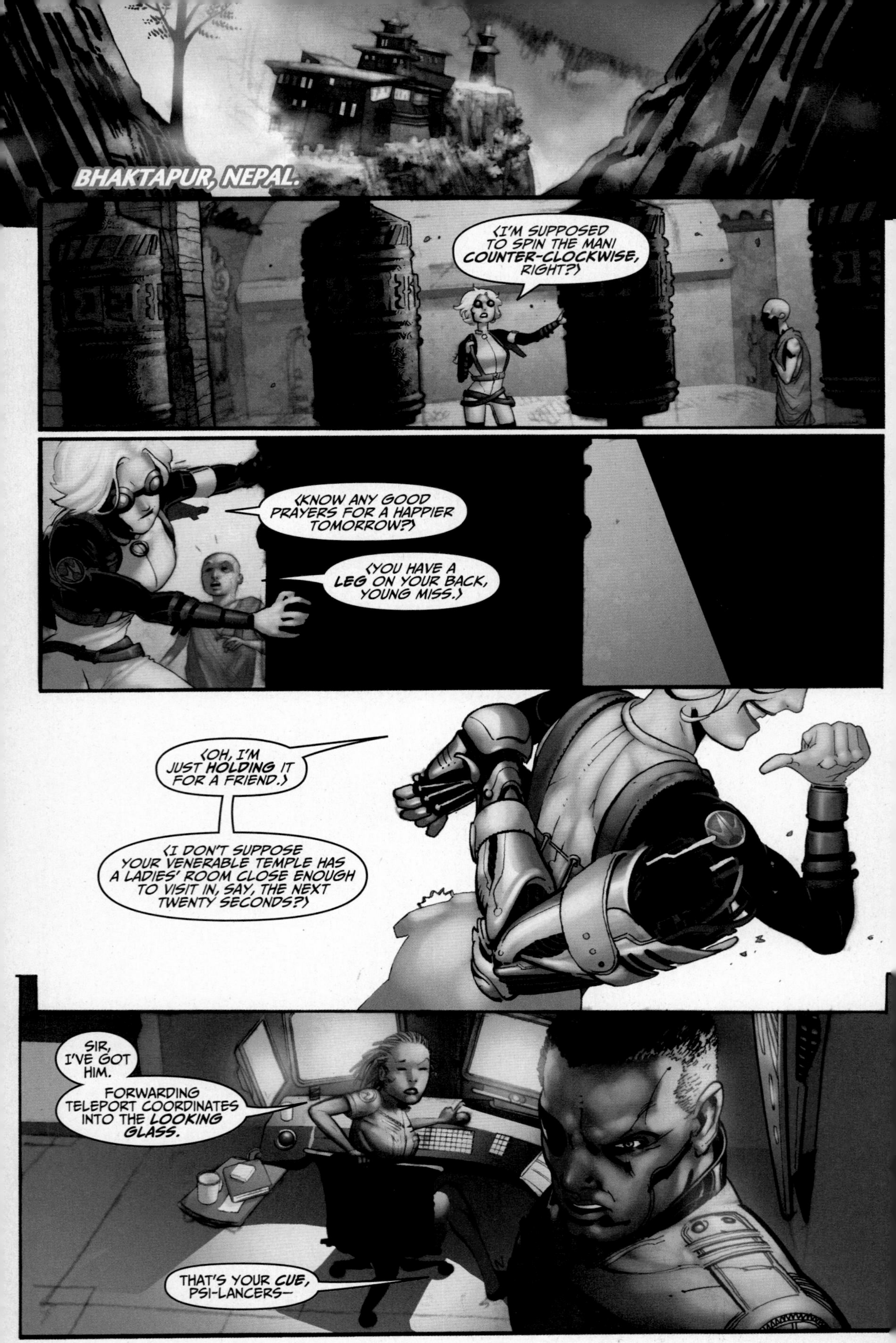
BHAKTAPUR, NEPAL.
⟨I'M SUPPOSED TO SPIN THE MANI COUNTER-CLOCKWISE, RIGHT?⟩
⟨KNOW ANY GOOD PRAYERS FOR A HAPPIER TOMORROW?⟩
⟨YOU HAVE A LEG ON YOUR BACK, YOUNG MISS.⟩
⟨OH, I'M JUST HOLDING IT FOR A FRIEND.⟩
⟨I DON'T SUPPOSE YOUR VENERABLE TEMPLE HAS A LADIES' ROOM CLOSE ENOUGH TO VISIT IN, SAY, THE NEXT TWENTY SECONDS?⟩
SIR, I'VE GOT HIM.
FORWARDING TELEPORT COORDINATES INTO THE LOOKING GLASS.
THAT'S YOUR CUE, PSI-LANCERS—

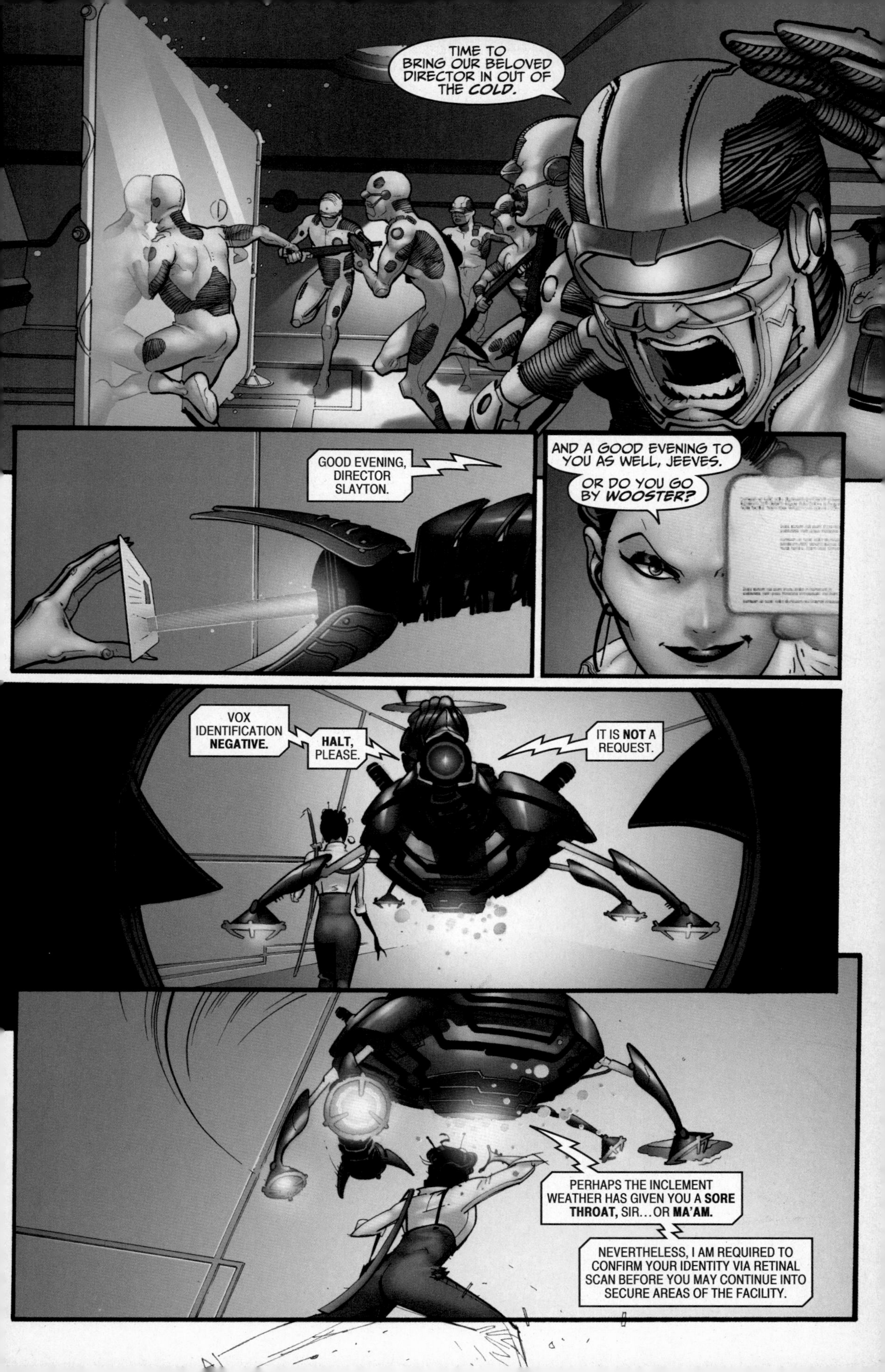
TIME TO BRING OUR BELOVED DIRECTOR IN OUT OF THE *COLD.*
GOOD EVENING, DIRECTOR SLAYTON.
AND A GOOD EVENING TO YOU AS WELL, JEEVES.
OR DO YOU GO BY *WOOSTER?*
VOX IDENTIFICATION **NEGATIVE.**
HALT, PLEASE.
IT IS **NOT** A REQUEST.
PERHAPS THE INCLEMENT WEATHER HAS GIVEN YOU A **SORE THROAT,** SIR...OR **MA'AM.**
NEVERTHELESS, I AM REQUIRED TO CONFIRM YOUR IDENTITY VIA RETINAL SCAN BEFORE YOU MAY CONTINUE INTO SECURE AREAS OF THE FACILITY.

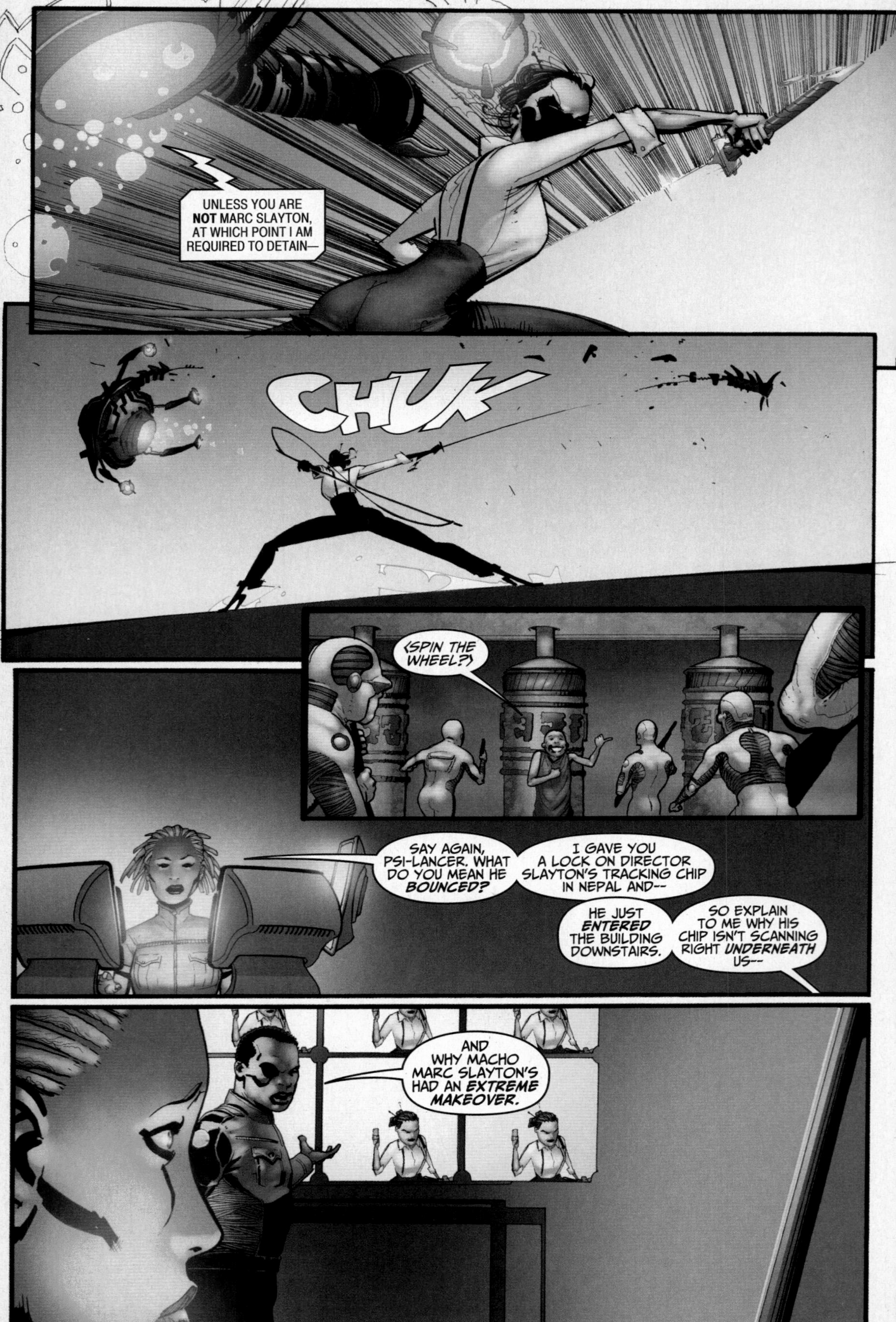

UNLESS YOU ARE NOT MARC SLAYTON, AT WHICH POINT I AM REQUIRED TO DETAIN—
CHUK
‹SPIN THE WHEEL?›
SAY AGAIN, PSI-LANCER. WHAT DO YOU MEAN HE BOUNCED?
I GAVE YOU A LOCK ON DIRECTOR SLAYTON'S TRACKING CHIP IN NEPAL AND--
HE JUST ENTERED THE BUILDING DOWNSTAIRS.
SO EXPLAIN TO ME WHY HIS CHIP ISN'T SCANNING RIGHT UNDERNEATH US--
AND WHY MACHO MARC SLAYTON'S HAD AN EXTREME MAKEOVER.

I AM *NOT AMUSED,* JODI LYN.

BUT WE WORKED SO HARD TO PLAN THIS EVENING, DADDY.

THERE'S A LOT AT STAKE HERE.

WHERE'S MY *DAMN* LEG?

I CAN'T SAY.

AND EVEN IF I KNEW *EXACTLY,* I'D BE SWORN TO SECRECY.

BUT I'M SURE IT'S HAVING A GOOD TIME WITH MY FRIEND, *WHEREVER* SHE IS...

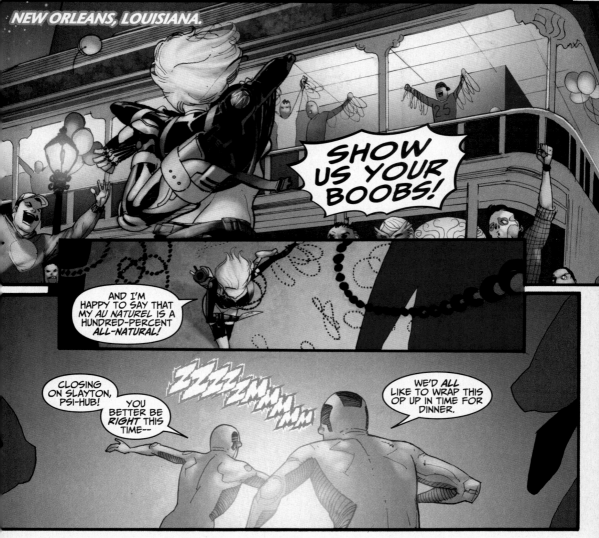

NEW ORLEANS, LOUISIANA.

SHOW US YOUR BOOBS!

AND I'M HAPPY TO SAY THAT MY *AU NATUREL* IS A HUNDRED-PERCENT *ALL-NATURAL!*

CLOSING ON SLAYTON, PSI-HUB! YOU BETTER BE *RIGHT* THIS TIME--

WE'D *ALL* LIKE TO WRAP THIS UP IN TIME FOR DINNER.

ZZZZMMMM

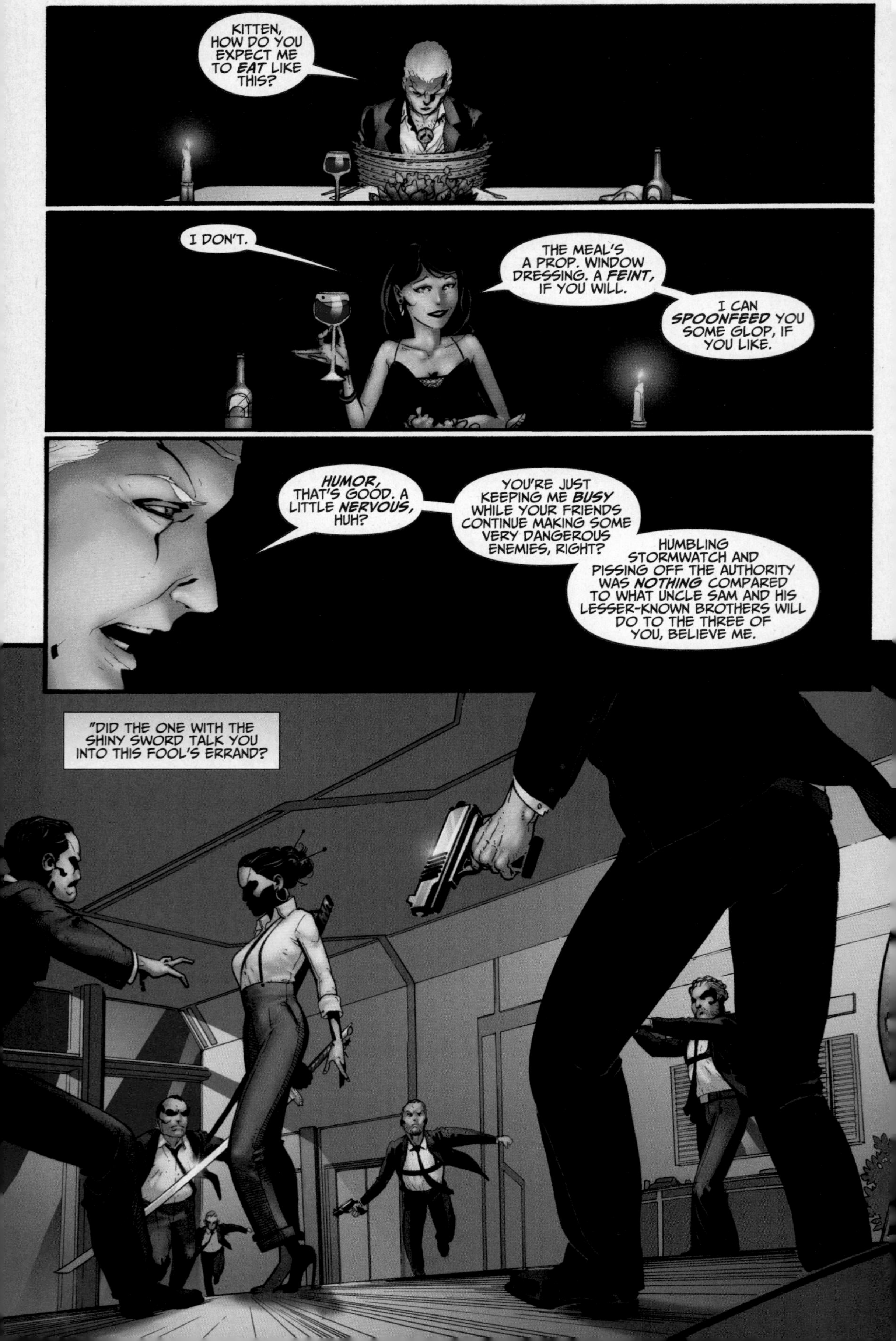
KITTEN, HOW DO YOU EXPECT ME TO EAT LIKE THIS?
I DON'T.
THE MEAL'S A PROP. WINDOW DRESSING. A FEINT, IF YOU WILL.
I CAN SPOONFEED YOU SOME GLOP, IF YOU LIKE.
HUMOR, THAT'S GOOD. A LITTLE NERVOUS, HUH?
YOU'RE JUST KEEPING ME BUSY WHILE YOUR FRIENDS CONTINUE MAKING SOME VERY DANGEROUS ENEMIES, RIGHT?
HUMBLING STORMWATCH AND PISSING OFF THE AUTHORITY WAS NOTHING COMPARED TO WHAT UNCLE SAM AND HIS LESSER-KNOWN BROTHERS WILL DO TO THE THREE OF YOU, BELIEVE ME.
"DID THE ONE WITH THE SHINY SWORD TALK YOU INTO THIS FOOL'S ERRAND?

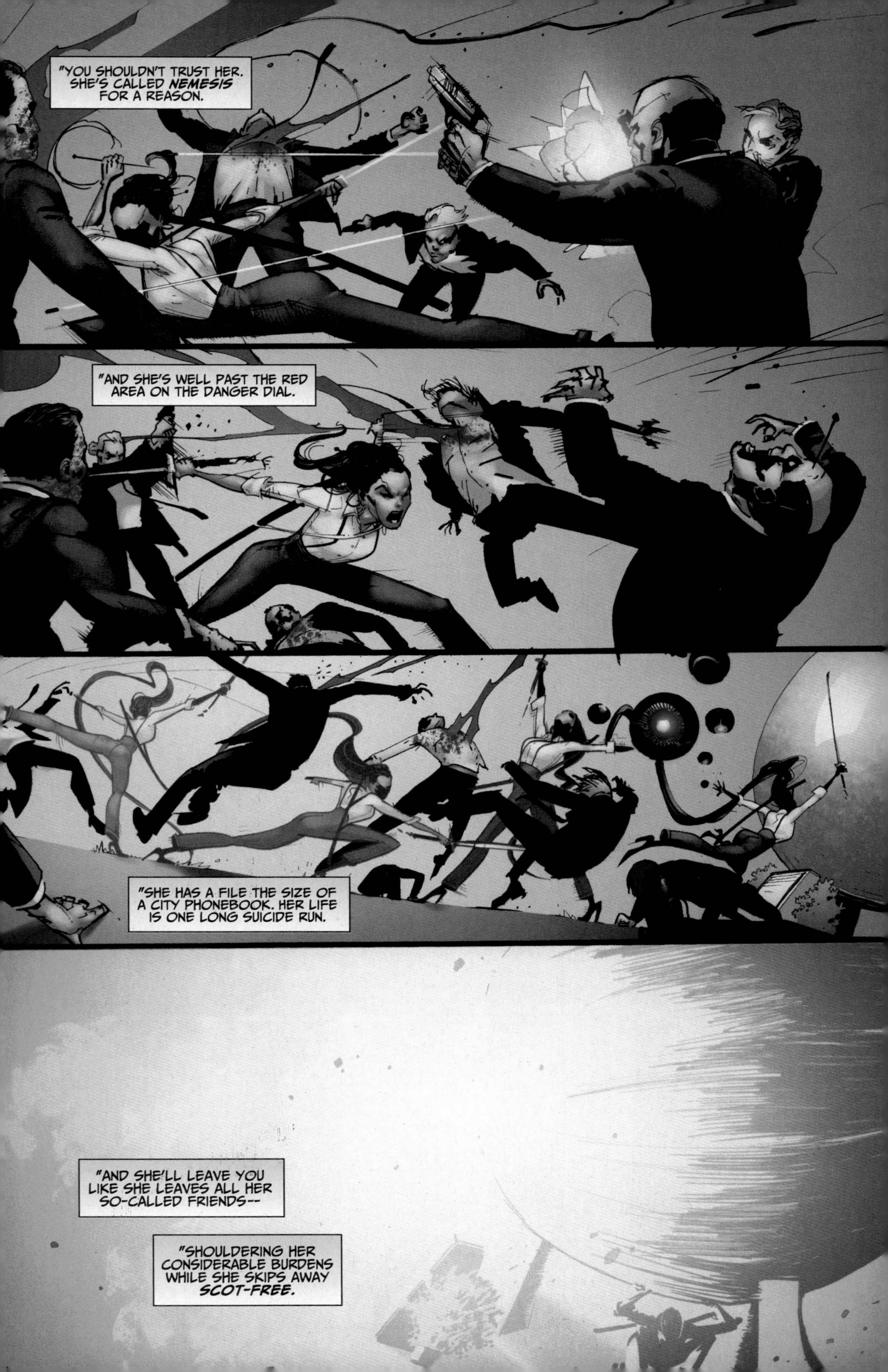
"YOU SHOULDN'T TRUST HER. SHE'S CALLED *NEMESIS* FOR A REASON.
"AND SHE'S WELL PAST THE RED AREA ON THE DANGER DIAL.
"SHE HAS A FILE THE SIZE OF A CITY PHONEBOOK. HER LIFE IS ONE LONG SUICIDE RUN.
"AND SHE'LL LEAVE YOU LIKE SHE LEAVES ALL HER SO-CALLED FRIENDS--
"SHOULDERING HER CONSIDERABLE BURDENS WHILE SHE SKIPS AWAY *SCOT-FREE*.

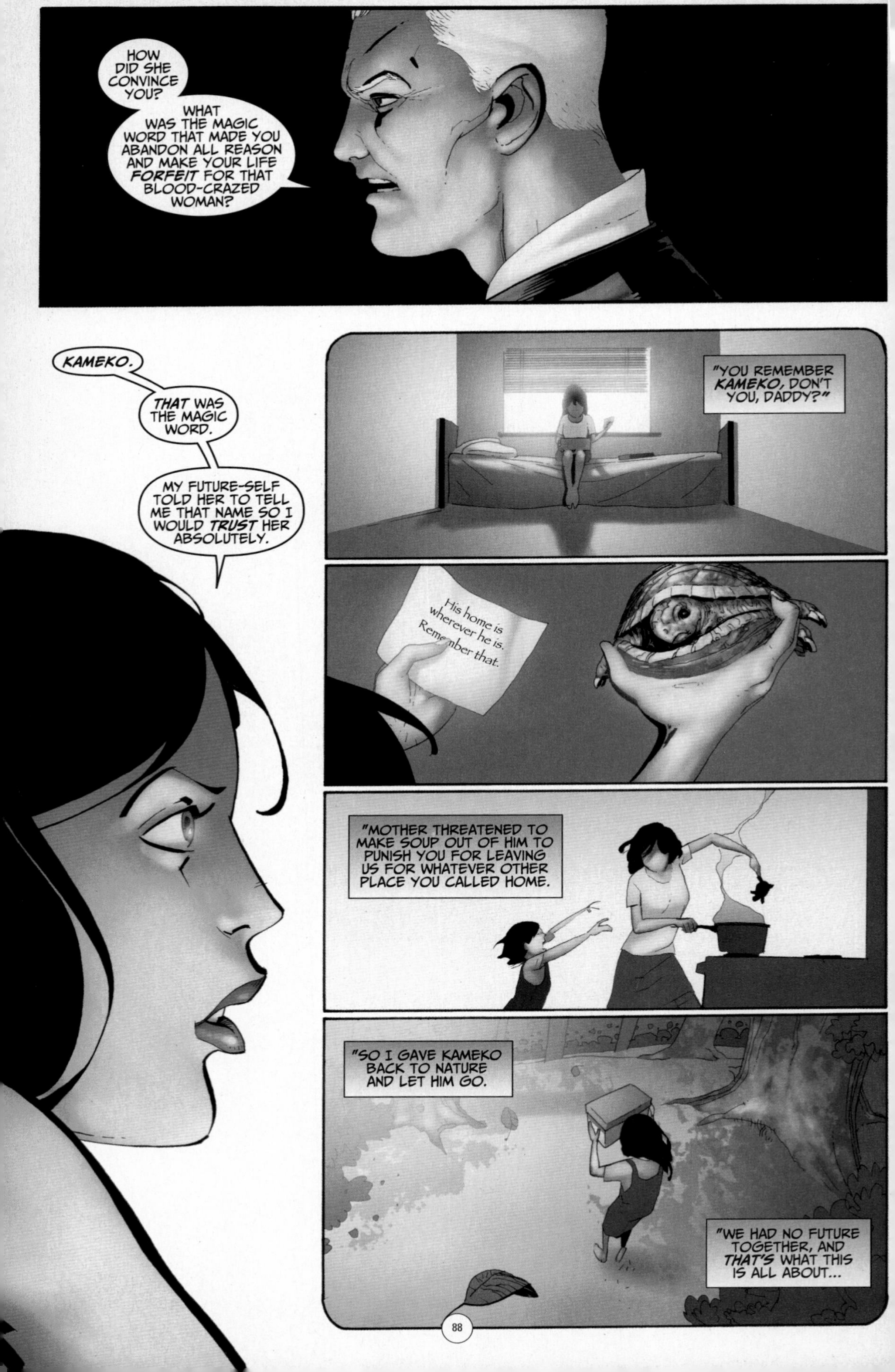
HOW DID SHE CONVINCE YOU?
WHAT WAS THE MAGIC WORD THAT MADE YOU ABANDON ALL REASON AND MAKE YOUR LIFE FORFEIT FOR THAT BLOOD-CRAZED WOMAN?
KAMEKO.
THAT WAS THE MAGIC WORD.
MY FUTURE-SELF TOLD HER TO TELL ME THAT NAME SO I WOULD TRUST HER ABSOLUTELY.
"YOU REMEMBER KAMEKO, DON'T YOU, DADDY?"
His home is wherever he is. Remember that.
"MOTHER THREATENED TO MAKE SOUP OUT OF HIM TO PUNISH YOU FOR LEAVING US FOR WHATEVER OTHER PLACE YOU CALLED HOME.
"SO I GAVE KAMEKO BACK TO NATURE AND LET HIM GO.
"WE HAD NO FUTURE TOGETHER, AND THAT'S WHAT THIS IS ALL ABOUT...

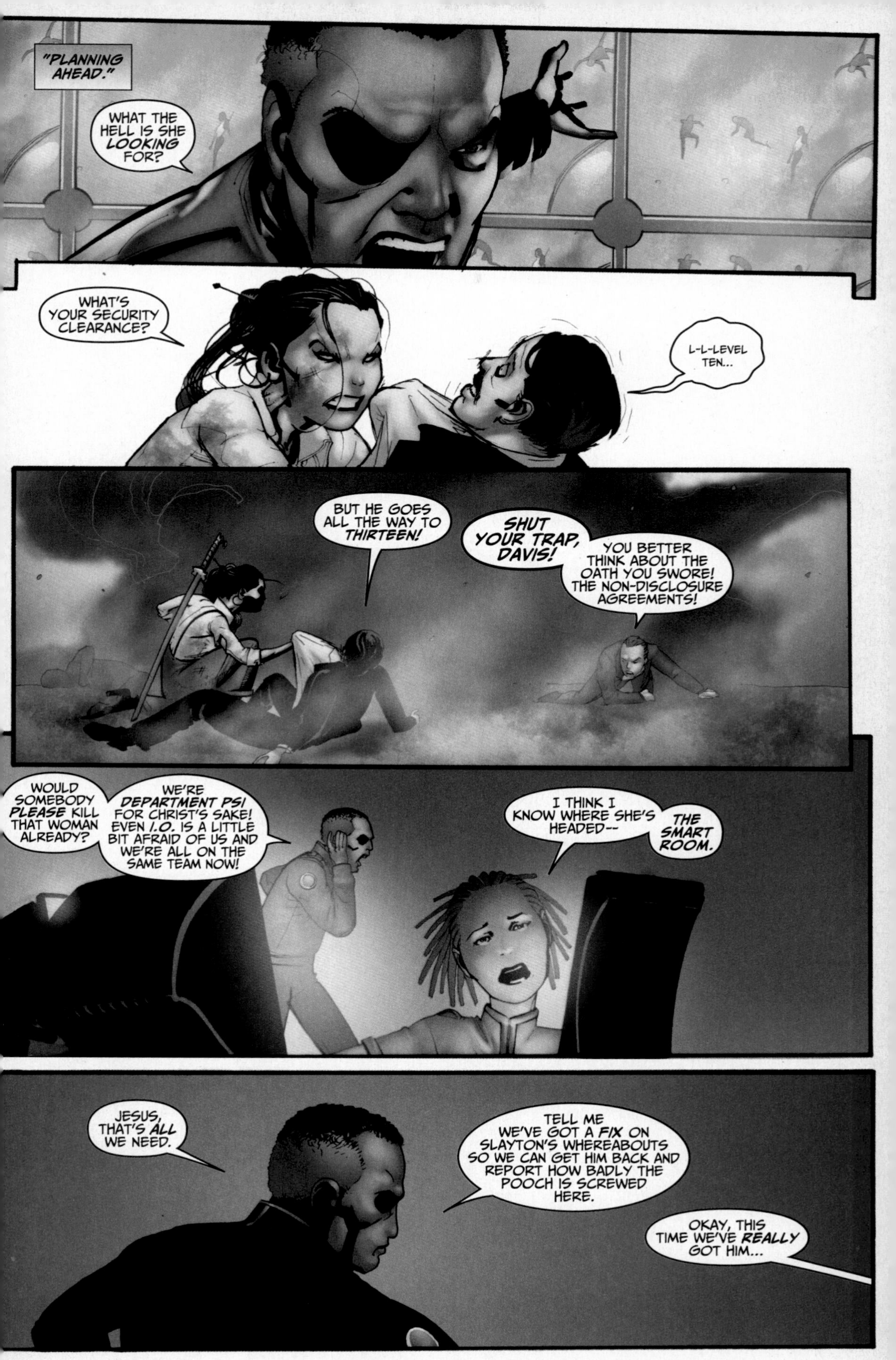
"PLANNING AHEAD."
WHAT THE HELL IS SHE LOOKING FOR?
WHAT'S YOUR SECURITY CLEARANCE?
L-L-LEVEL TEN...
BUT HE GOES ALL THE WAY TO THIRTEEN!
SHUT YOUR TRAP, DAVIS!
YOU BETTER THINK ABOUT THE OATH YOU SWORE! THE NON-DISCLOSURE AGREEMENTS!
WOULD SOMEBODY PLEASE KILL THAT WOMAN ALREADY?
WE'RE DEPARTMENT PSI FOR CHRIST'S SAKE! EVEN I.O. IS A LITTLE BIT AFRAID OF US AND WE'RE ALL ON THE SAME TEAM NOW!
I THINK I KNOW WHERE SHE'S HEADED-- THE SMART ROOM.
JESUS, THAT'S ALL WE NEED.
TELL ME WE'VE GOT A FIX ON SLAYTON'S WHEREABOUTS SO WE CAN GET HIM BACK AND REPORT HOW BADLY THE POOCH IS SCREWED HERE.
OKAY, THIS TIME WE'VE REALLY GOT HIM...

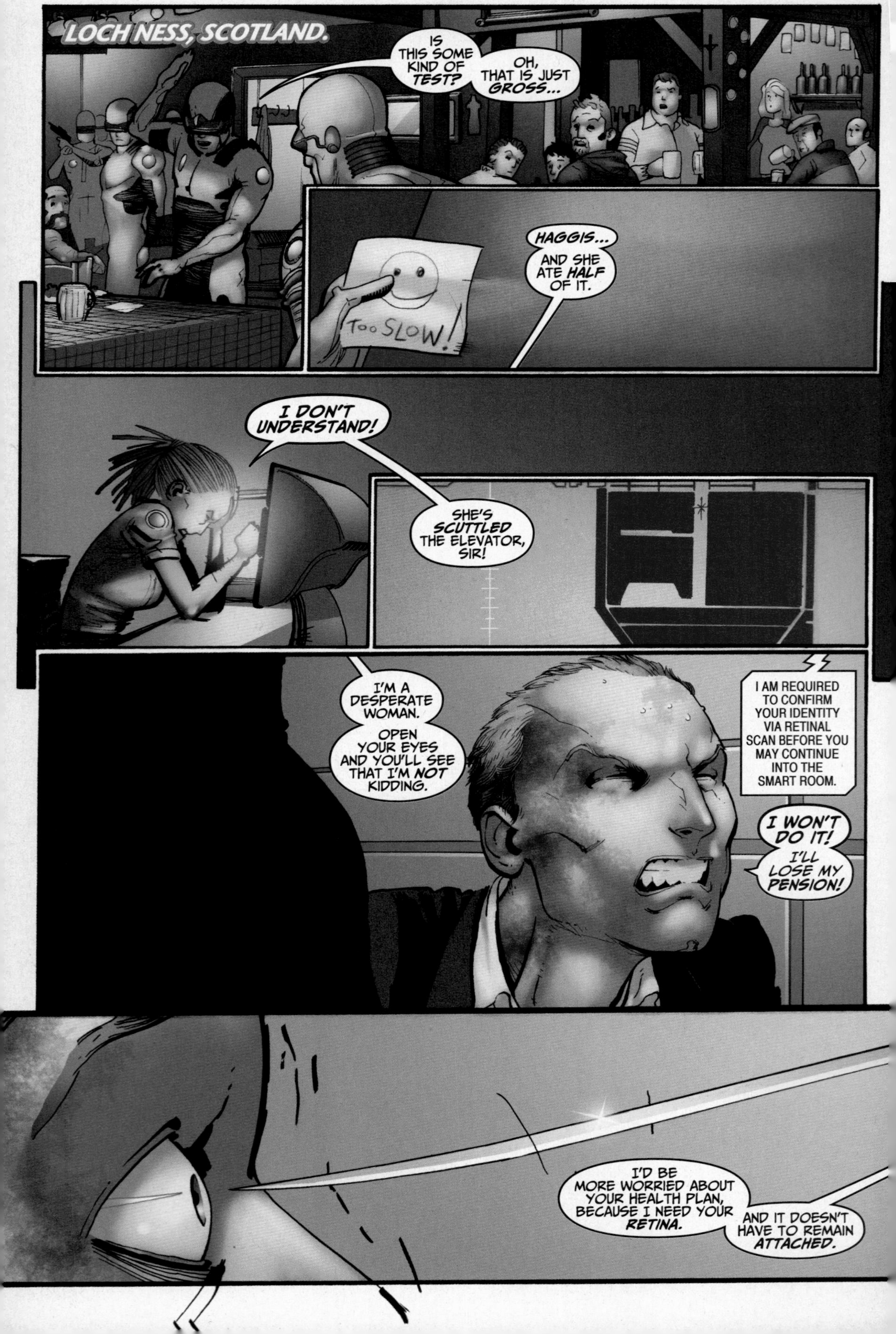

LOCH NESS, SCOTLAND.
IS THIS SOME KIND OF TEST?
OH, THAT IS JUST GROSS...
TOO SLOW!
HAGGIS...
AND SHE ATE HALF OF IT.
I DON'T UNDERSTAND!
SHE'S SCUTTLED THE ELEVATOR, SIR!
I'M A DESPERATE WOMAN.
OPEN YOUR EYES AND YOU'LL SEE THAT I'M NOT KIDDING.
I AM REQUIRED TO CONFIRM YOUR IDENTITY VIA RETINAL SCAN BEFORE YOU MAY CONTINUE INTO THE SMART ROOM.
I WON'T DO IT!
I'LL LOSE MY PENSION!
I'D BE MORE WORRIED ABOUT YOUR HEALTH PLAN, BECAUSE I NEED YOUR RETINA.
AND IT DOESN'T HAVE TO REMAIN ATTACHED.

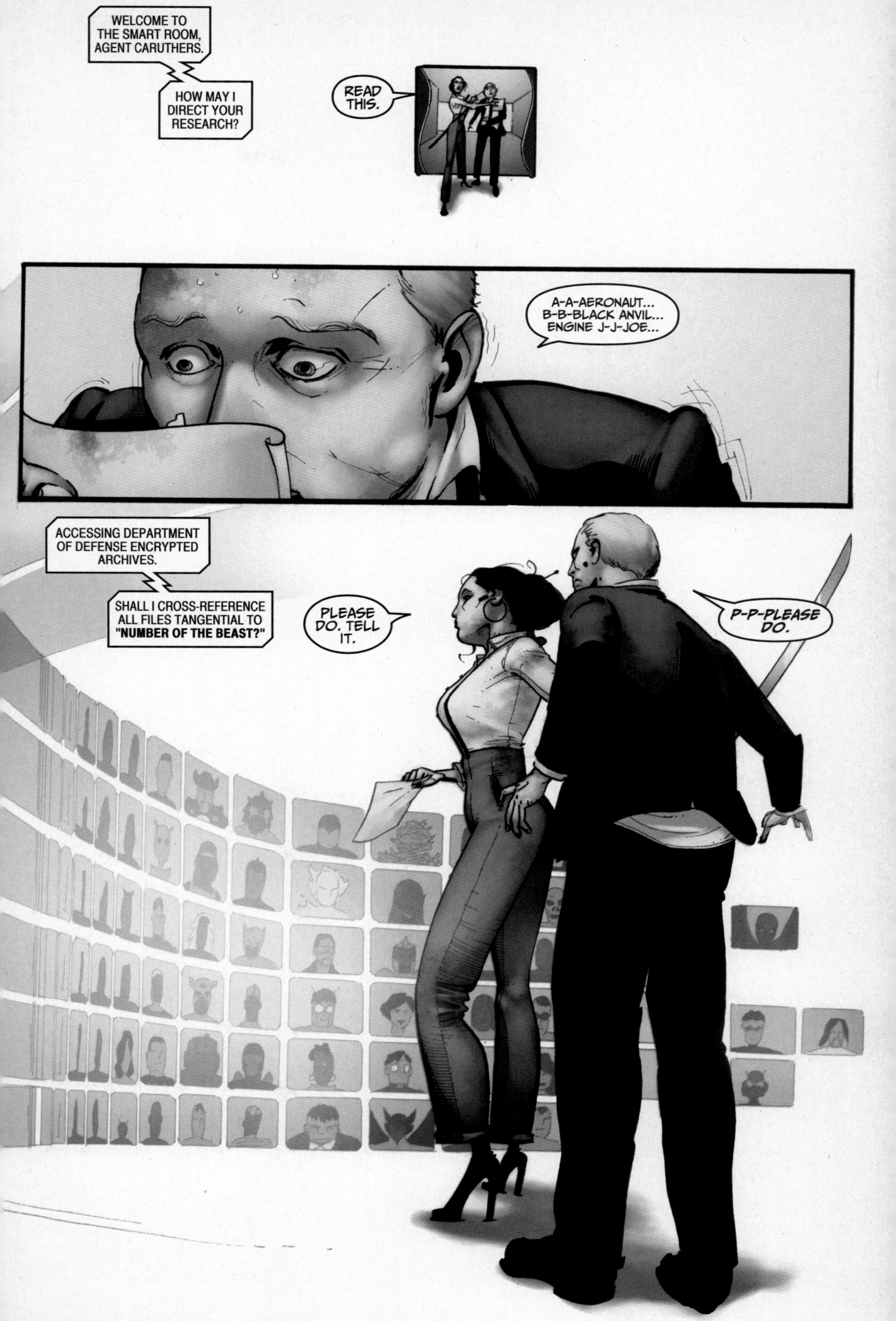
WELCOME TO THE SMART ROOM, AGENT CARUTHERS.
HOW MAY I DIRECT YOUR RESEARCH?
READ THIS.
A-A-AERONAUT... B-B-BLACK ANVIL... ENGINE J-J-JOE...
ACCESSING DEPARTMENT OF DEFENSE ENCRYPTED ARCHIVES.
SHALL I CROSS-REFERENCE ALL FILES TANGENTIAL TO **"NUMBER OF THE BEAST?"**
PLEASE DO. TELL IT.
P-P-PLEASE DO.

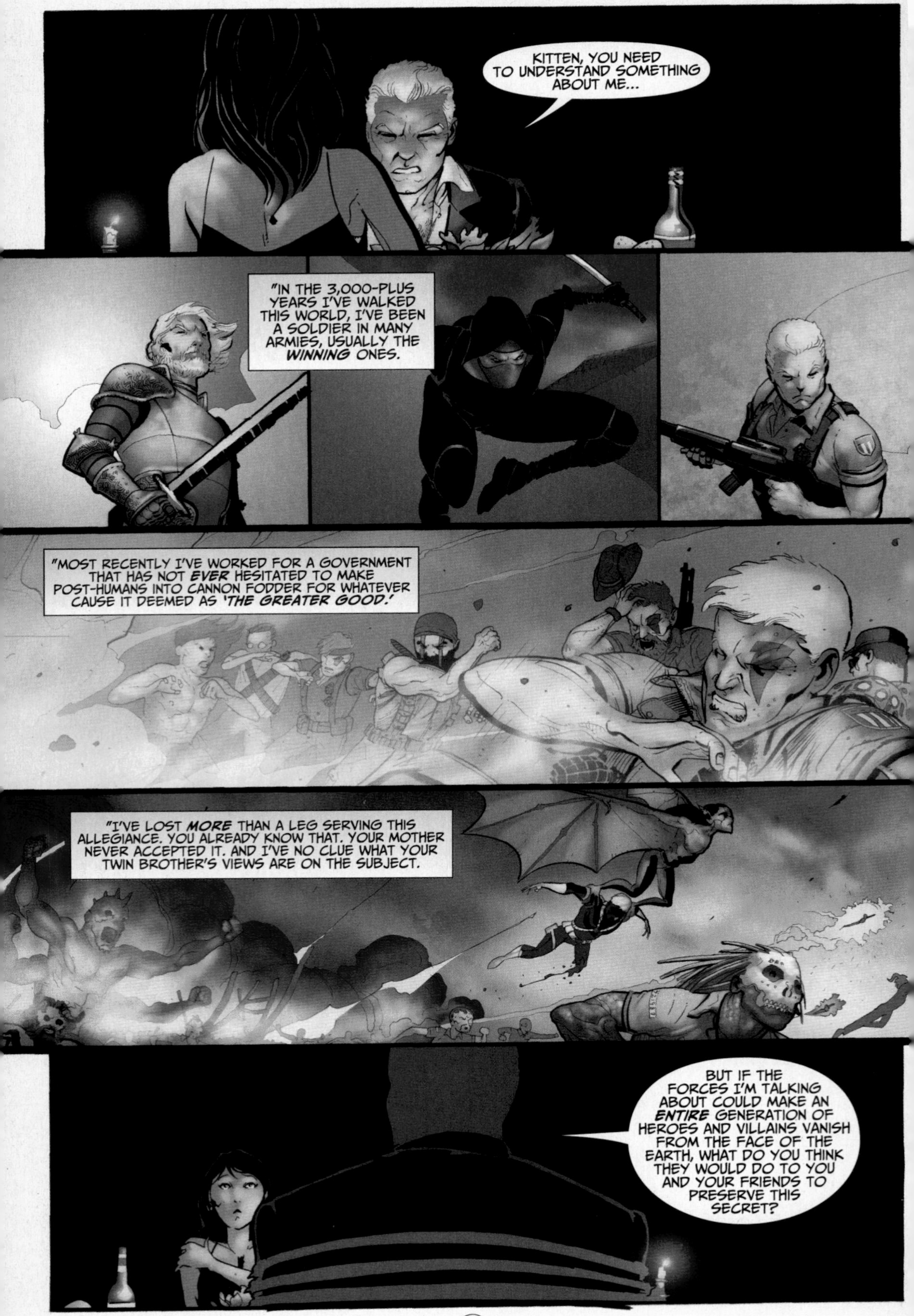
KITTEN, YOU NEED TO UNDERSTAND SOMETHING ABOUT ME...
"IN THE 3,000-PLUS YEARS I'VE WALKED THIS WORLD, I'VE BEEN A SOLDIER IN MANY ARMIES, USUALLY THE **WINNING** ONES.
"MOST RECENTLY I'VE WORKED FOR A GOVERNMENT THAT HAS NOT **EVER** HESITATED TO MAKE POST-HUMANS INTO CANNON FODDER FOR WHATEVER CAUSE IT DEEMED AS **'THE GREATER GOOD.'**
"I'VE LOST **MORE** THAN A LEG SERVING THIS ALLEGIANCE. YOU ALREADY KNOW THAT. YOUR MOTHER NEVER ACCEPTED IT. AND I'VE NO CLUE WHAT YOUR TWIN BROTHER'S VIEWS ARE ON THE SUBJECT.
BUT IF THE FORCES I'M TALKING ABOUT COULD MAKE AN **ENTIRE** GENERATION OF HEROES AND VILLAINS VANISH FROM THE FACE OF THE EARTH, WHAT DO YOU THINK THEY WOULD DO TO YOU AND YOUR FRIENDS TO PRESERVE THIS SECRET?

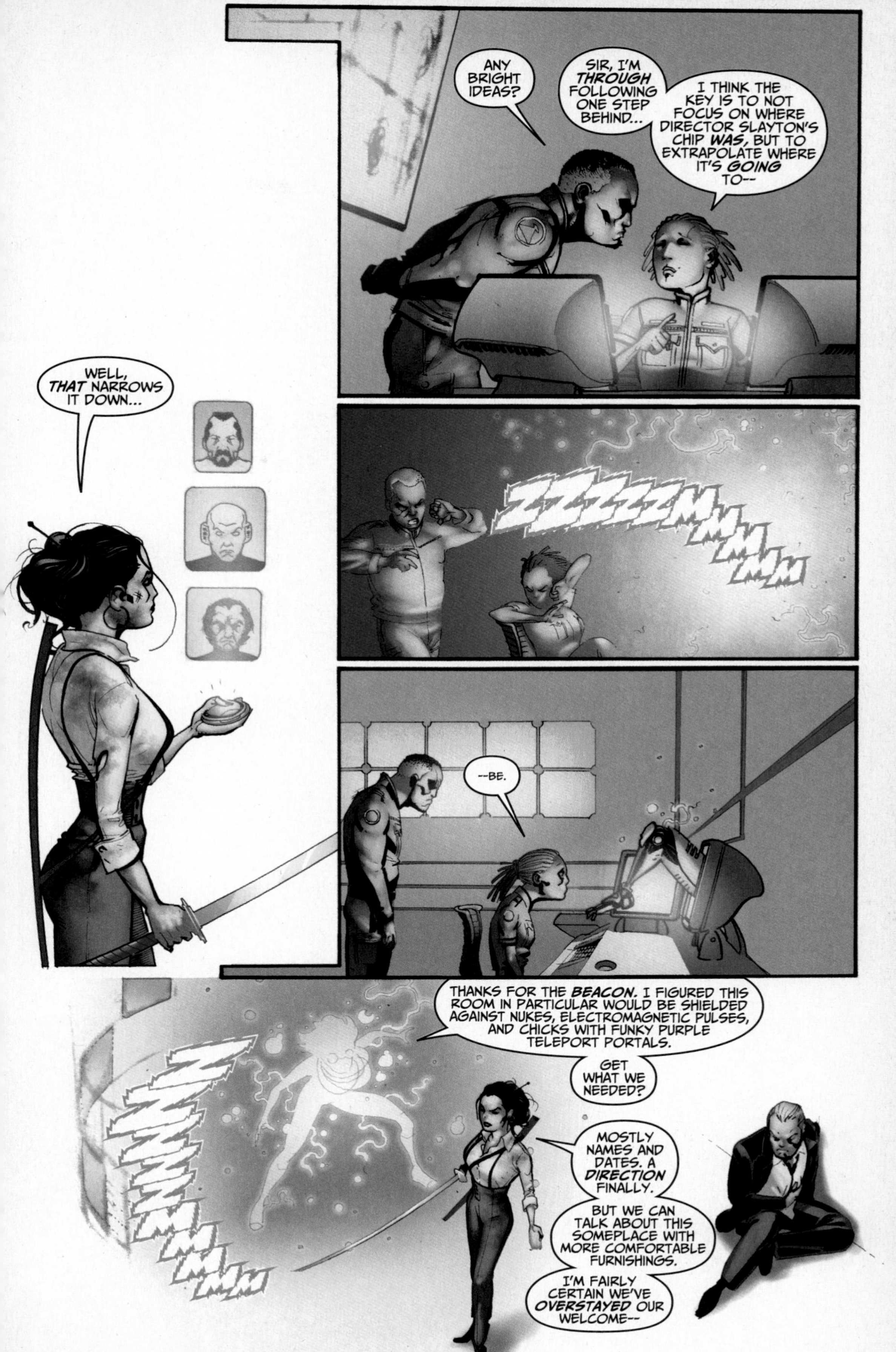

ANY BRIGHT IDEAS?
SIR, I'M THROUGH FOLLOWING ONE STEP BEHIND...
I THINK THE KEY IS TO NOT FOCUS ON WHERE DIRECTOR SLAYTON'S CHIP WAS, BUT TO EXTRAPOLATE WHERE IT'S GOING TO--
WELL, THAT NARROWS IT DOWN...
ZZZZZZMMMMMMMM
--BE.
THANKS FOR THE BEACON. I FIGURED THIS ROOM IN PARTICULAR WOULD BE SHIELDED AGAINST NUKES, ELECTROMAGNETIC PULSES, AND CHICKS WITH FUNKY PURPLE TELEPORT PORTALS.
GET WHAT WE NEEDED?
MOSTLY NAMES AND DATES. A DIRECTION FINALLY.
BUT WE CAN TALK ABOUT THIS SOMEPLACE WITH MORE COMFORTABLE FURNISHINGS.
I'M FAIRLY CERTAIN WE'VE OVERSTAYED OUR WELCOME--

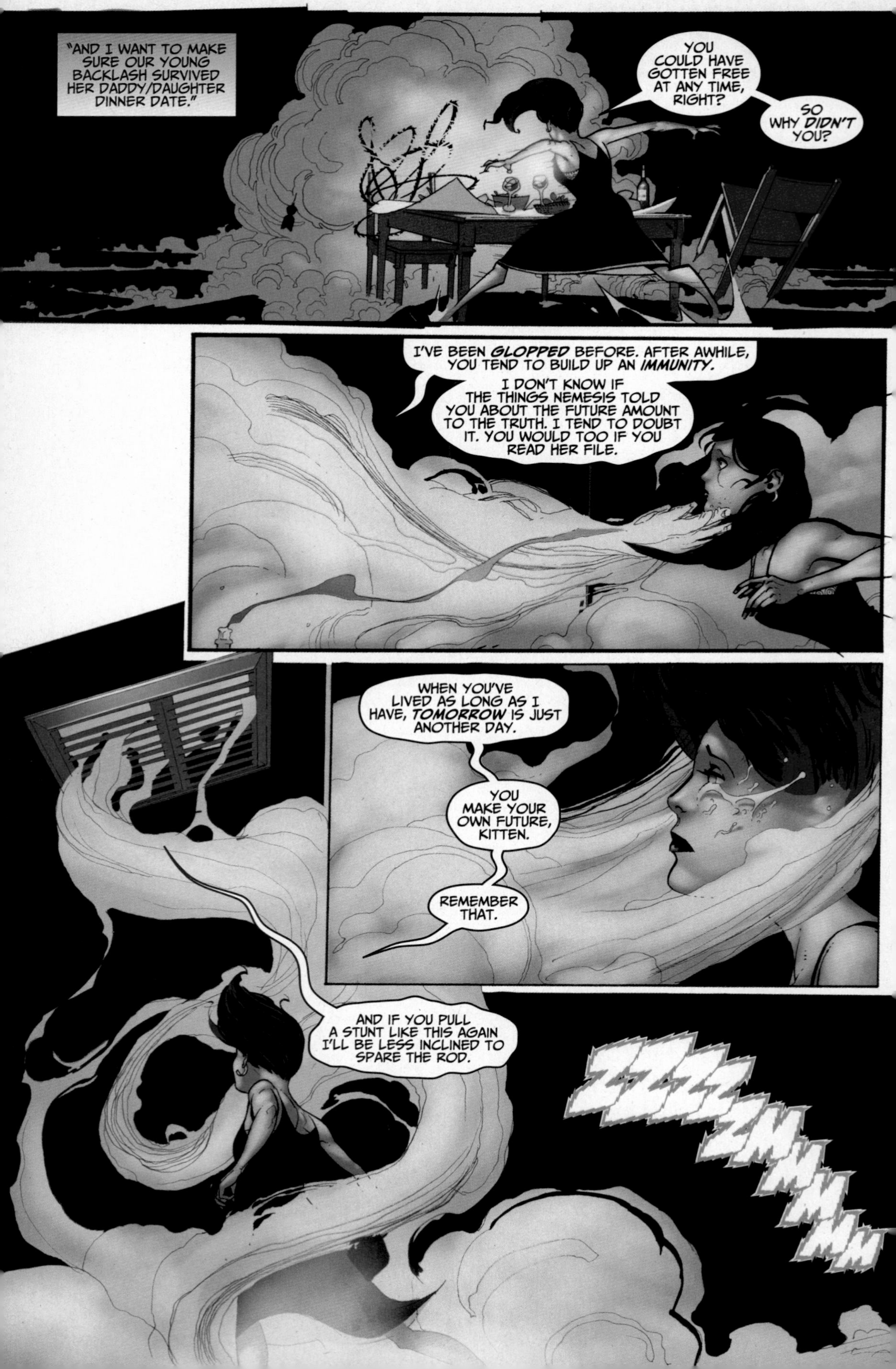
"AND I WANT TO MAKE SURE OUR YOUNG BACKLASH SURVIVED HER DADDY/DAUGHTER DINNER DATE."
YOU COULD HAVE GOTTEN FREE AT ANY TIME, RIGHT?
SO WHY DIDN'T YOU?
I'VE BEEN GLOPPED BEFORE. AFTER AWHILE, YOU TEND TO BUILD UP AN IMMUNITY.
I DON'T KNOW IF THE THINGS NEMESIS TOLD YOU ABOUT THE FUTURE AMOUNT TO THE TRUTH. I TEND TO DOUBT IT. YOU WOULD TOO IF YOU READ HER FILE.
WHEN YOU'VE LIVED AS LONG AS I HAVE, TOMORROW IS JUST ANOTHER DAY.
YOU MAKE YOUR OWN FUTURE, KITTEN.
REMEMBER THAT.
AND IF YOU PULL A STUNT LIKE THIS AGAIN I'LL BE LESS INCLINED TO SPARE THE ROD.
ZZZZZMMMMMM

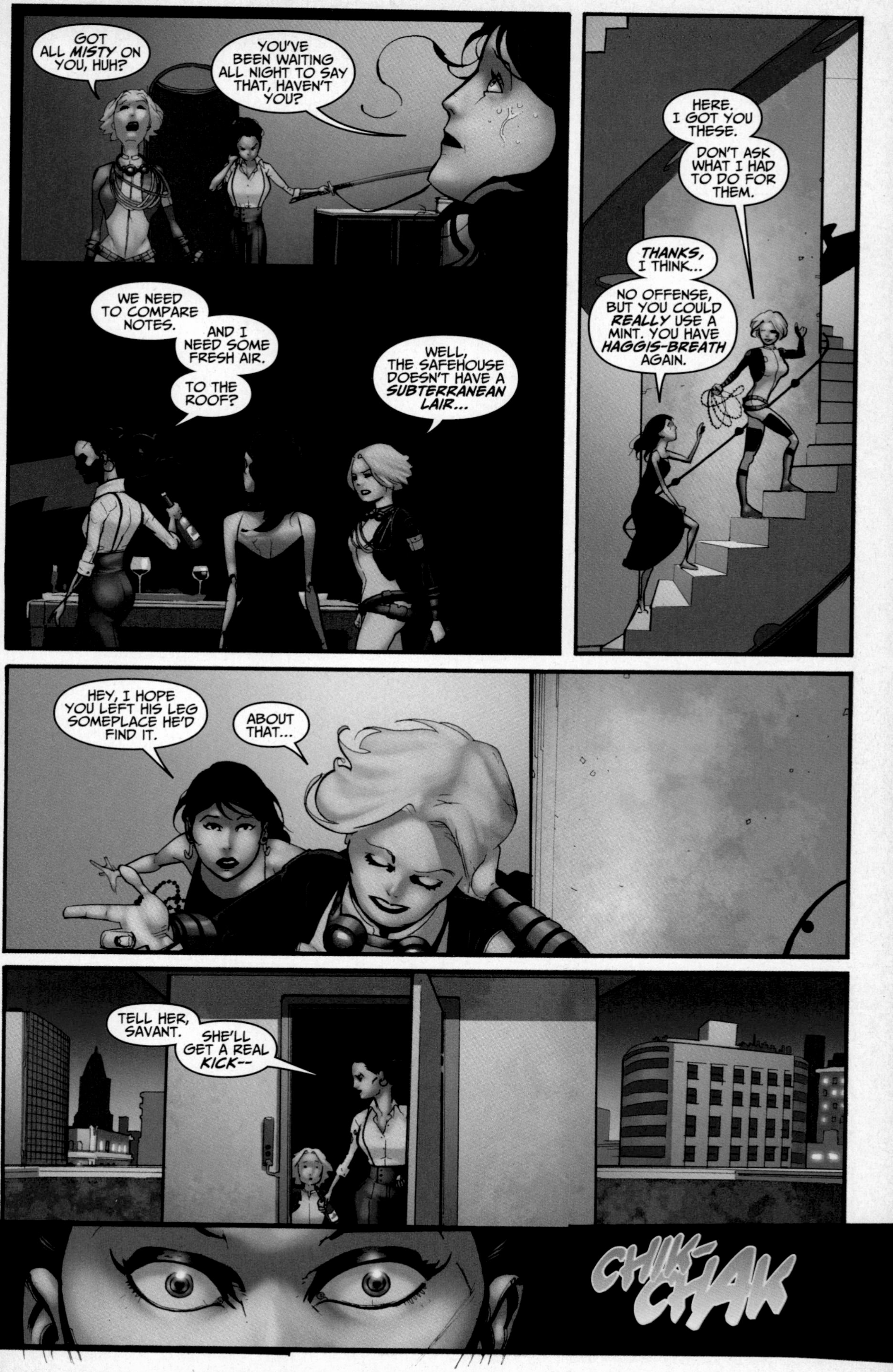
GOT ALL MISTY ON YOU, HUH?
YOU'VE BEEN WAITING ALL NIGHT TO SAY THAT, HAVEN'T YOU?
WE NEED TO COMPARE NOTES.
AND I NEED SOME FRESH AIR.
TO THE ROOF?
WELL, THE SAFEHOUSE DOESN'T HAVE A SUBTERRANEAN LAIR...
HERE. I GOT YOU THESE.
DON'T ASK WHAT I HAD TO DO FOR THEM.
THANKS, I THINK...
NO OFFENSE, BUT YOU COULD REALLY USE A MINT. YOU HAVE HAGGIS-BREATH AGAIN.
HEY, I HOPE YOU LEFT HIS LEG SOMEPLACE HE'D FIND IT.
ABOUT THAT...
TELL HER, SAVANT.
SHE'LL GET A REAL KICK--
CHIK-CHAK

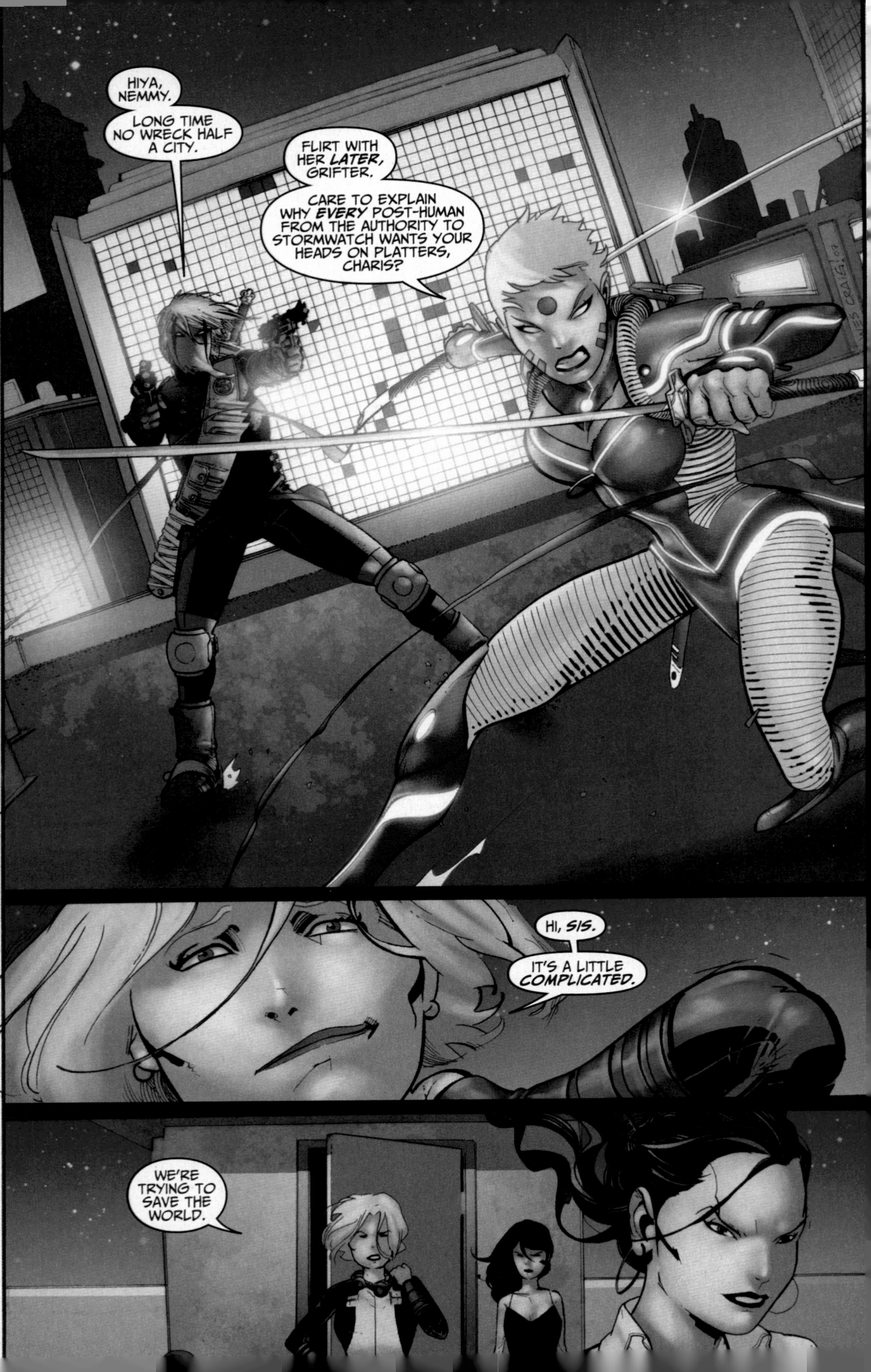
HIYA, NEMMY.
LONG TIME NO WRECK HALF A CITY.
FLIRT WITH HER LATER, GRIFTER.
CARE TO EXPLAIN WHY EVERY POST-HUMAN FROM THE AUTHORITY TO STORMWATCH WANTS YOUR HEADS ON PLATTERS, CHARIS?
HI, SIS.
IT'S A LITTLE COMPLICATED.
WE'RE TRYING TO SAVE THE WORLD.

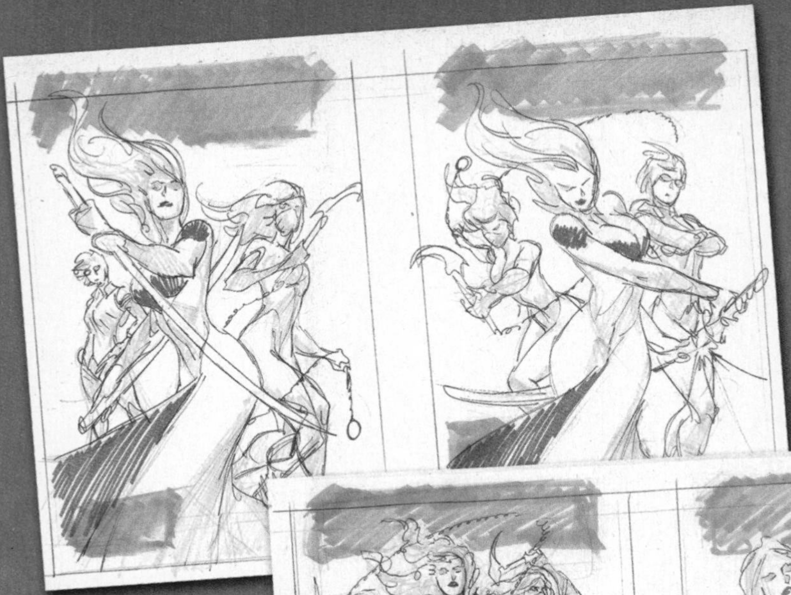

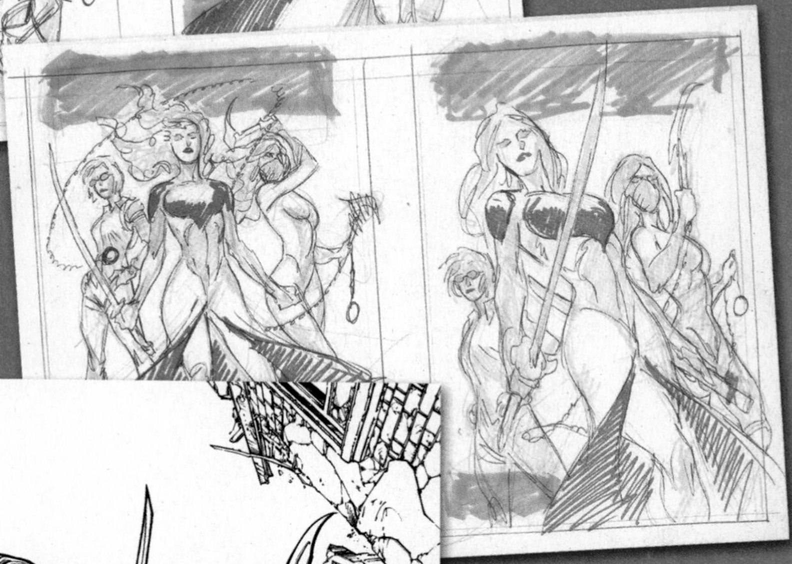

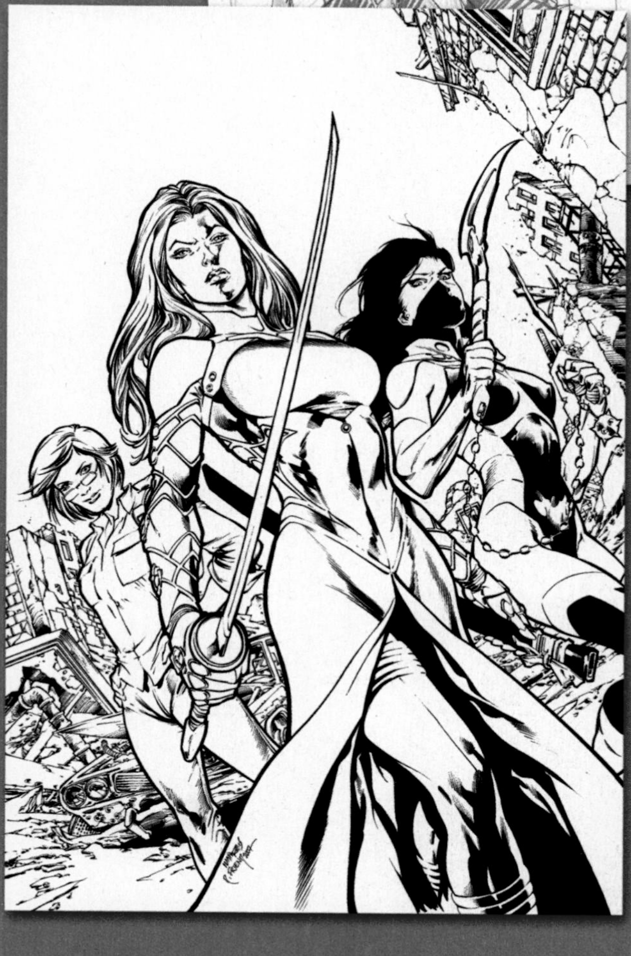

Cover Sketches
by Ivan Reis

Chapter 5

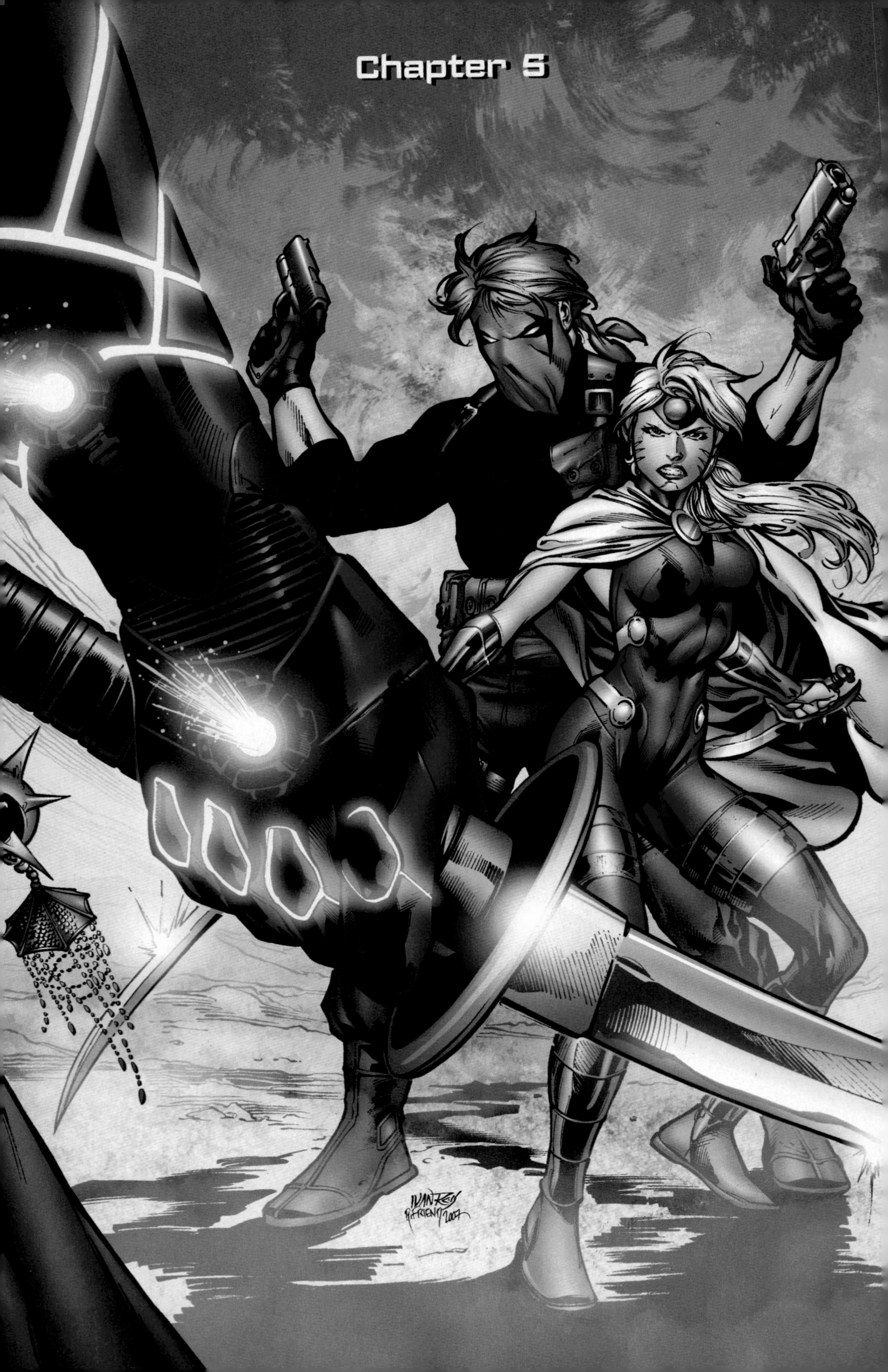

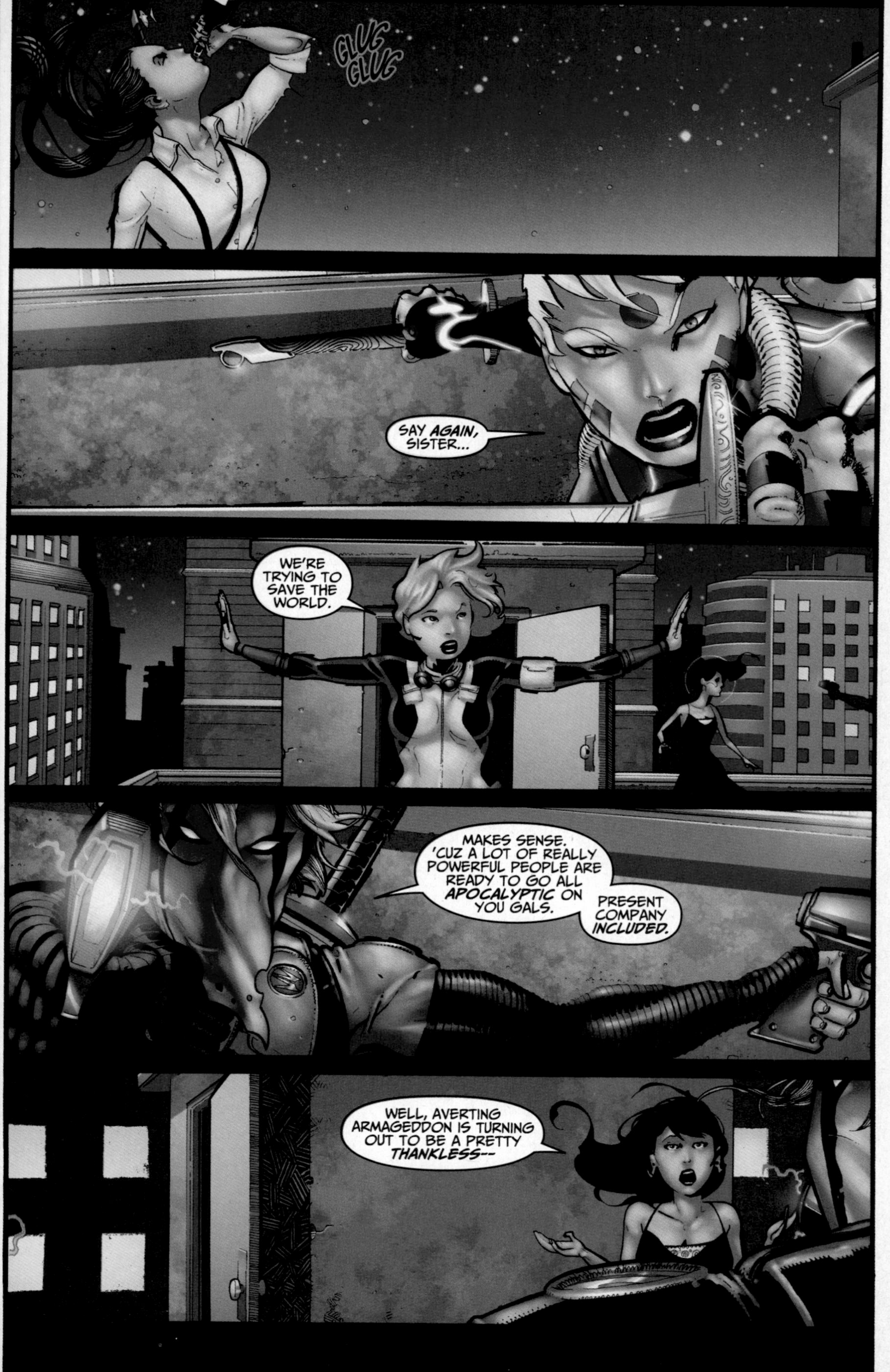
GLUG GLUG
SAY AGAIN, SISTER...
WE'RE TRYING TO SAVE THE WORLD.
MAKES SENSE. 'CUZ A LOT OF REALLY POWERFUL PEOPLE ARE READY TO GO ALL APOCALYPTIC ON YOU GALS.
PRESENT COMPANY INCLUDED.
WELL, AVERTING ARMAGEDDON IS TURNING OUT TO BE A PRETTY THANKLESS--

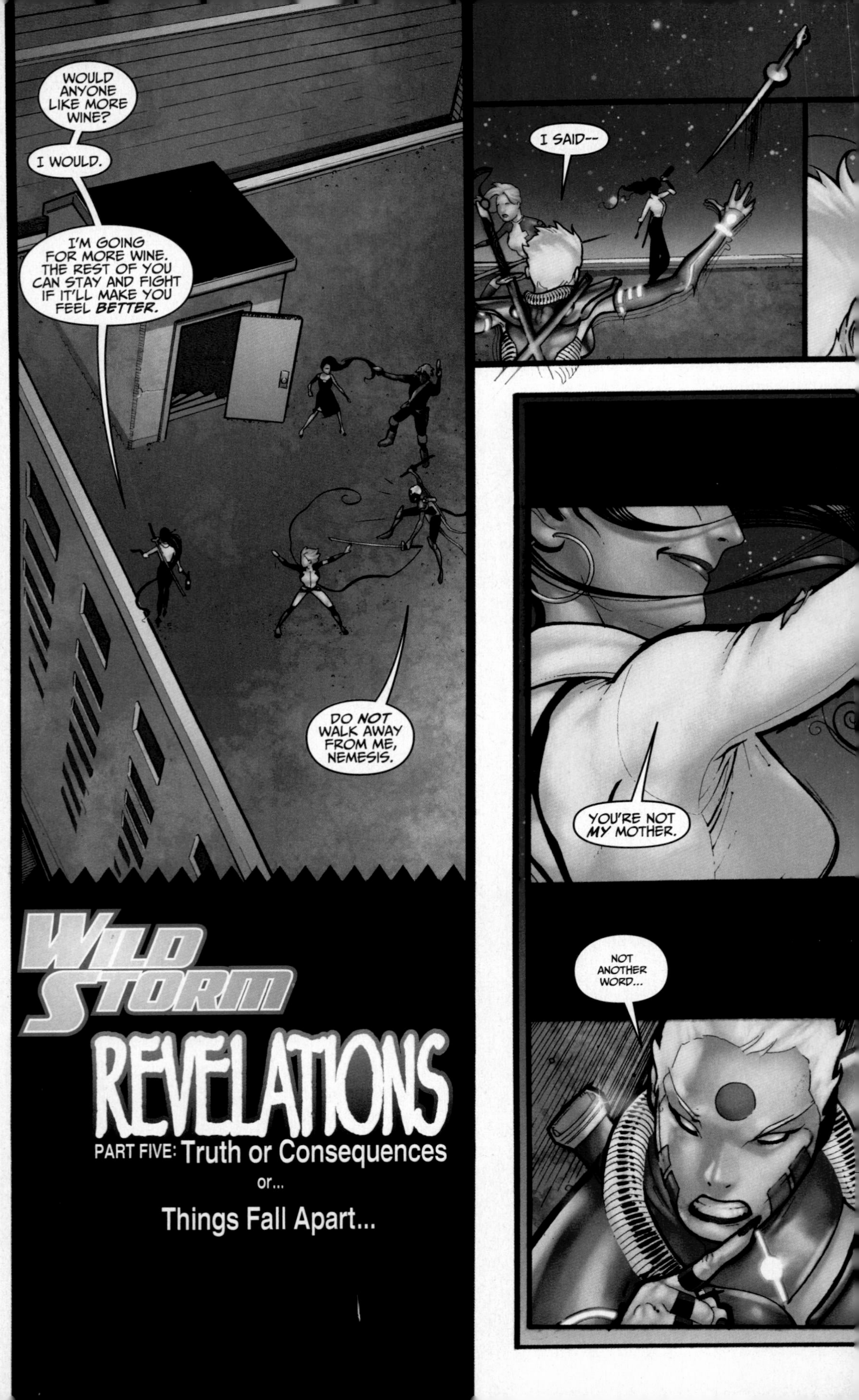
WOULD ANYONE LIKE MORE WINE?
I WOULD.
I'M GOING FOR MORE WINE. THE REST OF YOU CAN STAY AND FIGHT IF IT'LL MAKE YOU FEEL BETTER.
DO NOT WALK AWAY FROM ME, NEMESIS.
I SAID--
YOU'RE NOT MY MOTHER.
NOT ANOTHER WORD...
WILDSTORM
REVELATIONS
PART FIVE: Truth or Consequences
or...
Things Fall Apart...

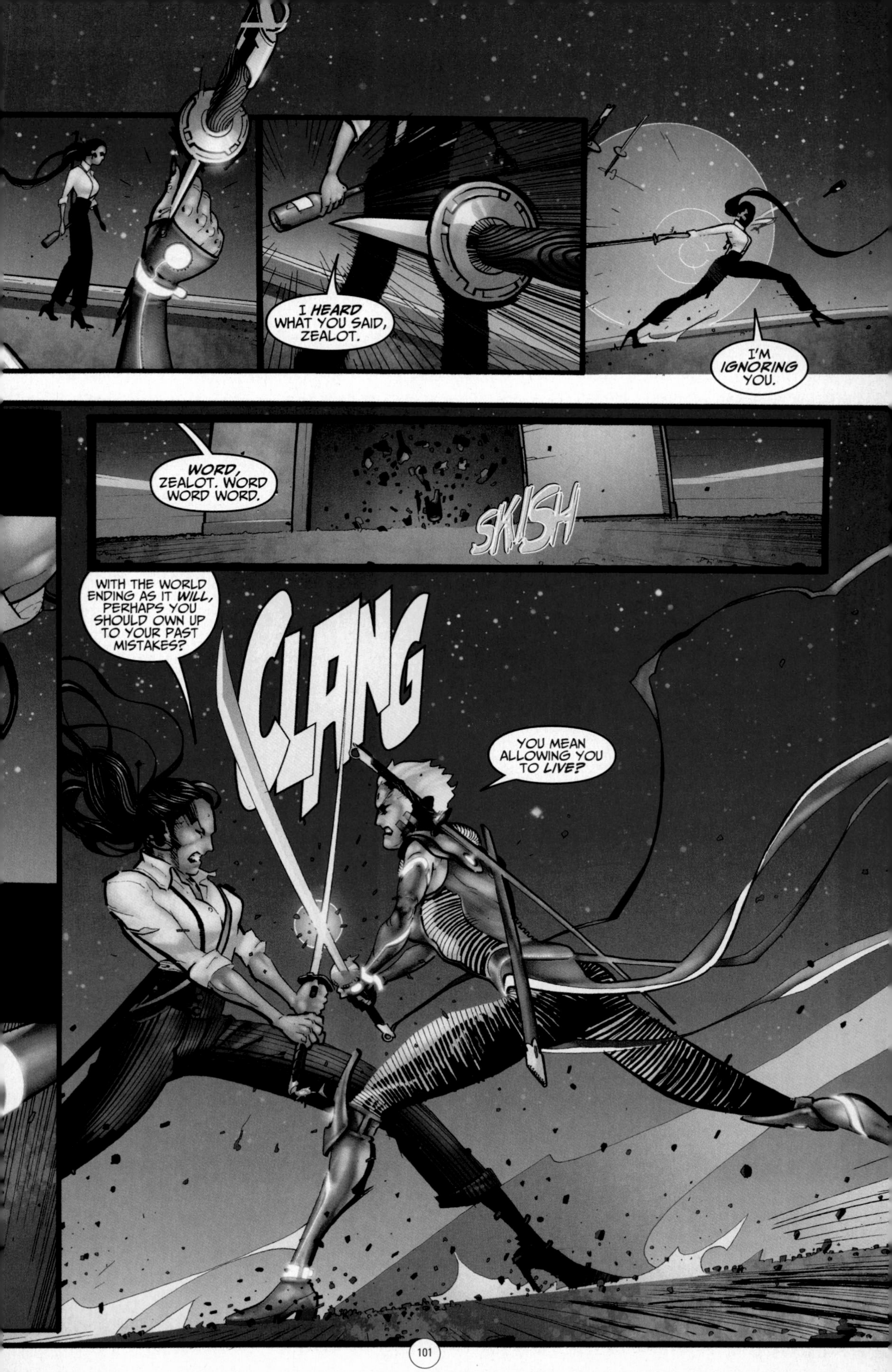
I HEARD WHAT YOU SAID, ZEALOT.
I'M IGNORING YOU.
WORD, ZEALOT. WORD WORD WORD.
SKISH
WITH THE WORLD ENDING AS IT WILL, PERHAPS YOU SHOULD OWN UP TO YOUR PAST MISTAKES?
CLANG
YOU MEAN ALLOWING YOU TO LIVE?

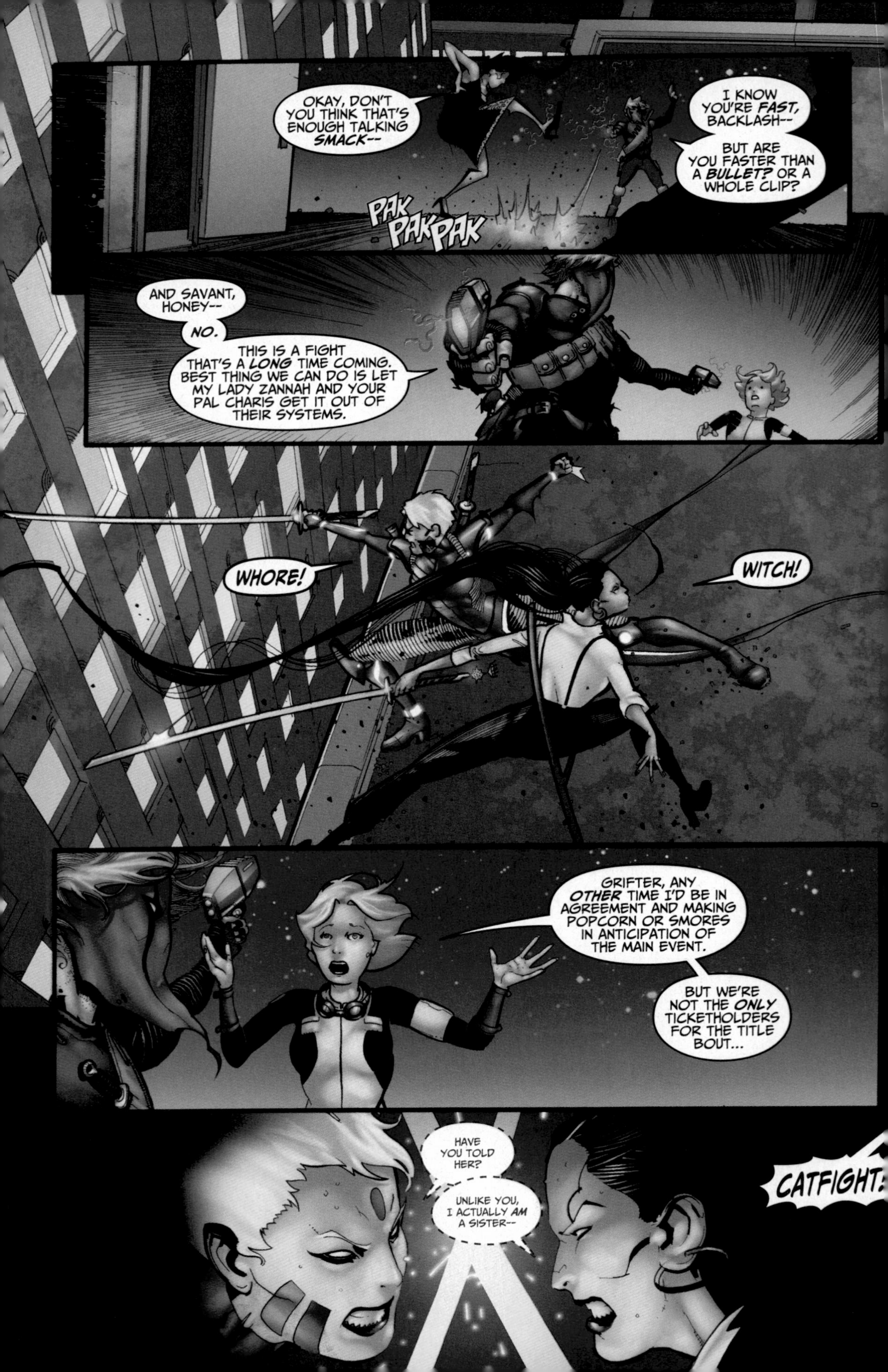
OKAY, DON'T YOU THINK THAT'S ENOUGH TALKING SMACK--
I KNOW YOU'RE FAST, BACKLASH--
BUT ARE YOU FASTER THAN A BULLET? OR A WHOLE CLIP?
PAK PAK PAK
AND SAVANT, HONEY--
NO.
THIS IS A FIGHT THAT'S A LONG TIME COMING. BEST THING WE CAN DO IS LET MY LADY ZANNAH AND YOUR PAL CHARIS GET IT OUT OF THEIR SYSTEMS.
WHORE!
WITCH!
GRIFTER, ANY OTHER TIME I'D BE IN AGREEMENT AND MAKING POPCORN OR SMORES IN ANTICIPATION OF THE MAIN EVENT.
BUT WE'RE NOT THE ONLY TICKETHOLDERS FOR THE TITLE BOUT...
HAVE YOU TOLD HER?
UNLIKE YOU, I ACTUALLY AM A SISTER--
CATFIGHT!

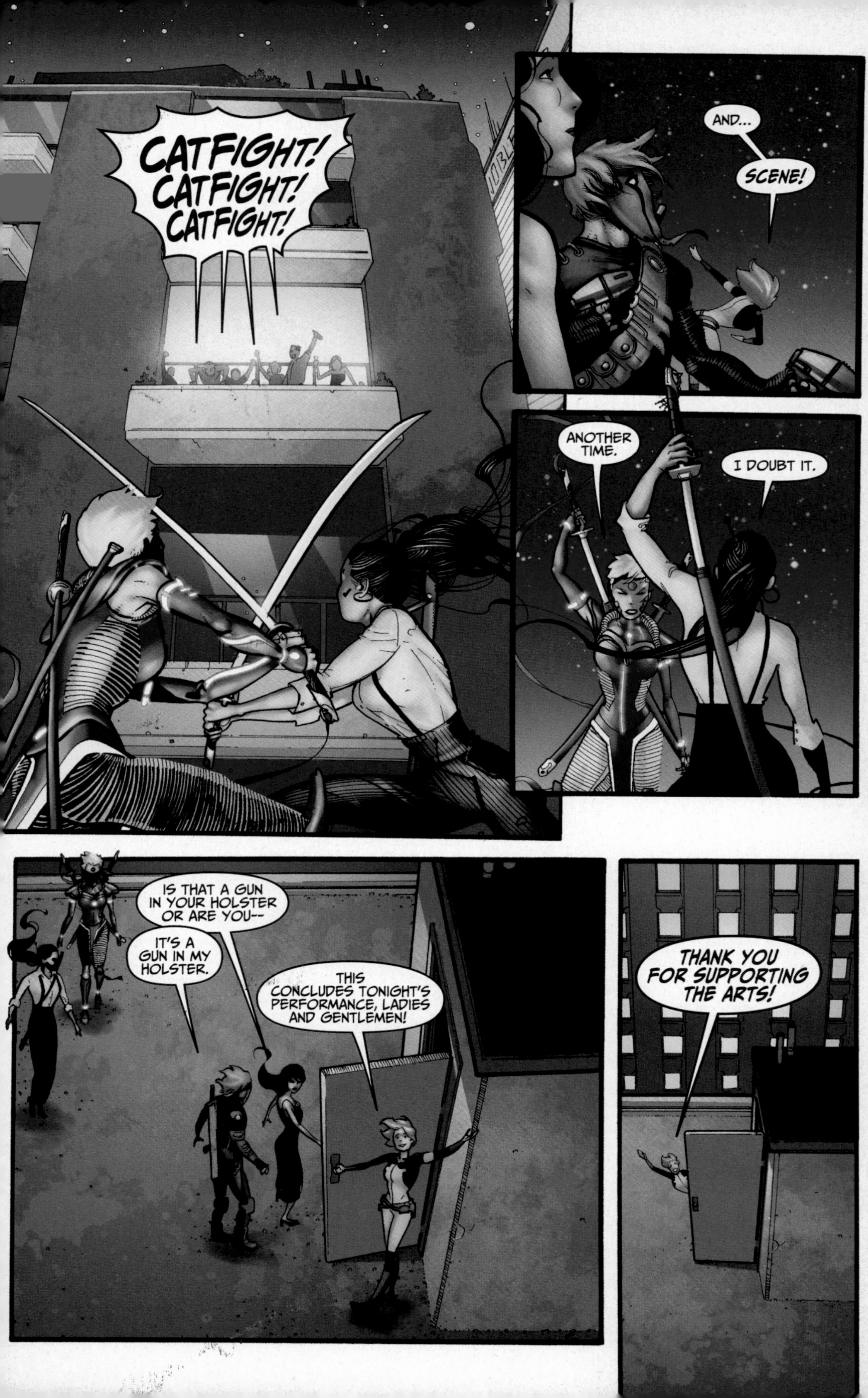
CATFIGHT! CATFIGHT! CATFIGHT!
AND...
SCENE!
ANOTHER TIME.
I DOUBT IT.
IS THAT A GUN IN YOUR HOLSTER OR ARE YOU--
IT'S A GUN IN MY HOLSTER.
THIS CONCLUDES TONIGHT'S PERFORMANCE, LADIES AND GENTLEMEN!
THANK YOU FOR SUPPORTING THE ARTS!

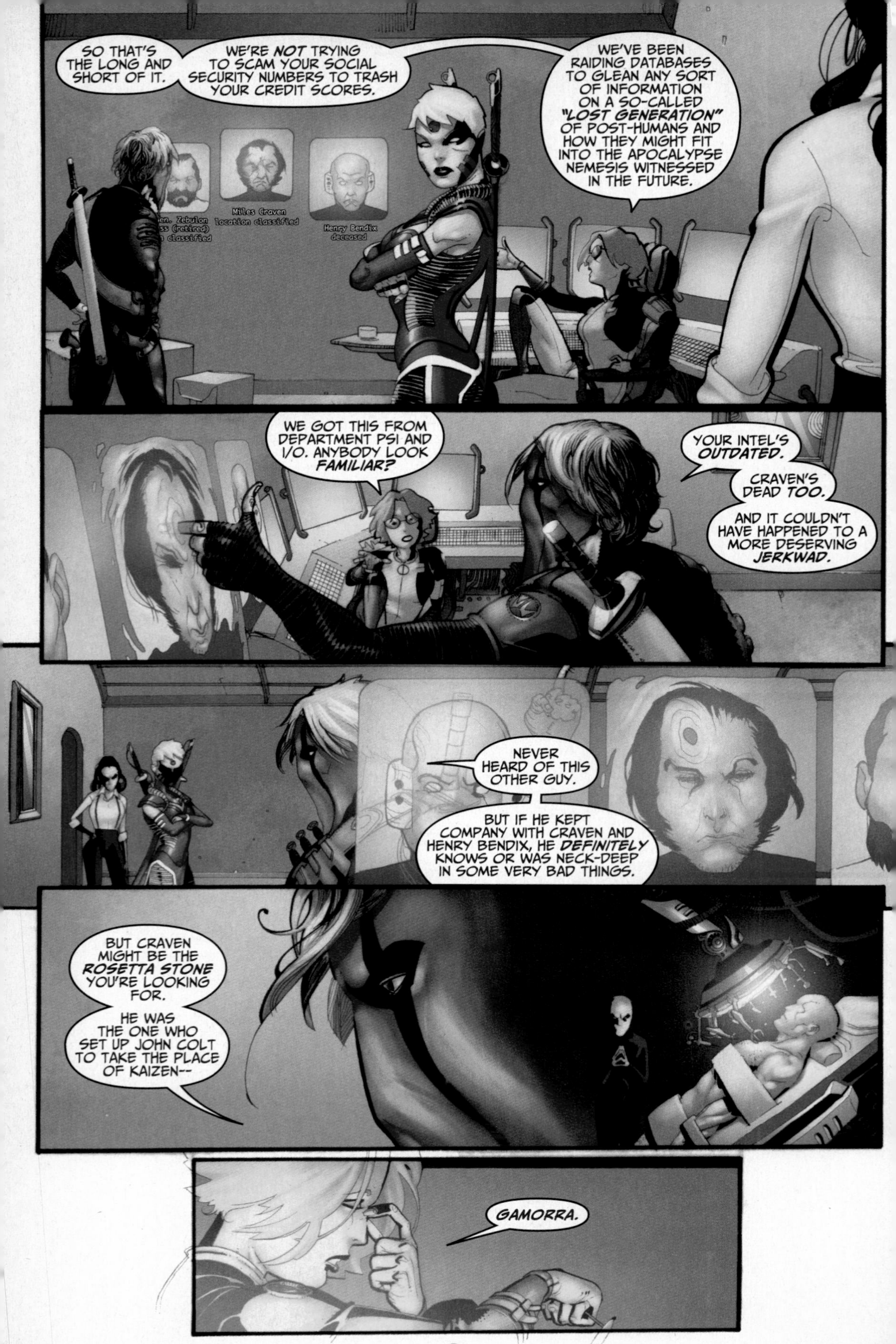
SO THAT'S THE LONG AND SHORT OF IT.
WE'RE NOT TRYING TO SCAM YOUR SOCIAL SECURITY NUMBERS TO TRASH YOUR CREDIT SCORES.
WE'VE BEEN RAIDING DATABASES TO GLEAN ANY SORT OF INFORMATION ON A SO-CALLED "LOST GENERATION" OF POST-HUMANS AND HOW THEY MIGHT FIT INTO THE APOCALYPSE NEMESIS WITNESSED IN THE FUTURE.
Miles Craven
location classified
Henry Bendix
deceased
WE GOT THIS FROM DEPARTMENT PSI AND I/O. ANYBODY LOOK FAMILIAR?
YOUR INTEL'S OUTDATED.
CRAVEN'S DEAD TOO.
AND IT COULDN'T HAVE HAPPENED TO A MORE DESERVING JERKWAD.
NEVER HEARD OF THIS OTHER GUY.
BUT IF HE KEPT COMPANY WITH CRAVEN AND HENRY BENDIX, HE DEFINITELY KNOWS OR WAS NECK-DEEP IN SOME VERY BAD THINGS.
BUT CRAVEN MIGHT BE THE ROSETTA STONE YOU'RE LOOKING FOR.
HE WAS THE ONE WHO SET UP JOHN COLT TO TAKE THE PLACE OF KAIZEN--
GAMORRA.

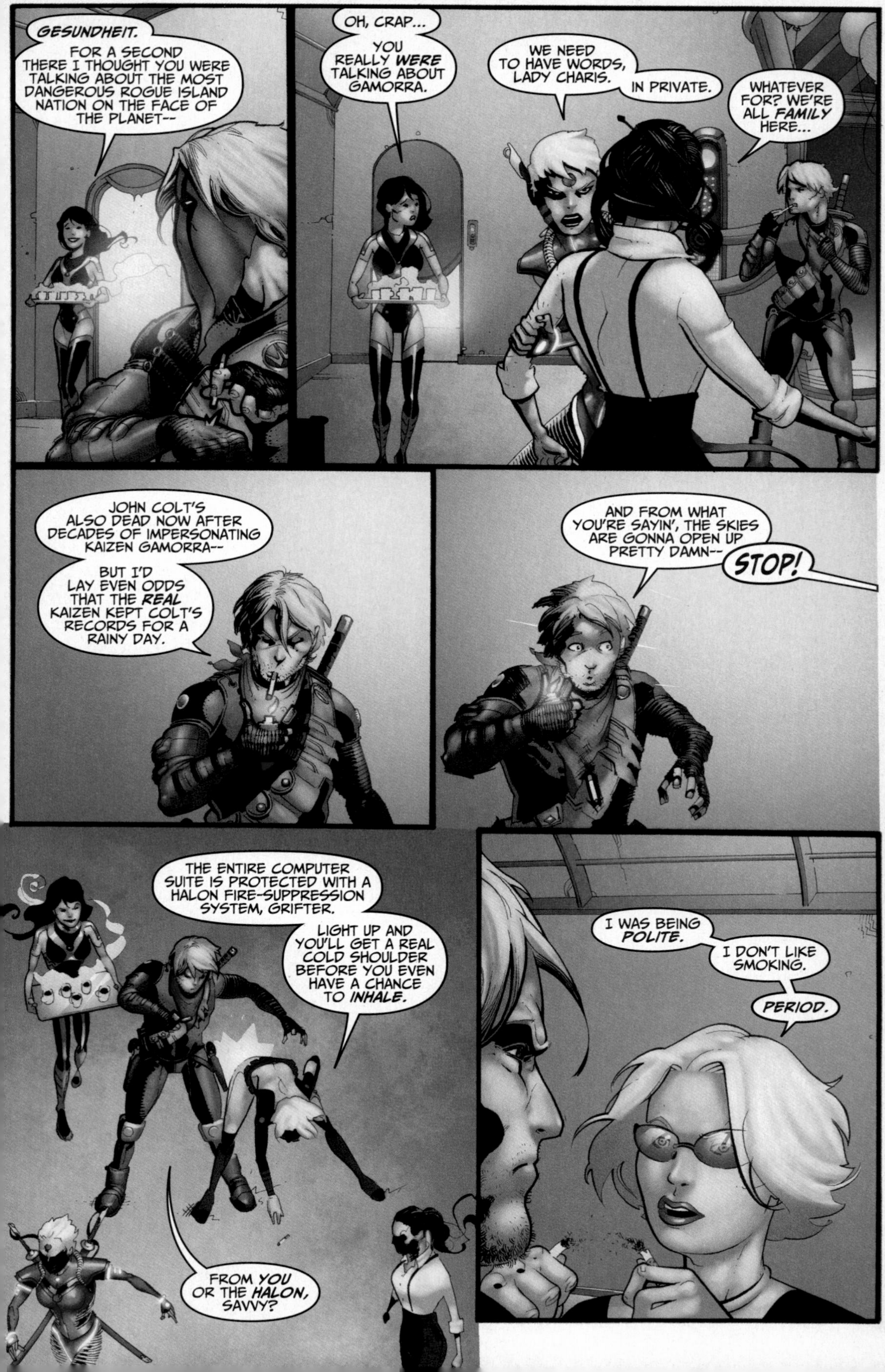
GESUNDHEIT.
FOR A SECOND THERE I THOUGHT YOU WERE TALKING ABOUT THE MOST DANGEROUS ROGUE ISLAND NATION ON THE FACE OF THE PLANET--
OH, CRAP...
YOU REALLY WERE TALKING ABOUT GAMORRA.
WE NEED TO HAVE WORDS, LADY CHARIS.
IN PRIVATE.
WHATEVER FOR? WE'RE ALL FAMILY HERE...
JOHN COLT'S ALSO DEAD NOW AFTER DECADES OF IMPERSONATING KAIZEN GAMORRA--
BUT I'D LAY EVEN ODDS THAT THE REAL KAIZEN KEPT COLT'S RECORDS FOR A RAINY DAY.
AND FROM WHAT YOU'RE SAYIN', THE SKIES ARE GONNA OPEN UP PRETTY DAMN--
STOP!
THE ENTIRE COMPUTER SUITE IS PROTECTED WITH A HALON FIRE-SUPPRESSION SYSTEM, GRIFTER.
LIGHT UP AND YOU'LL GET A REAL COLD SHOULDER BEFORE YOU EVEN HAVE A CHANCE TO INHALE.
FROM YOU OR THE HALON, SAVVY?
I WAS BEING POLITE.
I DON'T LIKE SMOKING.
PERIOD.

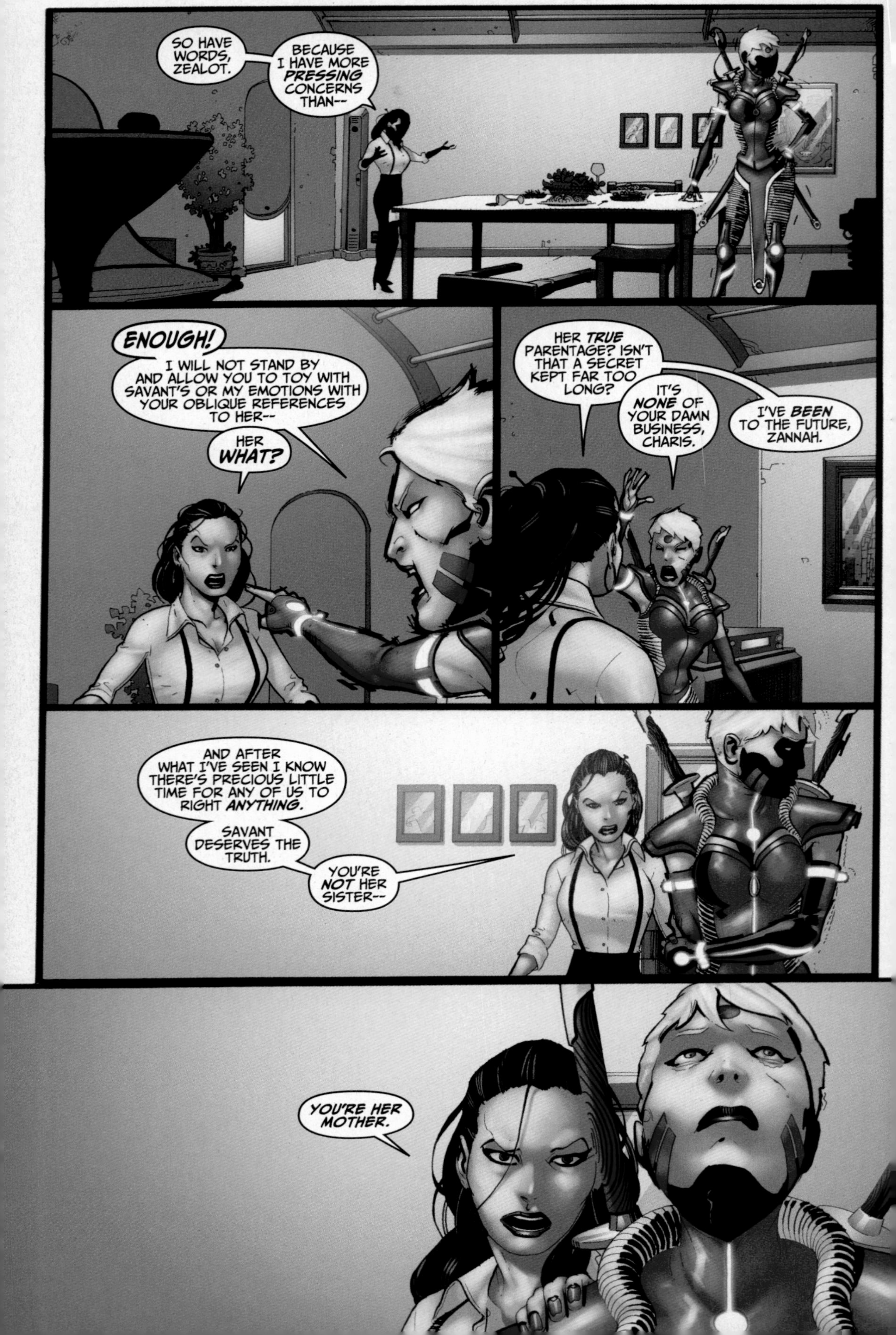
SO HAVE WORDS, ZEALOT.
BECAUSE I HAVE MORE PRESSING CONCERNS THAN--
ENOUGH!
I WILL NOT STAND BY AND ALLOW YOU TO TOY WITH SAVANT'S OR MY EMOTIONS WITH YOUR OBLIQUE REFERENCES TO HER--
HER WHAT?
HER TRUE PARENTAGE? ISN'T THAT A SECRET KEPT FAR TOO LONG?
IT'S NONE OF YOUR DAMN BUSINESS, CHARIS.
I'VE BEEN TO THE FUTURE, ZANNAH.
AND AFTER WHAT I'VE SEEN I KNOW THERE'S PRECIOUS LITTLE TIME FOR ANY OF US TO RIGHT ANYTHING.
SAVANT DESERVES THE TRUTH.
YOU'RE NOT HER SISTER--
YOU'RE HER MOTHER.

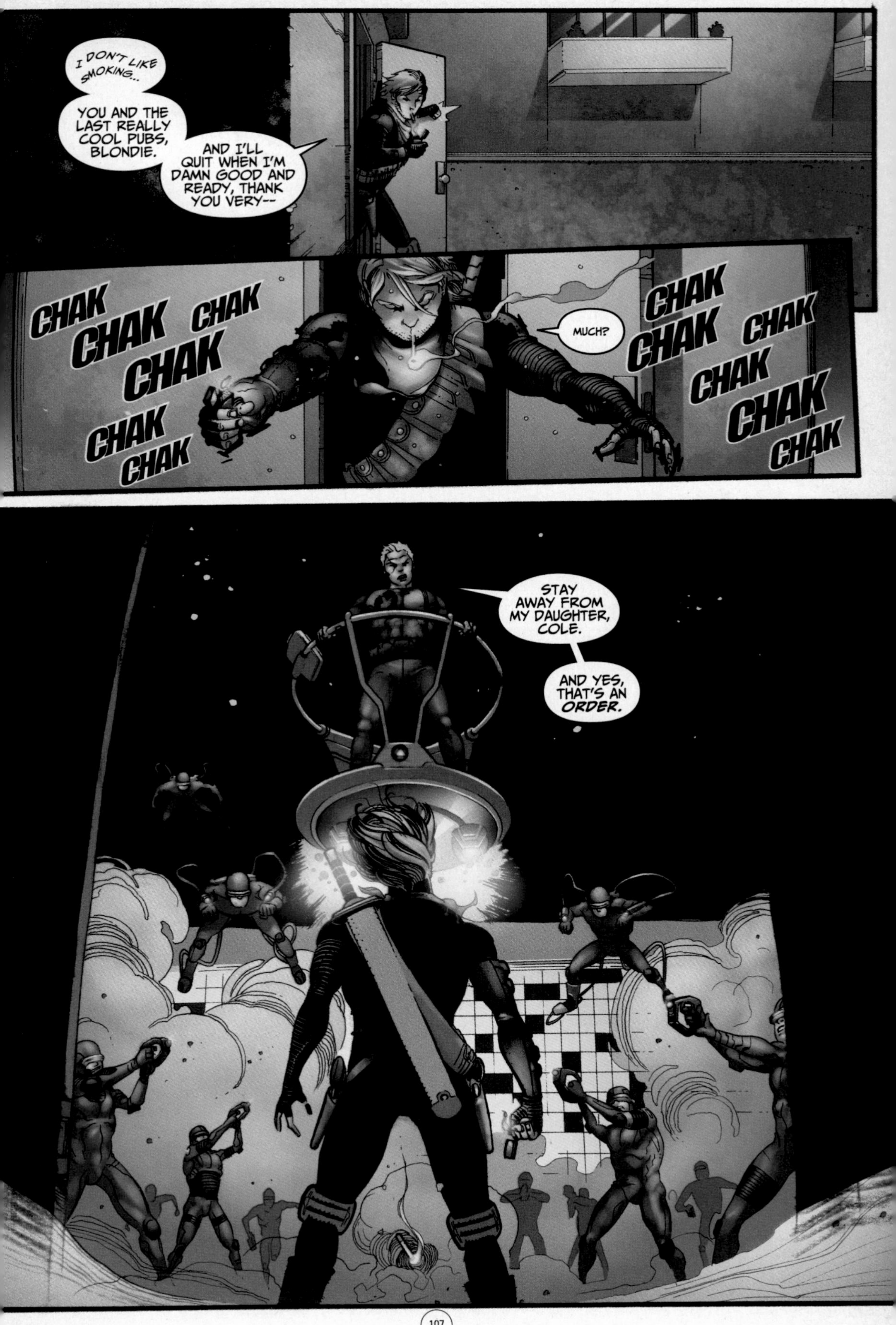
I DON'T LIKE SMOKING...
YOU AND THE LAST REALLY COOL PUBS, BLONDIE.
AND I'LL QUIT WHEN I'M DAMN GOOD AND READY, THANK YOU VERY--
CHAK CHAK CHAK CHAK CHAK CHAK
MUCH?
CHAK CHAK CHAK CHAK CHAK CHAK
STAY AWAY FROM MY DAUGHTER, COLE.
AND YES, THAT'S AN ORDER.

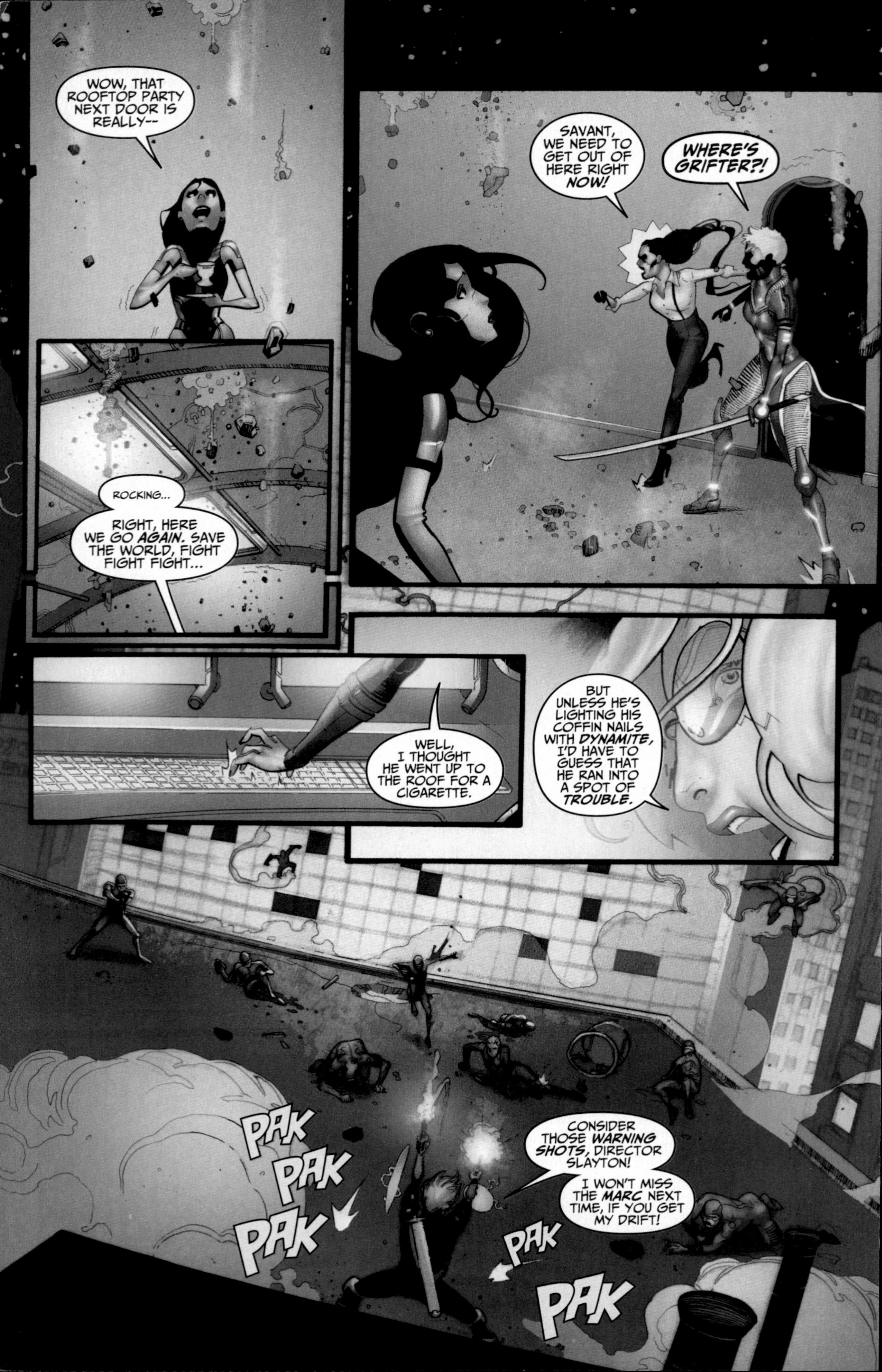
WOW, THAT ROOFTOP PARTY NEXT DOOR IS REALLY--
SAVANT, WE NEED TO GET OUT OF HERE RIGHT NOW!
WHERE'S GRIFTER?!
ROCKING...
RIGHT, HERE WE GO AGAIN. SAVE THE WORLD, FIGHT FIGHT FIGHT...
WELL, I THOUGHT HE WENT UP TO THE ROOF FOR A CIGARETTE.
BUT UNLESS HE'S LIGHTING HIS COFFIN NAILS WITH DYNAMITE, I'D HAVE TO GUESS THAT HE RAN INTO A SPOT OF TROUBLE.
PAK
PAK
PAK
CONSIDER THOSE WARNING SHOTS, DIRECTOR SLAYTON!
I WON'T MISS THE MARC NEXT TIME, IF YOU GET MY DRIFT!
PAK
PAK

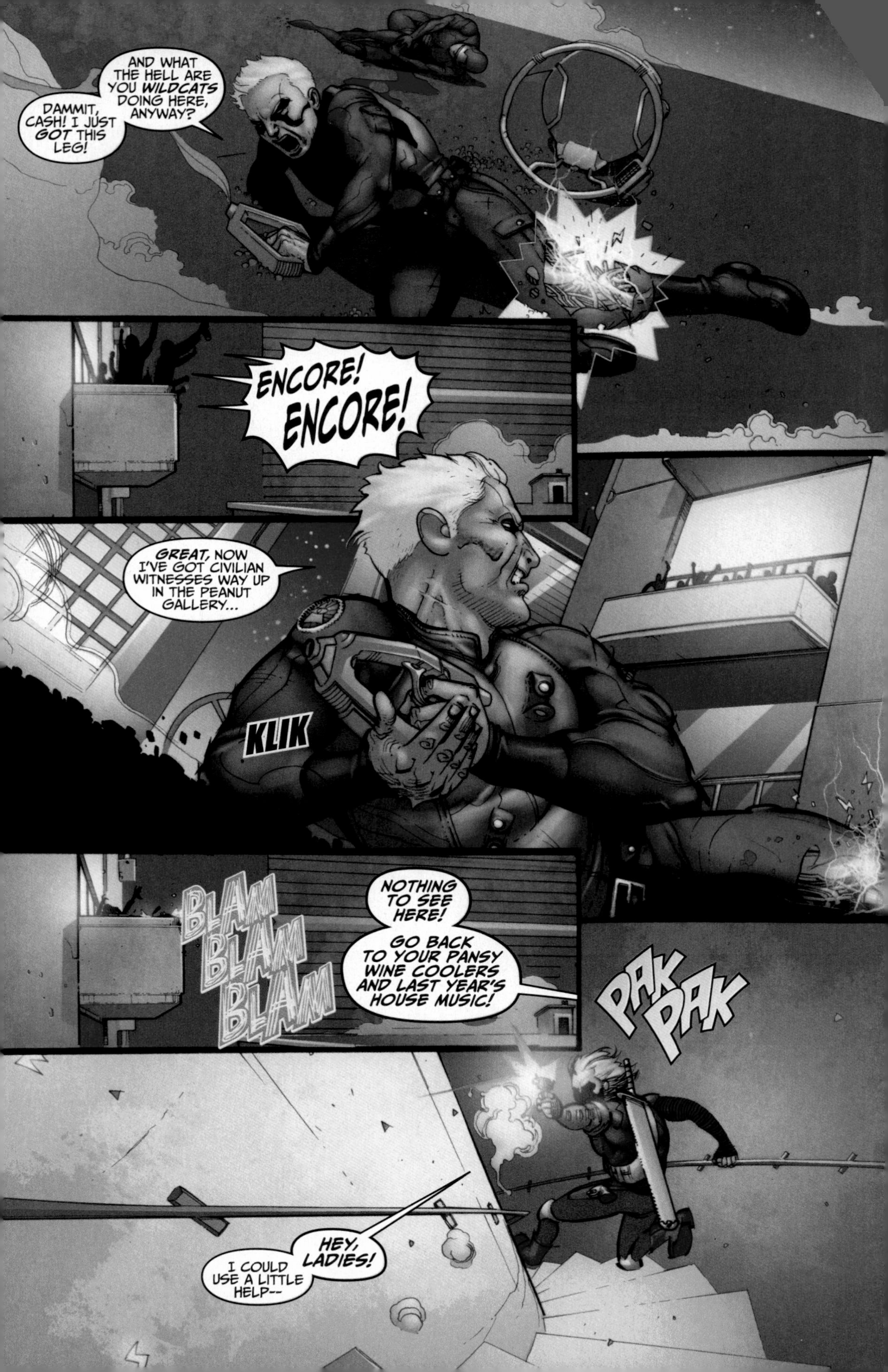
AND WHAT THE HELL ARE YOU *WILDCATS* DOING HERE, ANYWAY?
DAMMIT, CASH! I JUST *GOT* THIS LEG!
ENCORE! ENCORE!
GREAT, NOW I'VE GOT CIVILIAN WITNESSES WAY UP IN THE PEANUT GALLERY...
KLIK
BLAM BLAM BLAM
NOTHING TO SEE HERE!
GO BACK TO YOUR PANSY WINE COOLERS AND LAST YEAR'S HOUSE MUSIC!
PAK PAK
HEY, LADIES!
I COULD USE A LITTLE HELP--

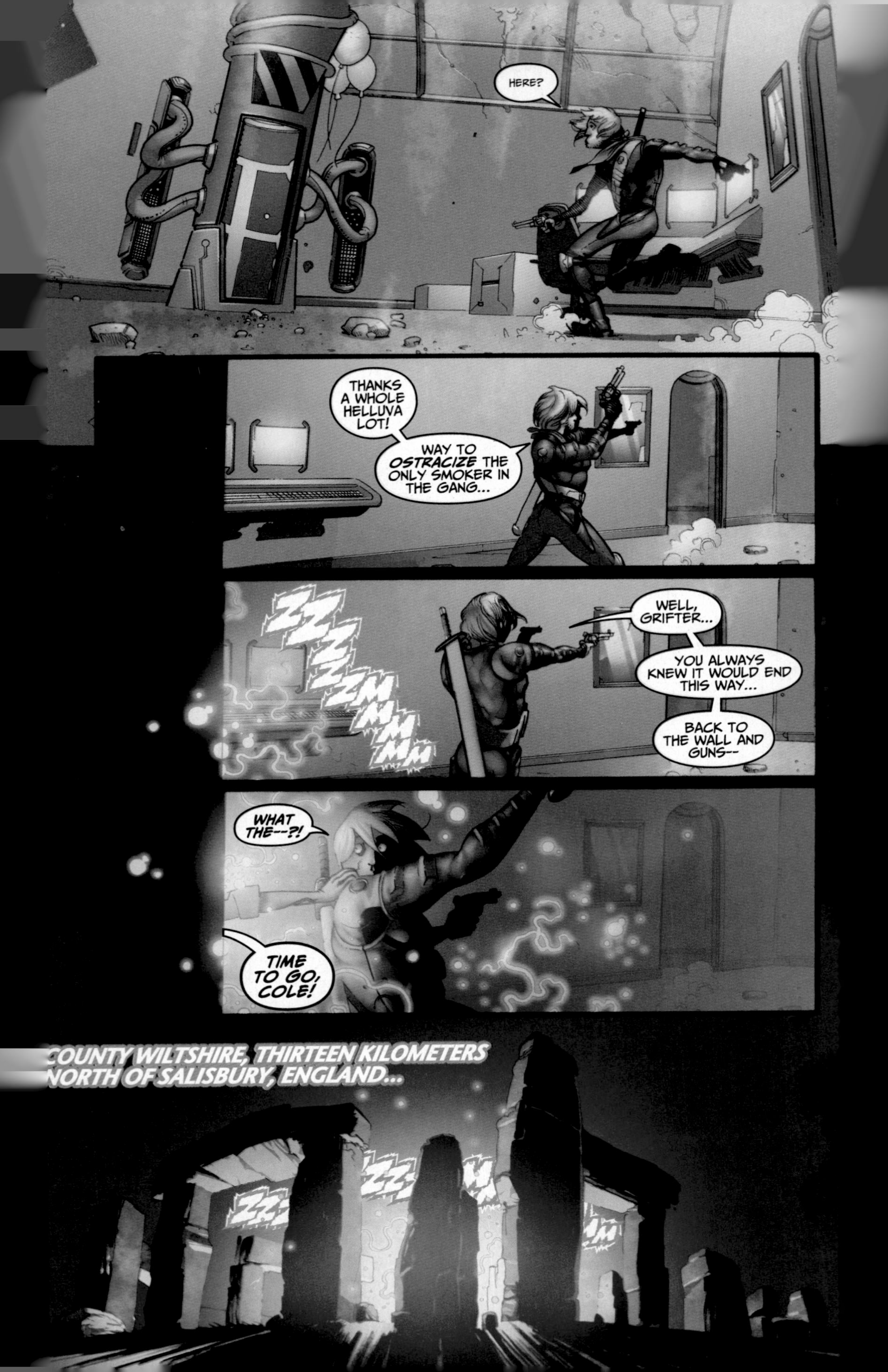
HERE?
THANKS A WHOLE HELLUVA LOT!
WAY TO OSTRACIZE THE ONLY SMOKER IN THE GANG...
ZZZZMMMMMM
WELL, GRIFTER...
YOU ALWAYS KNEW IT WOULD END THIS WAY...
BACK TO THE WALL AND GUNS--
WHAT THE--?!
TIME TO GO, COLE!
COUNTY WILTSHIRE, THIRTEEN KILOMETERS NORTH OF SALISBURY, ENGLAND...

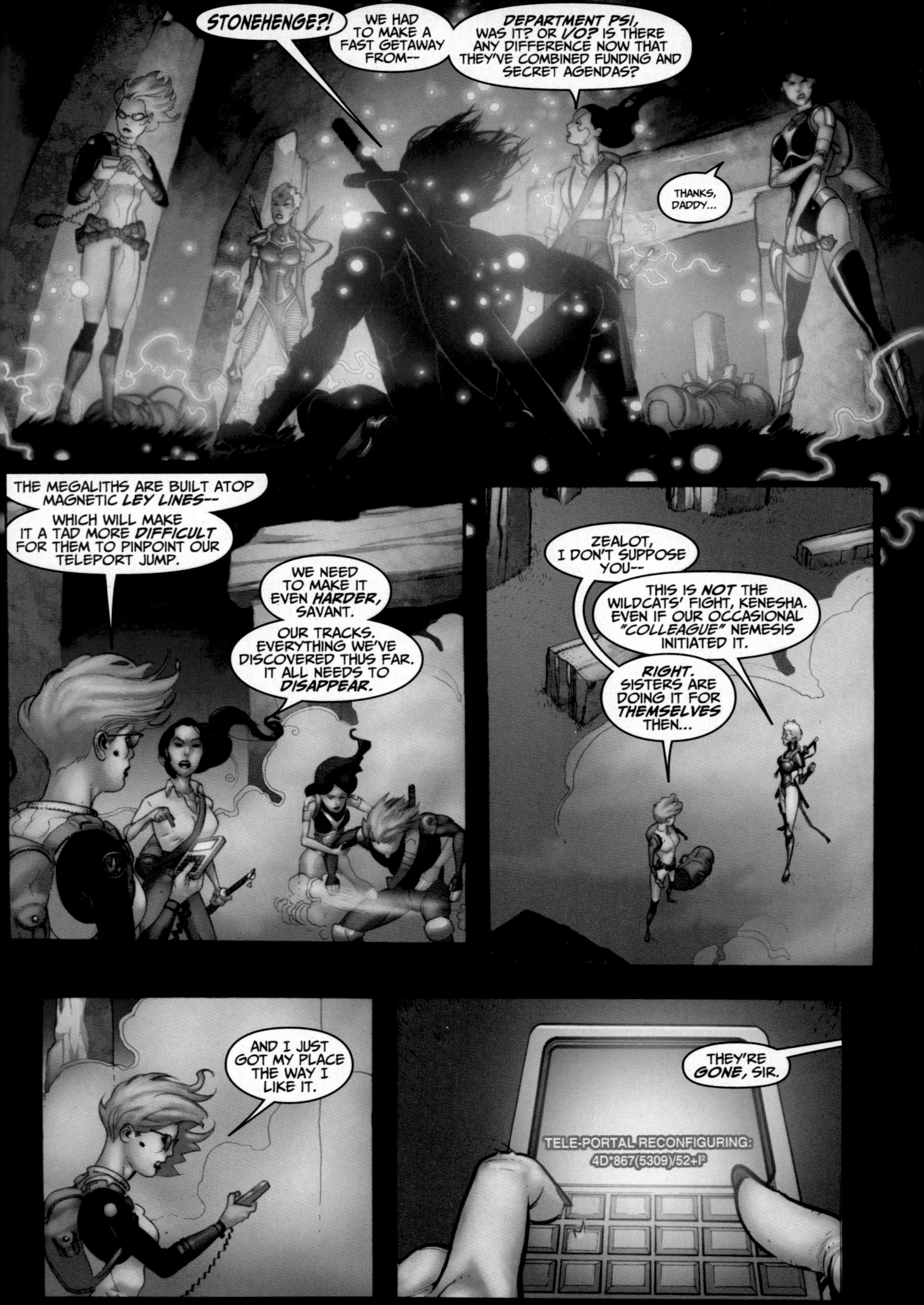
STONEHENGE?!
WE HAD TO MAKE A FAST GETAWAY FROM--
DEPARTMENT PSI, WAS IT? OR I/O? IS THERE ANY DIFFERENCE NOW THAT THEY'VE COMBINED FUNDING AND SECRET AGENDAS?
THANKS, DADDY...
THE MEGALITHS ARE BUILT ATOP MAGNETIC LEY LINES--
WHICH WILL MAKE IT A TAD MORE DIFFICULT FOR THEM TO PINPOINT OUR TELEPORT JUMP.
WE NEED TO MAKE IT EVEN HARDER, SAVANT.
OUR TRACKS. EVERYTHING WE'VE DISCOVERED THUS FAR. IT ALL NEEDS TO DISAPPEAR.
ZEALOT, I DON'T SUPPOSE YOU--
THIS IS NOT THE WILDCATS' FIGHT, KENESHA. EVEN IF OUR OCCASIONAL "COLLEAGUE" NEMESIS INITIATED IT.
RIGHT. SISTERS ARE DOING IT FOR THEMSELVES THEN...
AND I JUST GOT MY PLACE THE WAY I LIKE IT.
THEY'RE GONE, SIR.
TELE-PORTAL RECONFIGURING:
4D*867(5309)/52+I²

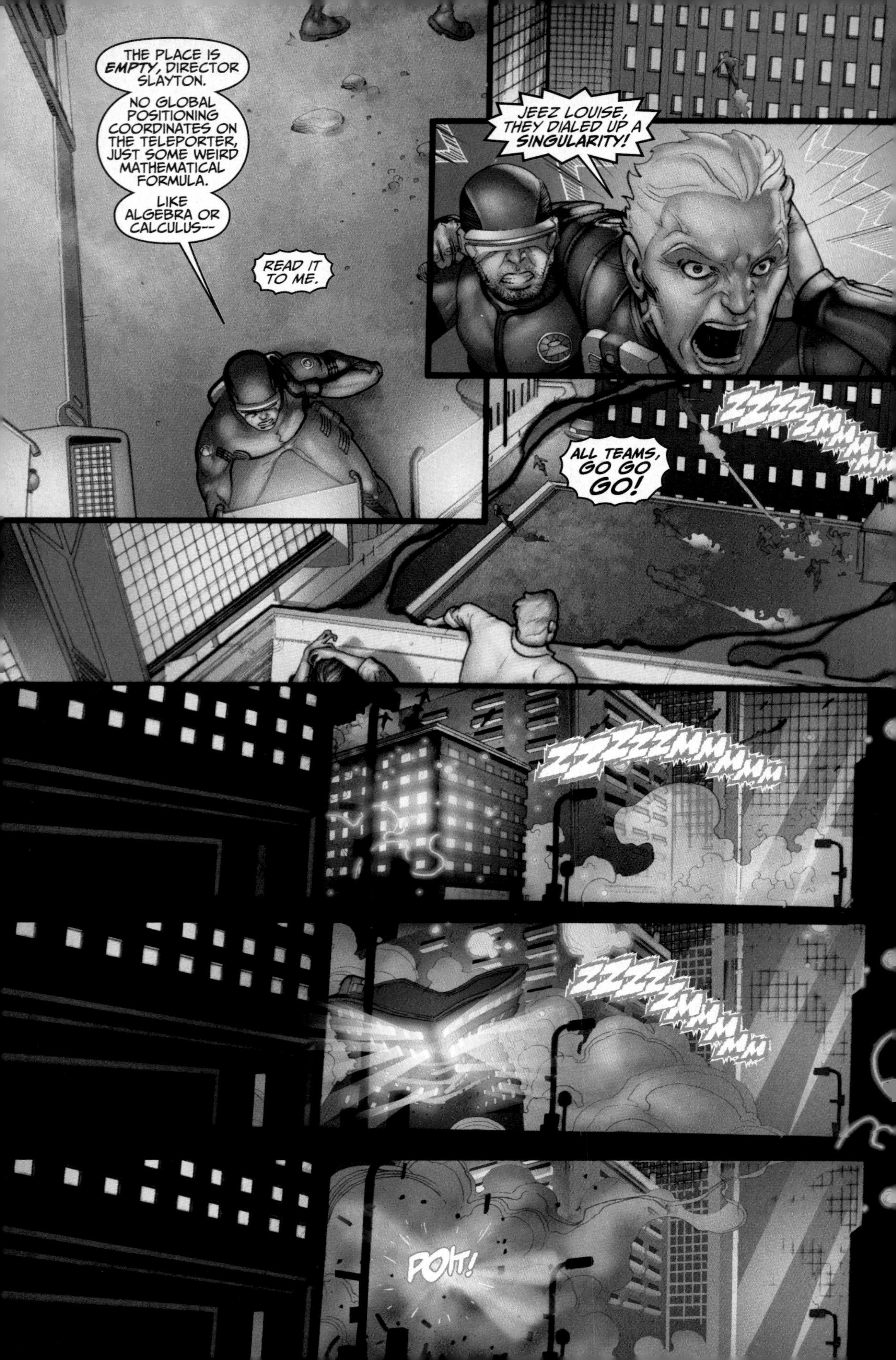
THE PLACE IS EMPTY, DIRECTOR SLAYTON.
NO GLOBAL POSITIONING COORDINATES ON THE TELEPORTER, JUST SOME WEIRD MATHEMATICAL FORMULA.
LIKE ALGEBRA OR CALCULUS--
READ IT TO ME.
JEEZ LOUISE, THEY DIALED UP A SINGULARITY!
ZZZZZMMMMM
ALL TEAMS, GO GO GO!
ZZZZZMMMMMM
ZZZZZMMMMM
POIT!

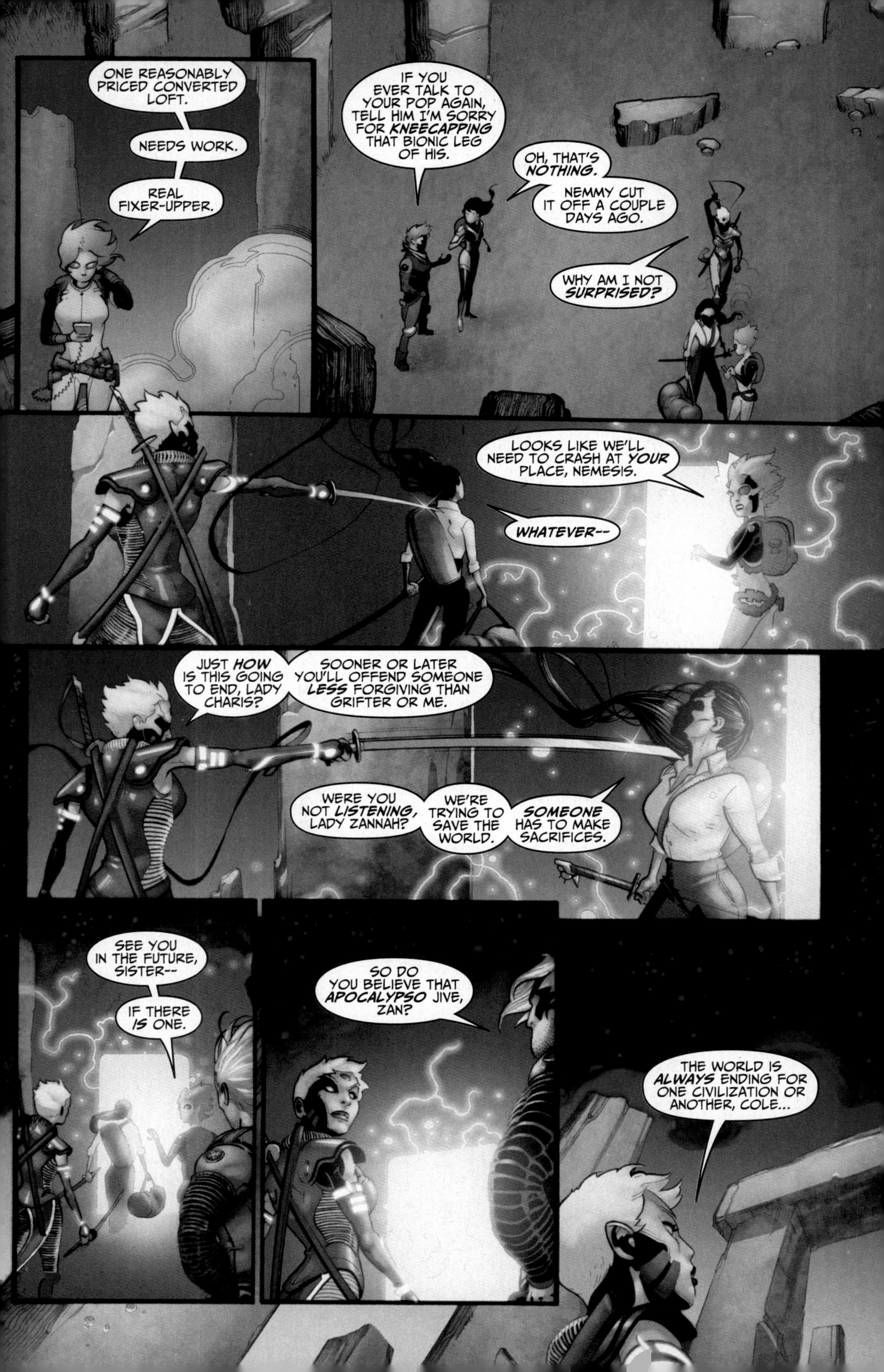
ONE REASONABLY PRICED CONVERTED LOFT.
NEEDS WORK.
REAL FIXER-UPPER.
IF YOU EVER TALK TO YOUR POP AGAIN, TELL HIM I'M SORRY FOR *KNEECAPPING* THAT BIONIC LEG OF HIS.
OH, THAT'S *NOTHING.*
NEMMY CUT IT OFF A COUPLE DAYS AGO.
WHY AM I NOT *SURPRISED?*
LOOKS LIKE WE'LL NEED TO CRASH AT *YOUR* PLACE, NEMESIS.
WHATEVER--
JUST *HOW* IS THIS GOING TO END, LADY CHARIS?
SOONER OR LATER YOU'LL OFFEND SOMEONE *LESS* FORGIVING THAN GRIFTER OR ME.
WERE YOU NOT *LISTENING,* LADY ZANNAH?
WE'RE TRYING TO SAVE THE WORLD.
SOMEONE HAS TO MAKE SACRIFICES.
SEE YOU IN THE FUTURE, SISTER--
IF THERE *IS* ONE.
SO DO YOU BELIEVE THAT *APOCALYPSO* JIVE, ZAN?
THE WORLD IS *ALWAYS* ENDING FOR ONE CIVILIZATION OR ANOTHER, COLE...

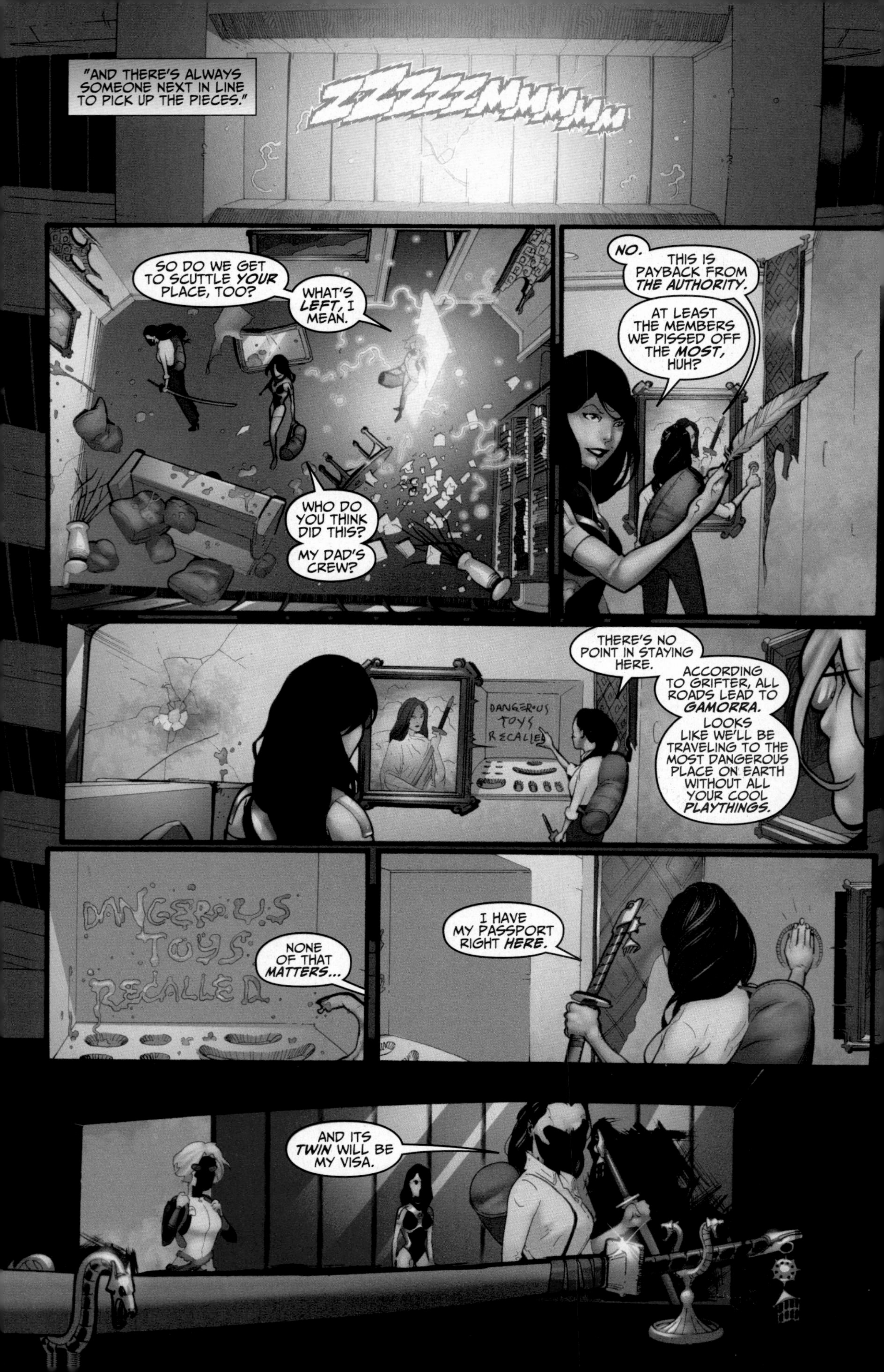
"AND THERE'S ALWAYS SOMEONE NEXT IN LINE TO PICK UP THE PIECES."
ZZZZZMMMMM
SO DO WE GET TO SCUTTLE *YOUR* PLACE, TOO?
WHAT'S *LEFT*, I MEAN.
WHO DO YOU THINK DID THIS?
MY DAD'S CREW?
NO.
THIS IS PAYBACK FROM *THE AUTHORITY*.
AT LEAST THE MEMBERS WE PISSED OFF THE *MOST*, HUH?
DANGEROUS TOYS RECALLED
THERE'S NO POINT IN STAYING HERE.
ACCORDING TO GRIFTER, ALL ROADS LEAD TO *GAMORRA.*
LOOKS LIKE WE'LL BE TRAVELING TO THE MOST DANGEROUS PLACE ON EARTH WITHOUT ALL YOUR COOL *PLAYTHINGS*.
DANGEROUS TOYS RECALLED
NONE OF THAT *MATTERS...*
I HAVE MY PASSPORT RIGHT *HERE*.
AND ITS *TWIN* WILL BE MY VISA.

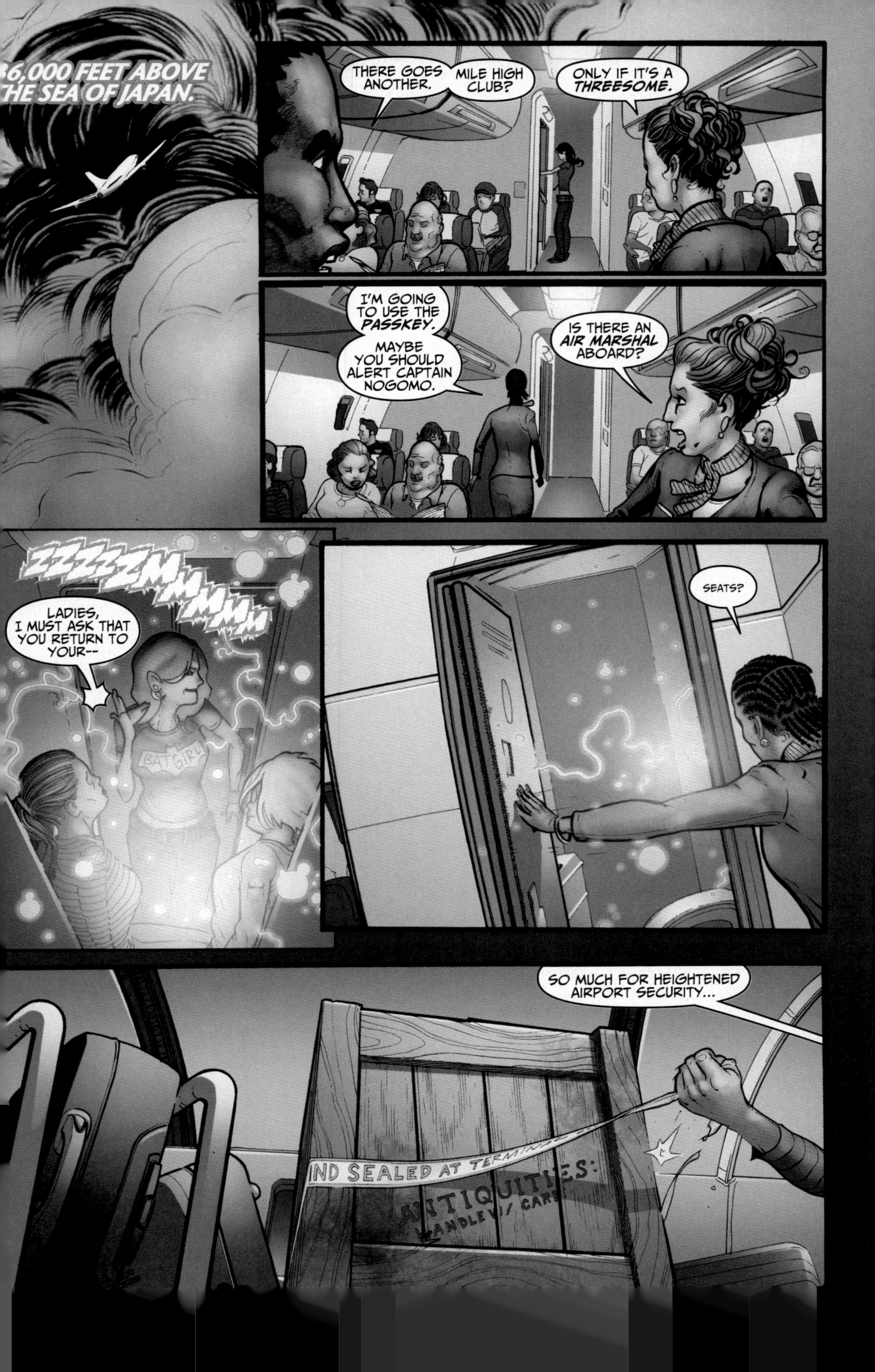
36,000 FEET ABOVE THE SEA OF JAPAN.
THERE GOES ANOTHER.
MILE HIGH CLUB?
ONLY IF IT'S A THREESOME.
I'M GOING TO USE THE PASSKEY.
MAYBE YOU SHOULD ALERT CAPTAIN NOGOMO.
IS THERE AN AIR MARSHAL ABOARD?
ZZZZZMMMMMM
LADIES, I MUST ASK THAT YOU RETURN TO YOUR--
BATGIRL
SEATS?
SO MUCH FOR HEIGHTENED AIRPORT SECURITY...
ND SEALED AT TERM
ANTIQUITIES:
HANDLE W/ CARE

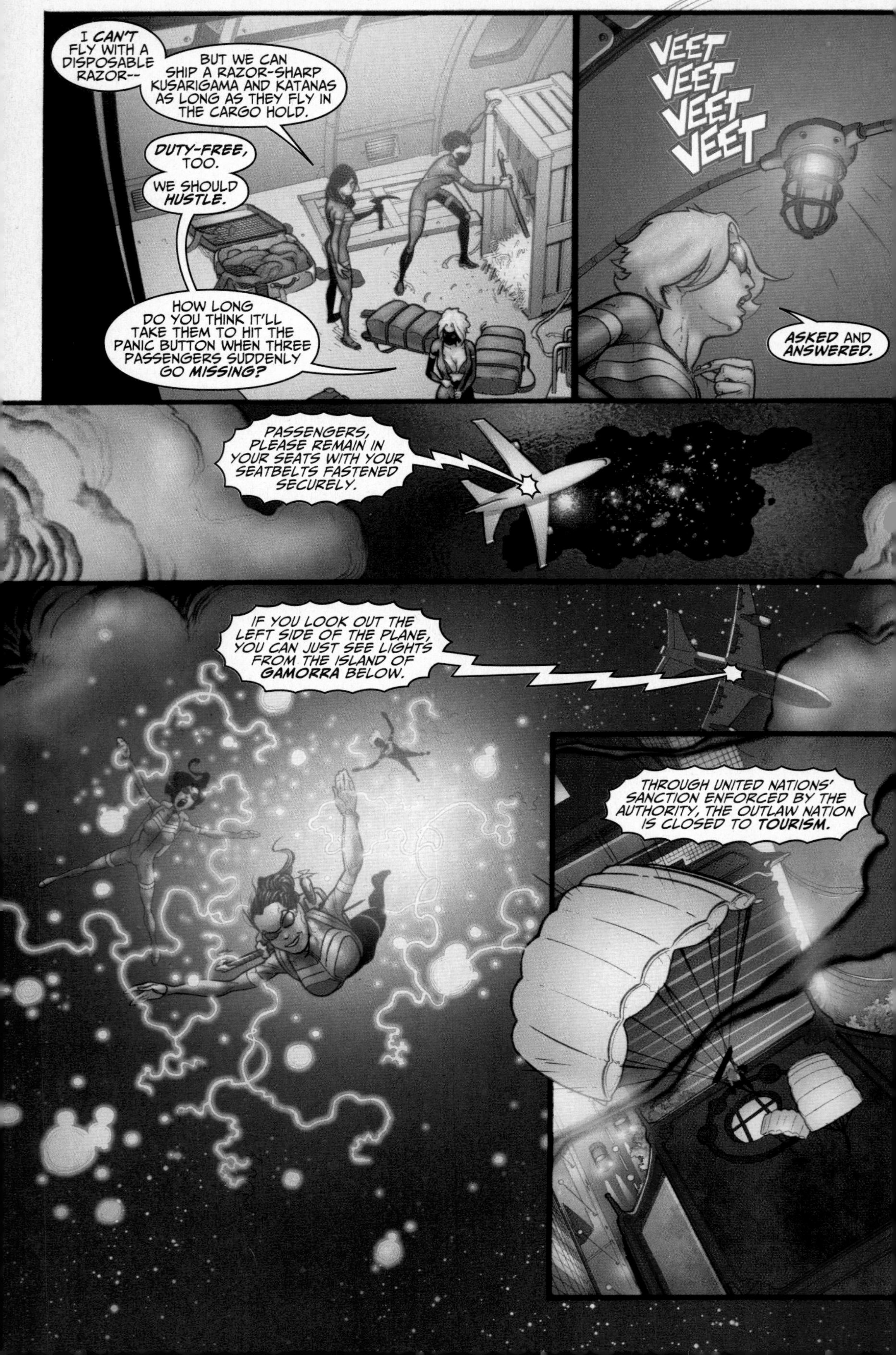
I CAN'T FLY WITH A DISPOSABLE RAZOR--
BUT WE CAN SHIP A RAZOR-SHARP KUSARIGAMA AND KATANAS AS LONG AS THEY FLY IN THE CARGO HOLD.
DUTY-FREE, TOO.
WE SHOULD HUSTLE.
HOW LONG DO YOU THINK IT'LL TAKE THEM TO HIT THE PANIC BUTTON WHEN THREE PASSENGERS SUDDENLY GO MISSING?
VEET VEET VEET VEET
ASKED AND ANSWERED.
PASSENGERS, PLEASE REMAIN IN YOUR SEATS WITH YOUR SEATBELTS FASTENED SECURELY.
IF YOU LOOK OUT THE LEFT SIDE OF THE PLANE, YOU CAN JUST SEE LIGHTS FROM THE ISLAND OF GAMORRA BELOW.
THROUGH UNITED NATIONS' SANCTION ENFORCED BY THE AUTHORITY, THE OUTLAW NATION IS CLOSED TO TOURISM.

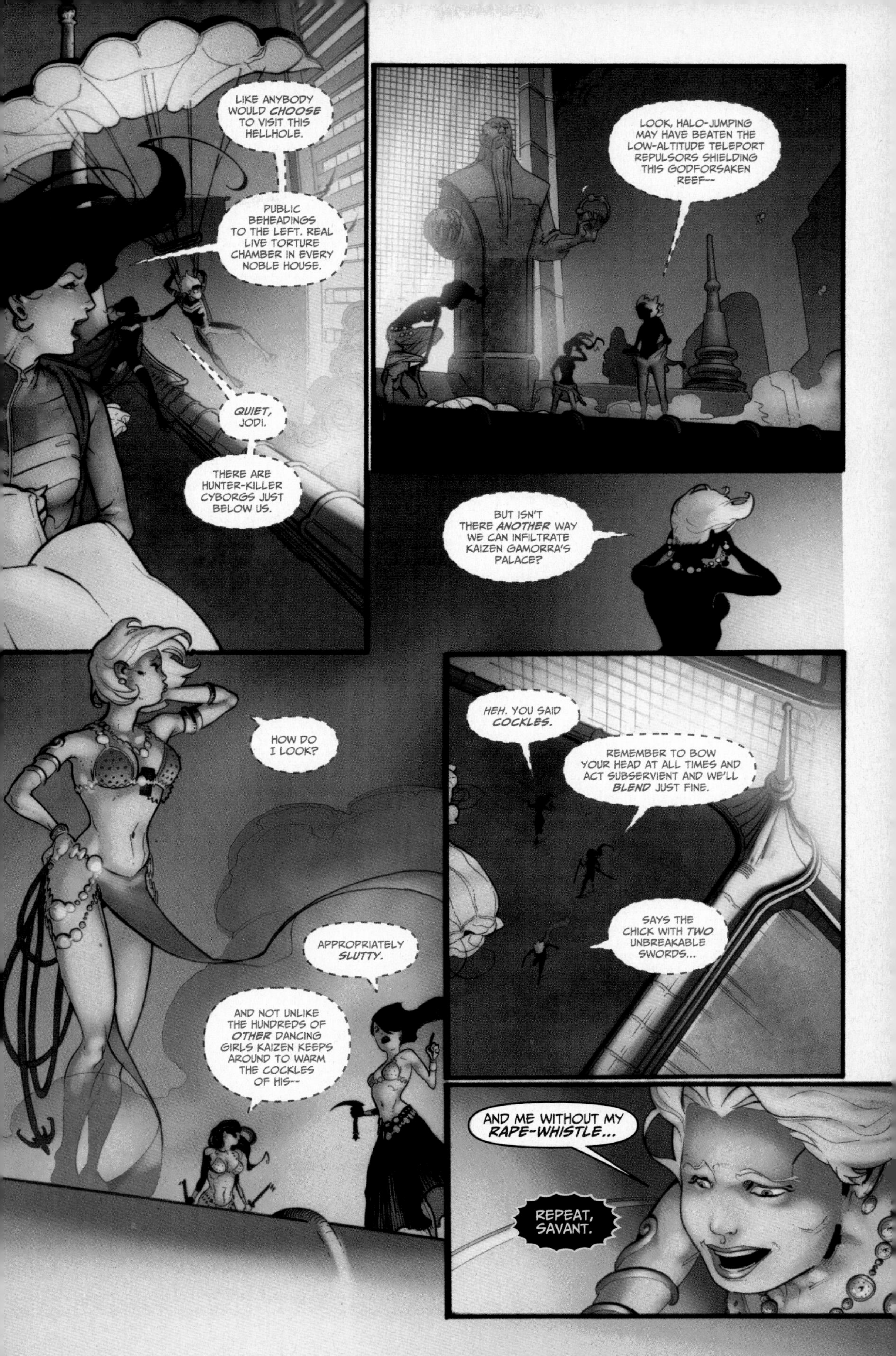
LIKE ANYBODY WOULD CHOOSE TO VISIT THIS HELLHOLE.
PUBLIC BEHEADINGS TO THE LEFT. REAL LIVE TORTURE CHAMBER IN EVERY NOBLE HOUSE.
QUIET, JODI.
THERE ARE HUNTER-KILLER CYBORGS JUST BELOW US.
LOOK, HALO-JUMPING MAY HAVE BEATEN THE LOW-ALTITUDE TELEPORT REPULSORS SHIELDING THIS GODFORSAKEN REEF--
BUT ISN'T THERE ANOTHER WAY WE CAN INFILTRATE KAIZEN GAMORRA'S PALACE?
HOW DO I LOOK?
APPROPRIATELY SLUTTY.
AND NOT UNLIKE THE HUNDREDS OF OTHER DANCING GIRLS KAIZEN KEEPS AROUND TO WARM THE COCKLES OF HIS--
HEH. YOU SAID COCKLES.
REMEMBER TO BOW YOUR HEAD AT ALL TIMES AND ACT SUBSERVIENT AND WE'LL BLEND JUST FINE.
SAYS THE CHICK WITH TWO UNBREAKABLE SWORDS...
AND ME WITHOUT MY RAPE-WHISTLE...
REPEAT, SAVANT.

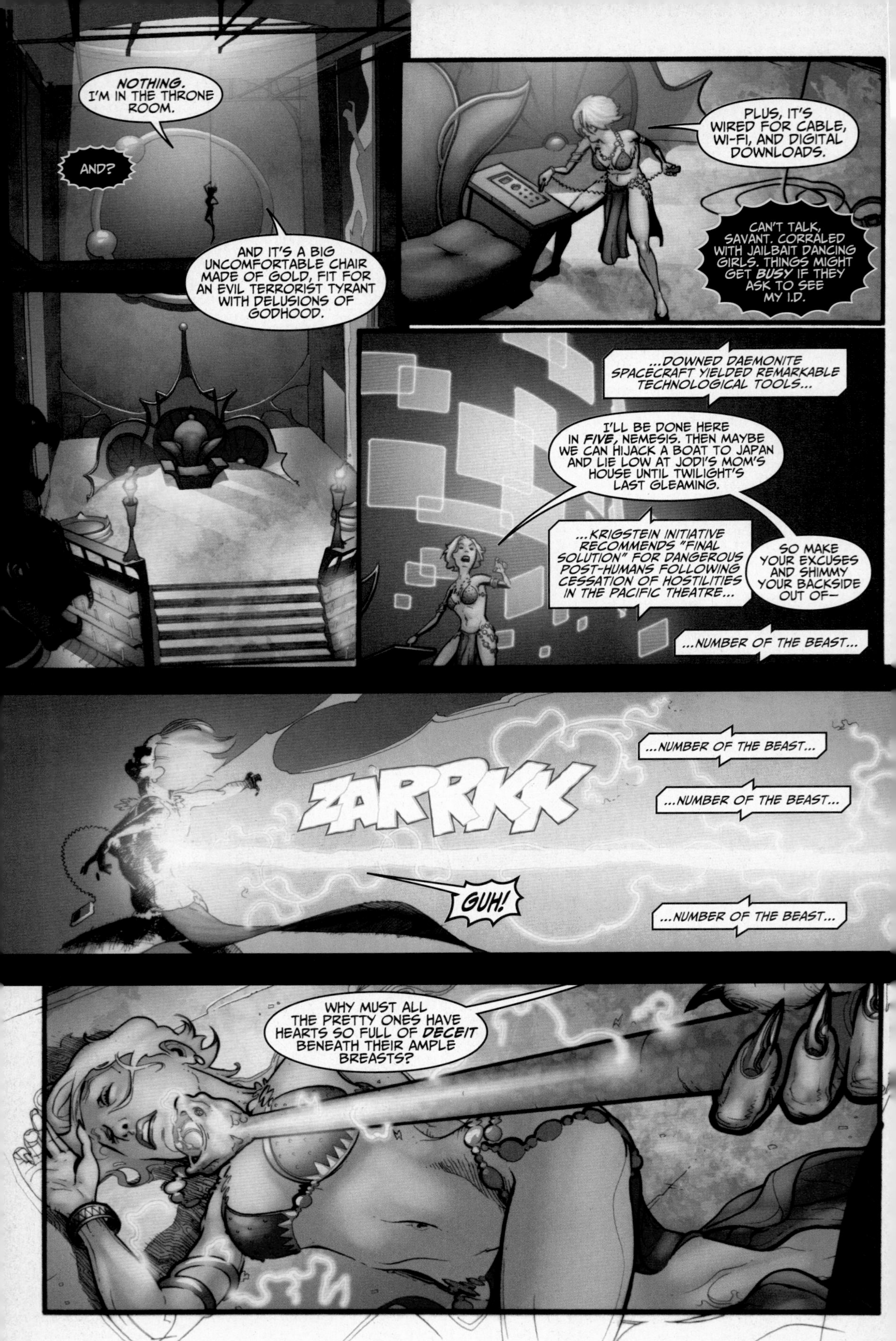
NOTHING. I'M IN THE THRONE ROOM.
AND?
AND IT'S A BIG UNCOMFORTABLE CHAIR MADE OF GOLD, FIT FOR AN EVIL TERRORIST TYRANT WITH DELUSIONS OF GODHOOD.
PLUS, IT'S WIRED FOR CABLE, WI-FI, AND DIGITAL DOWNLOADS.
CAN'T TALK, SAVANT. CORRALED WITH JAILBAIT DANCING GIRLS. THINGS MIGHT GET BUSY IF THEY ASK TO SEE MY I.D.
...DOWNED DAEMONITE SPACECRAFT YIELDED REMARKABLE TECHNOLOGICAL TOOLS...
I'LL BE DONE HERE IN FIVE, NEMESIS. THEN MAYBE WE CAN HIJACK A BOAT TO JAPAN AND LIE LOW AT JODI'S MOM'S HOUSE UNTIL TWILIGHT'S LAST GLEAMING.
...KRIGSTEIN INITIATIVE RECOMMENDS "FINAL SOLUTION" FOR DANGEROUS POST-HUMANS FOLLOWING CESSATION OF HOSTILITIES IN THE PACIFIC THEATRE...
SO MAKE YOUR EXCUSES AND SHIMMY YOUR BACKSIDE OUT OF—
...NUMBER OF THE BEAST...
...NUMBER OF THE BEAST...
ZARRKK
...NUMBER OF THE BEAST...
GUH!
...NUMBER OF THE BEAST...
WHY MUST ALL THE PRETTY ONES HAVE HEARTS SO FULL OF DECEIT BENEATH THEIR AMPLE BREASTS?

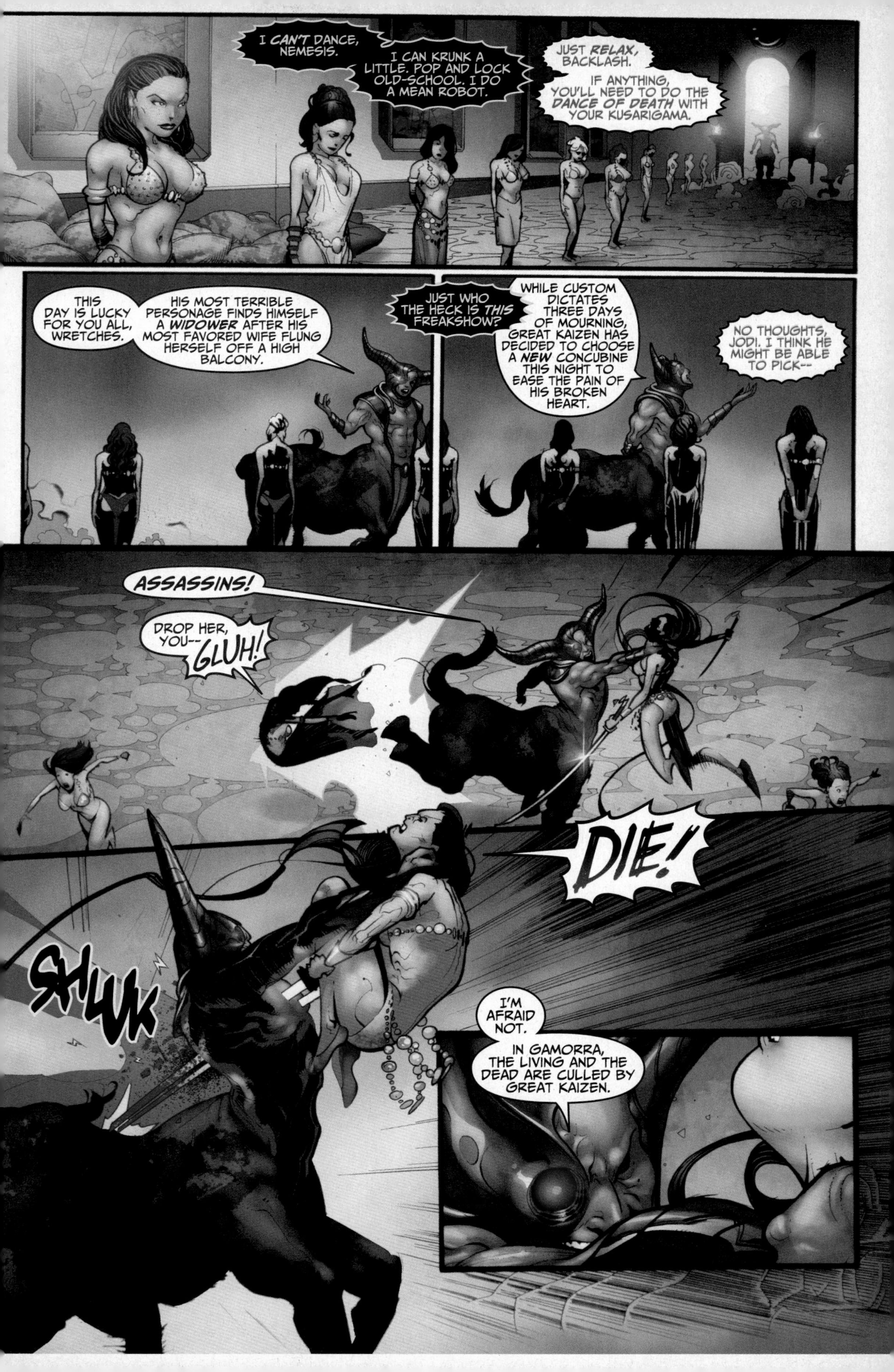
I CAN'T DANCE, NEMESIS.
I CAN KRUNK A LITTLE. POP AND LOCK OLD-SCHOOL. I DO A MEAN ROBOT.
JUST RELAX, BACKLASH.
IF ANYTHING, YOU'LL NEED TO DO THE DANCE OF DEATH WITH YOUR KUSARIGAMA.
THIS DAY IS LUCKY FOR YOU ALL, WRETCHES.
HIS MOST TERRIBLE PERSONAGE FINDS HIMSELF A WIDOWER AFTER HIS MOST FAVORED WIFE FLUNG HERSELF OFF A HIGH BALCONY.
JUST WHO THE HECK IS THIS FREAKSHOW?
WHILE CUSTOM DICTATES THREE DAYS OF MOURNING, GREAT KAIZEN HAS DECIDED TO CHOOSE A NEW CONCUBINE THIS NIGHT TO EASE THE PAIN OF HIS BROKEN HEART.
NO THOUGHTS, JODI. I THINK HE MIGHT BE ABLE TO PICK--
ASSASSINS!
DROP HER, YOU-- GLUH!
DIE!
SHLUK
I'M AFRAID NOT.
IN GAMORRA, THE LIVING AND THE DEAD ARE CULLED BY GREAT KAIZEN.

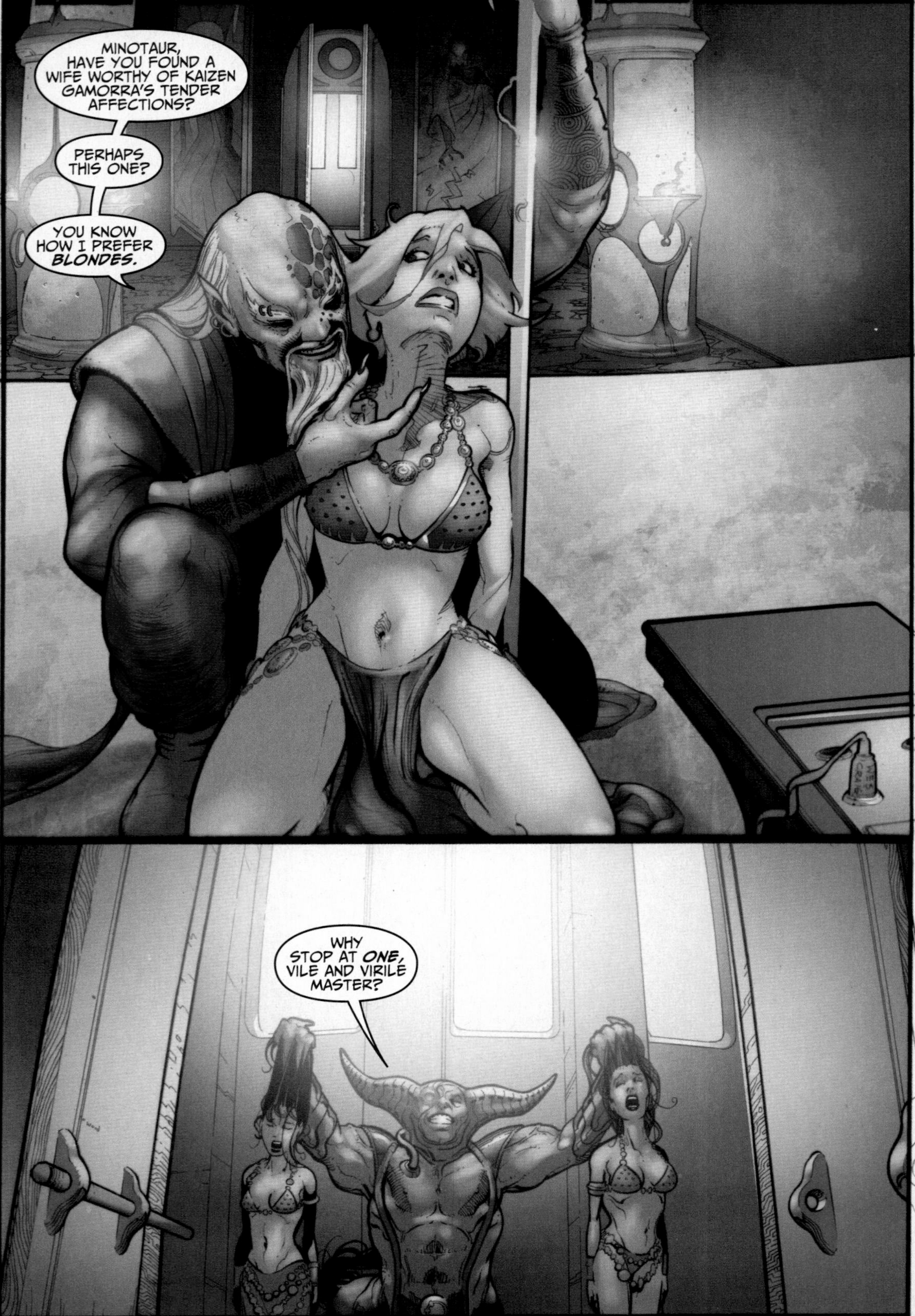
MINOTAUR, HAVE YOU FOUND A WIFE WORTHY OF KAIZEN GAMORRA'S TENDER AFFECTIONS?
PERHAPS THIS ONE?
YOU KNOW HOW I PREFER *BLONDES.*
WHY STOP AT *ONE,* VILE AND VIRILE MASTER?

Chapter 6

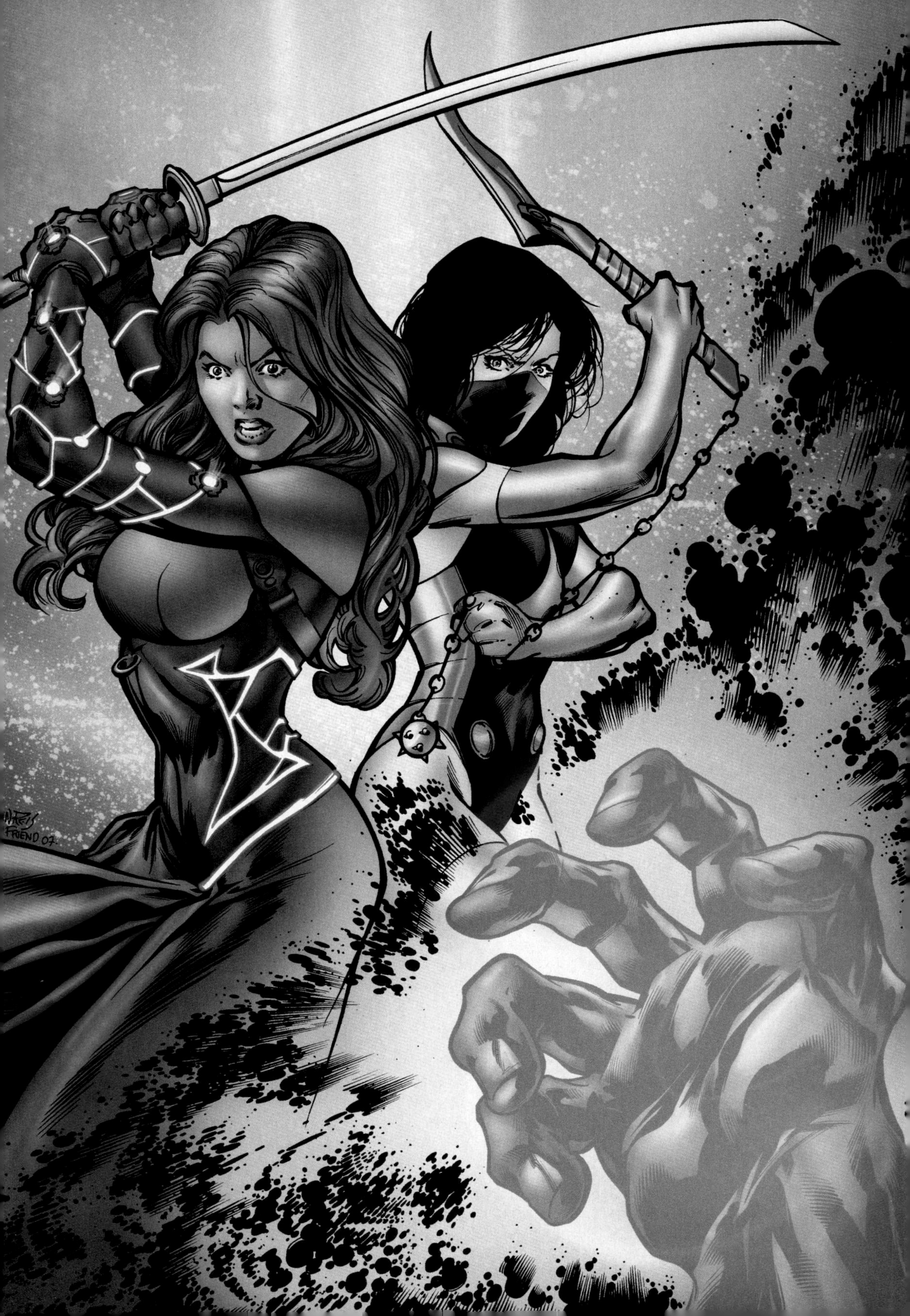

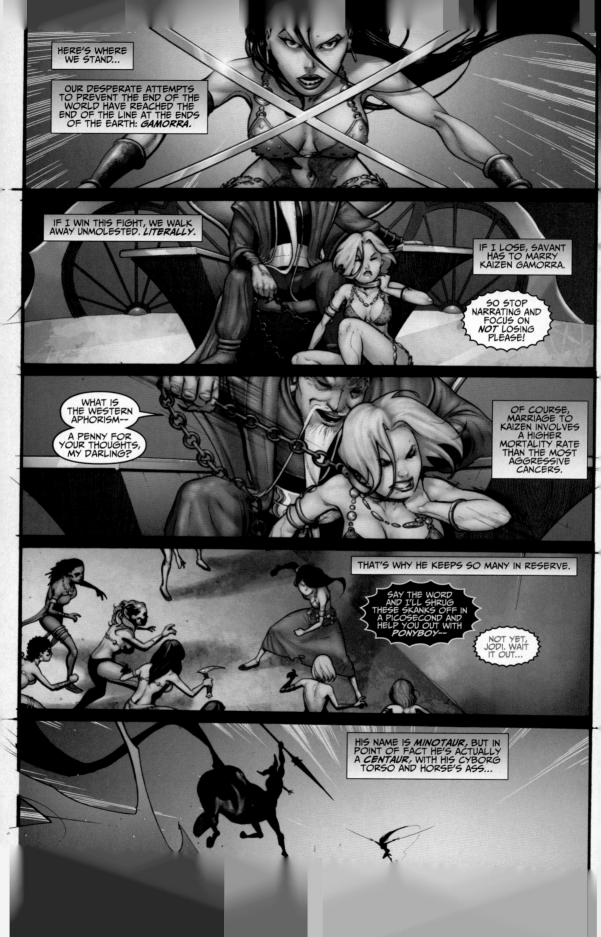

HERE'S WHERE WE STAND...

OUR DESPERATE ATTEMPTS TO PREVENT THE END OF THE WORLD HAVE REACHED THE END OF THE LINE AT THE ENDS OF THE EARTH: *GAMORRA*.

IF I WIN THIS FIGHT, WE WALK AWAY UNMOLESTED. *LITERALLY*.

IF I LOSE, SAVANT HAS TO MARRY KAIZEN GAMORRA.

SO STOP NARRATING AND FOCUS ON *NOT* LOSING PLEASE!

WHAT IS THE WESTERN APHORISM--

A PENNY FOR YOUR THOUGHTS, MY DARLING?

OF COURSE, MARRIAGE TO KAIZEN INVOLVES A HIGHER MORTALITY RATE THAN THE MOST AGGRESSIVE CANCERS.

THAT'S WHY HE KEEPS SO MANY IN RESERVE.

SAY THE WORD AND I'LL SHRUG THESE SKANKS OFF IN A PICOSECOND AND HELP YOU OUT WITH *PONYBOY*--

NOT YET, JODI. WAIT IT OUT...

HIS NAME IS *MINOTAUR*, BUT IN POINT OF FACT HE'S ACTUALLY A *CENTAUR*, WITH HIS CYBORG TORSO AND HORSE'S ASS...

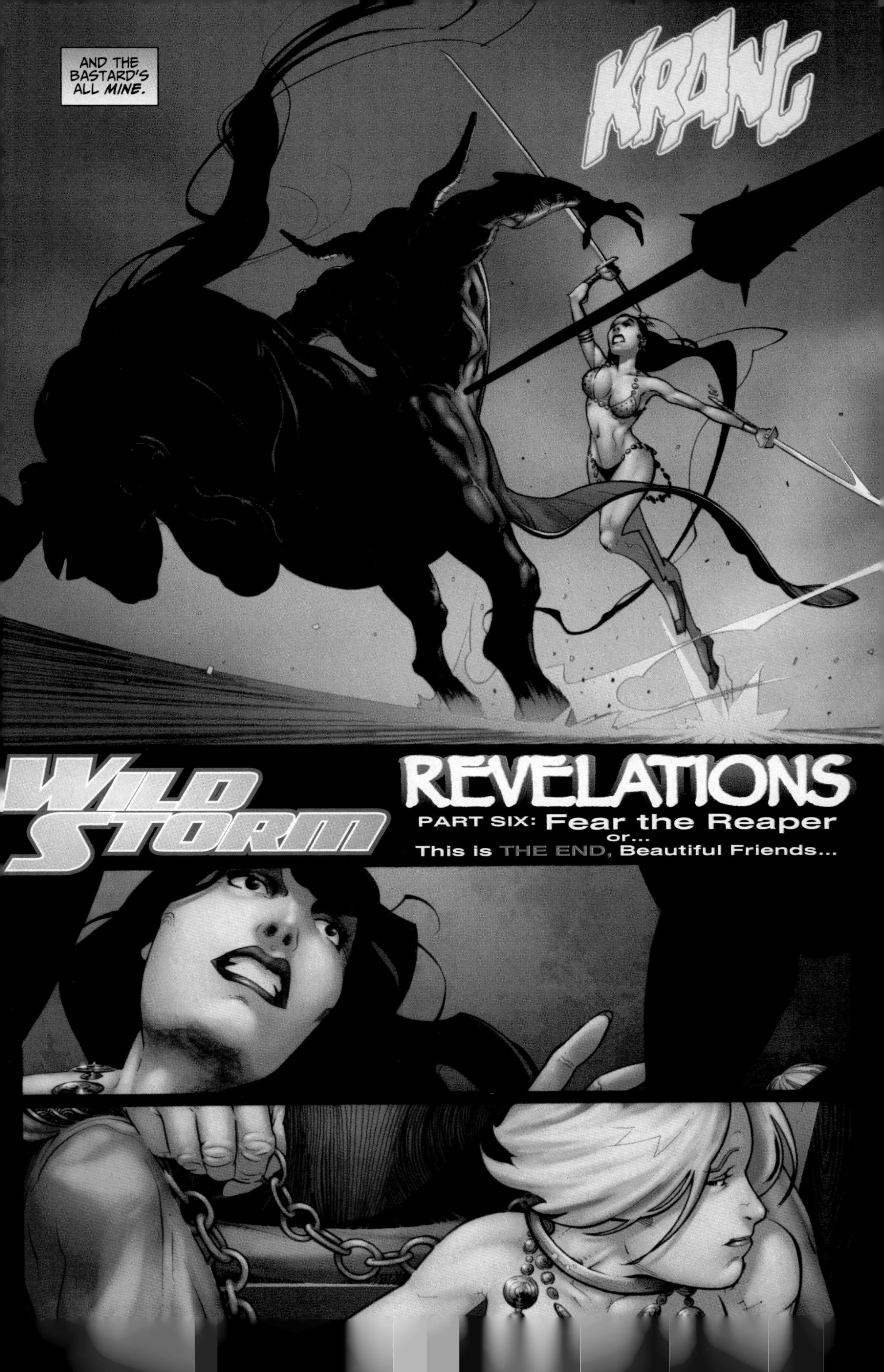
AND THE BASTARD'S ALL *MINE.*
KRANG
WILD STORM
REVELATIONS
PART SIX: Fear the Reaper
or...
This is THE END, Beautiful Friends...

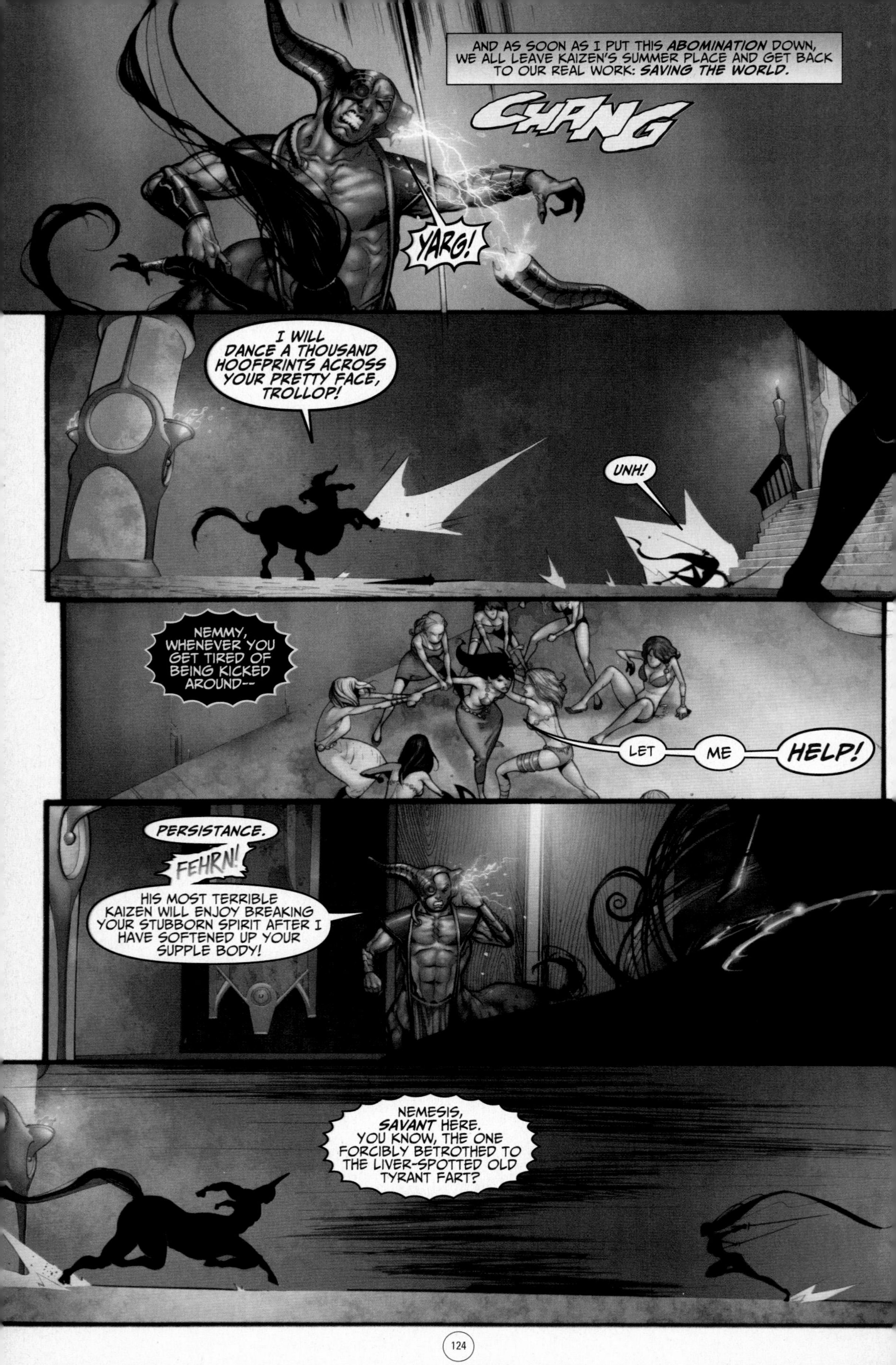

AND AS SOON AS I PUT THIS ABOMINATION DOWN, WE ALL LEAVE KAIZEN'S SUMMER PLACE AND GET BACK TO OUR REAL WORK: SAVING THE WORLD.
CHANG
YARG!
I WILL DANCE A THOUSAND HOOFPRINTS ACROSS YOUR PRETTY FACE, TROLLOP!
UNH!
NEMMY, WHENEVER YOU GET TIRED OF BEING KICKED AROUND--
LET
ME
HELP!
PERSISTANCE.
FEHRN!
HIS MOST TERRIBLE KAIZEN WILL ENJOY BREAKING YOUR STUBBORN SPIRIT AFTER I HAVE SOFTENED UP YOUR SUPPLE BODY!
NEMESIS, SAVANT HERE. YOU KNOW, THE ONE FORCIBLY BETROTHED TO THE LIVER-SPOTTED OLD TYRANT FART?

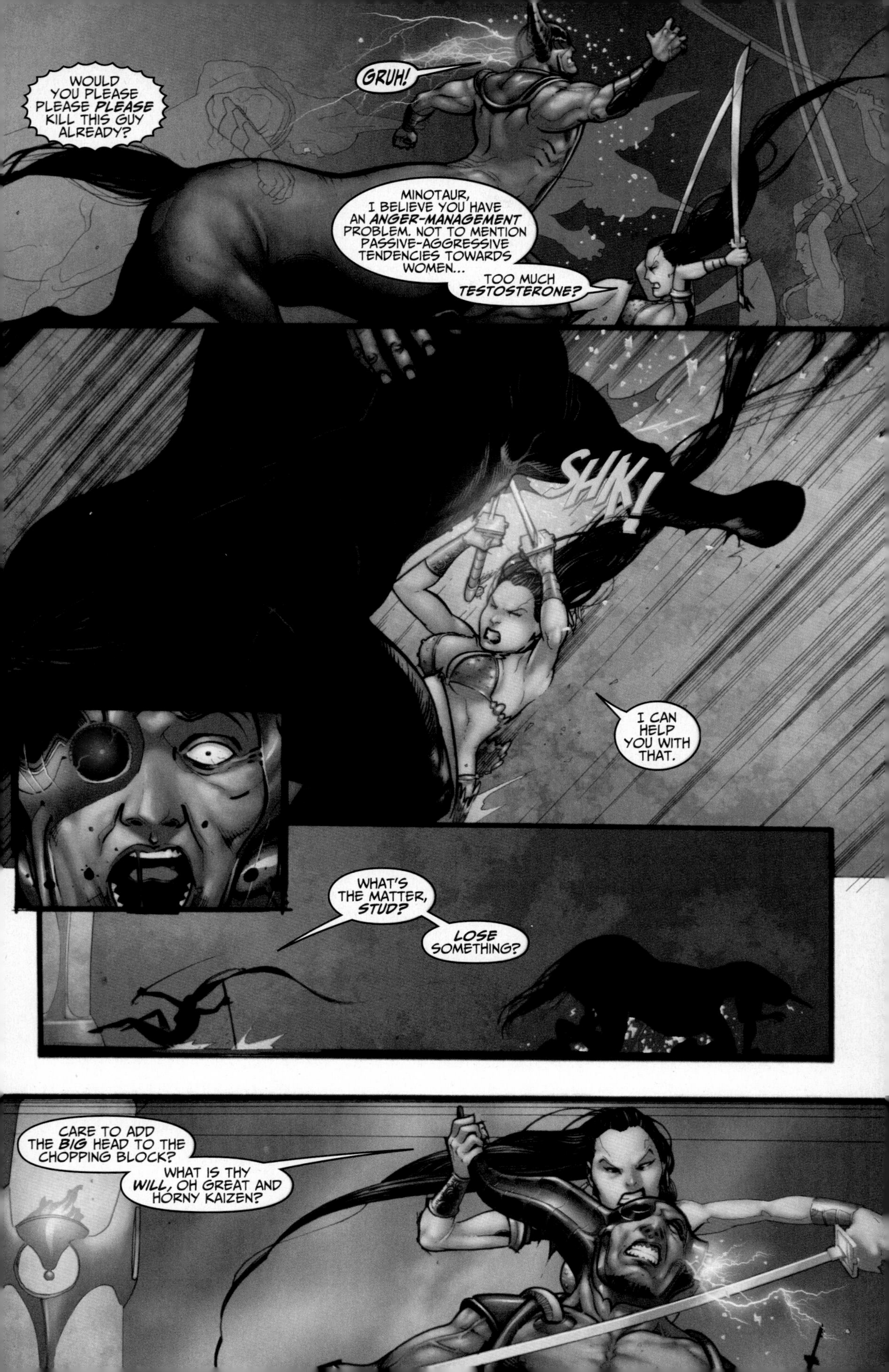

WOULD YOU PLEASE PLEASE PLEASE KILL THIS GUY ALREADY?
GRUH!
MINOTAUR, I BELIEVE YOU HAVE AN ANGER-MANAGEMENT PROBLEM. NOT TO MENTION PASSIVE-AGGRESSIVE TENDENCIES TOWARDS WOMEN...
TOO MUCH TESTOSTERONE?
SHK!
I CAN HELP YOU WITH THAT.
WHAT'S THE MATTER, STUD?
LOSE SOMETHING?
CARE TO ADD THE BIG HEAD TO THE CHOPPING BLOCK?
WHAT IS THY WILL, OH GREAT AND HORNY KAIZEN?

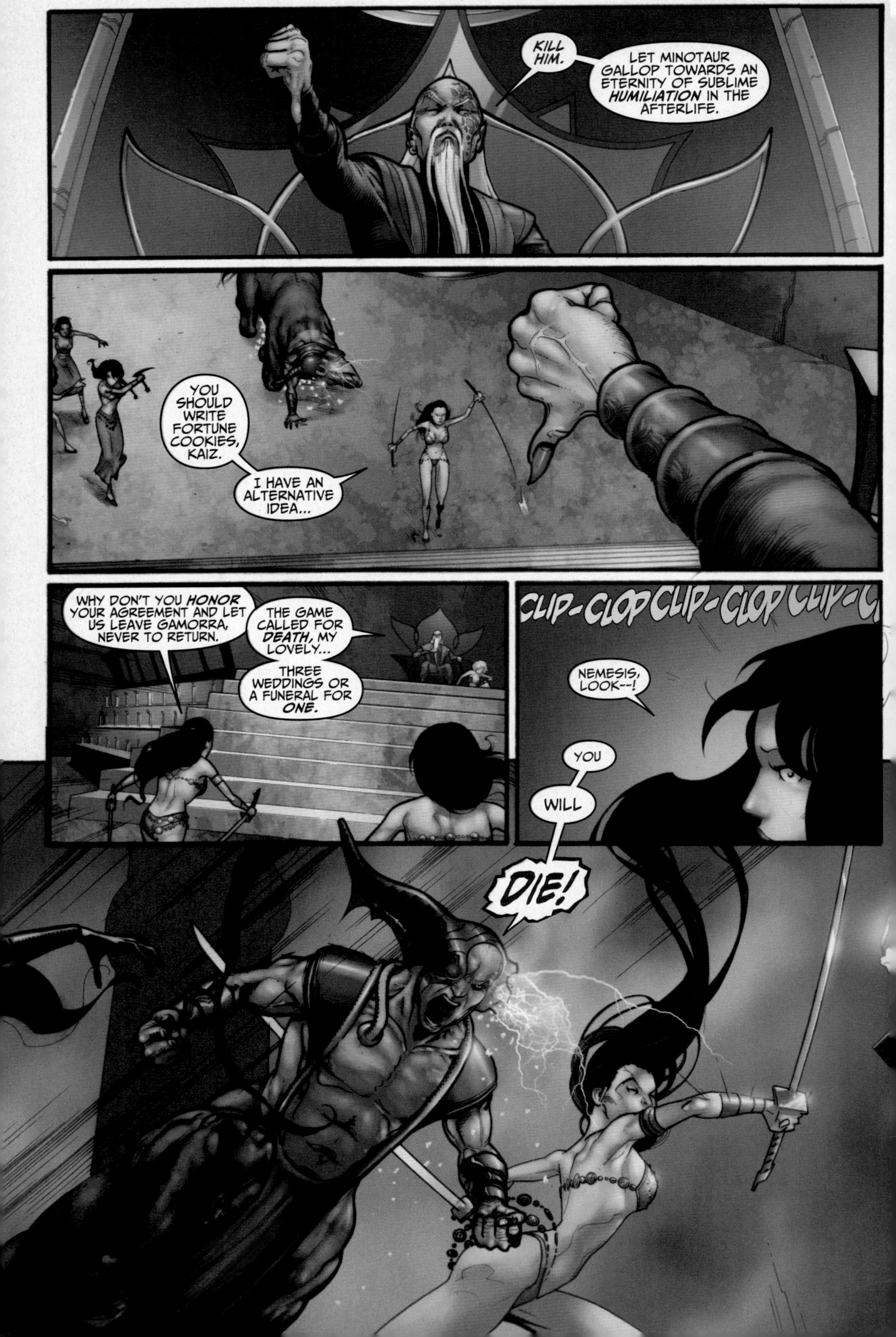
KILL HIM.
LET MINOTAUR GALLOP TOWARDS AN ETERNITY OF SUBLIME HUMILIATION IN THE AFTERLIFE.
YOU SHOULD WRITE FORTUNE COOKIES, KAIZ.
I HAVE AN ALTERNATIVE IDEA...
WHY DON'T YOU HONOR YOUR AGREEMENT AND LET US LEAVE GAMORRA, NEVER TO RETURN.
THE GAME CALLED FOR DEATH, MY LOVELY...
THREE WEDDINGS OR A FUNERAL FOR ONE.
CLIP-CLOP CLIP-CLOP CLIP-C
NEMESIS, LOOK--!
YOU
WILL
DIE!

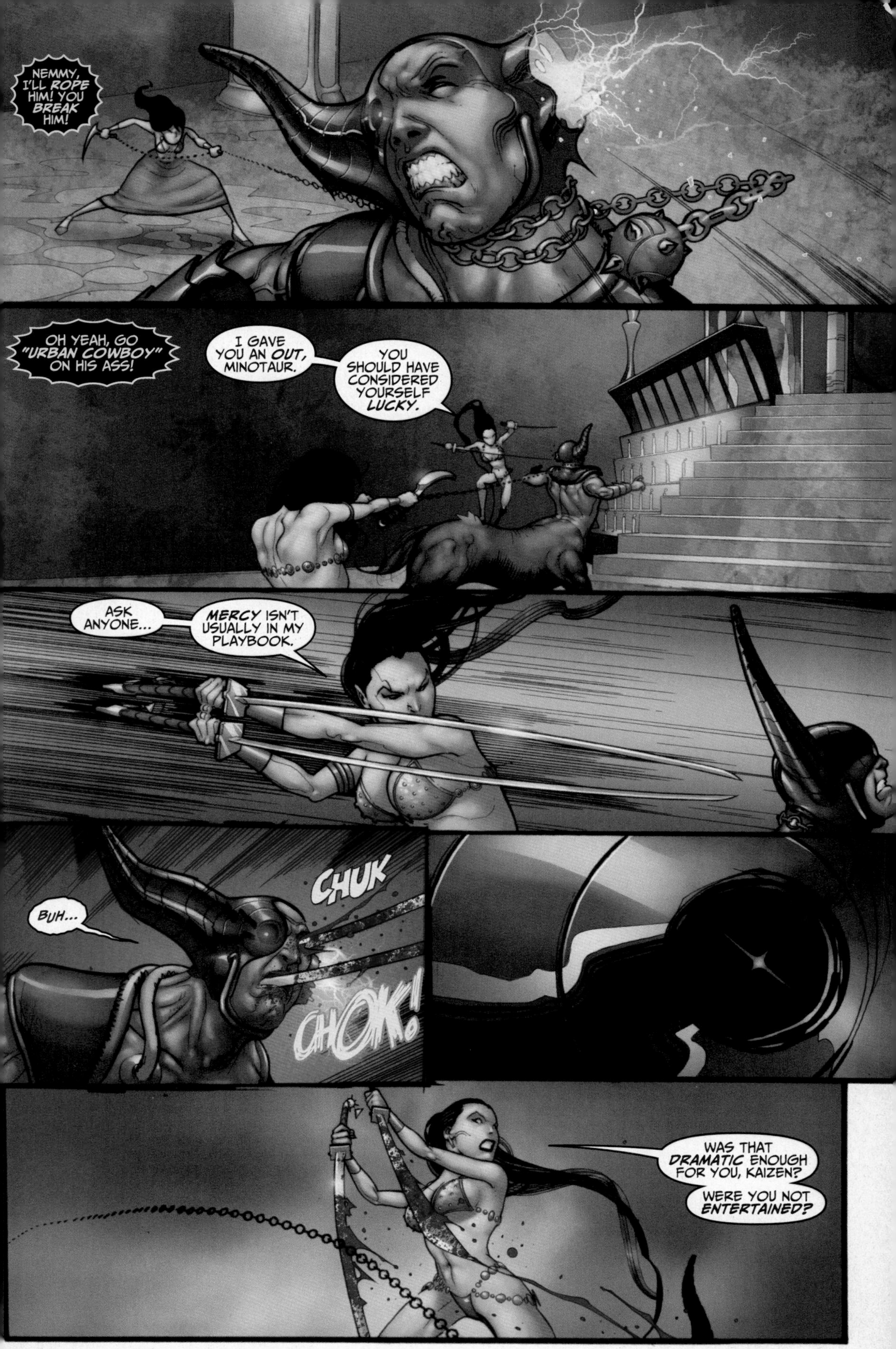

NEMMY, I'LL ROPE HIM! YOU BREAK HIM!
OH YEAH, GO "URBAN COWBOY" ON HIS ASS!
I GAVE YOU AN OUT, MINOTAUR.
YOU SHOULD HAVE CONSIDERED YOURSELF LUCKY.
ASK ANYONE...
MERCY ISN'T USUALLY IN MY PLAYBOOK.
CHUK
BUH...
CHOK!
WAS THAT DRAMATIC ENOUGH FOR YOU, KAIZEN?
WERE YOU NOT ENTERTAINED?

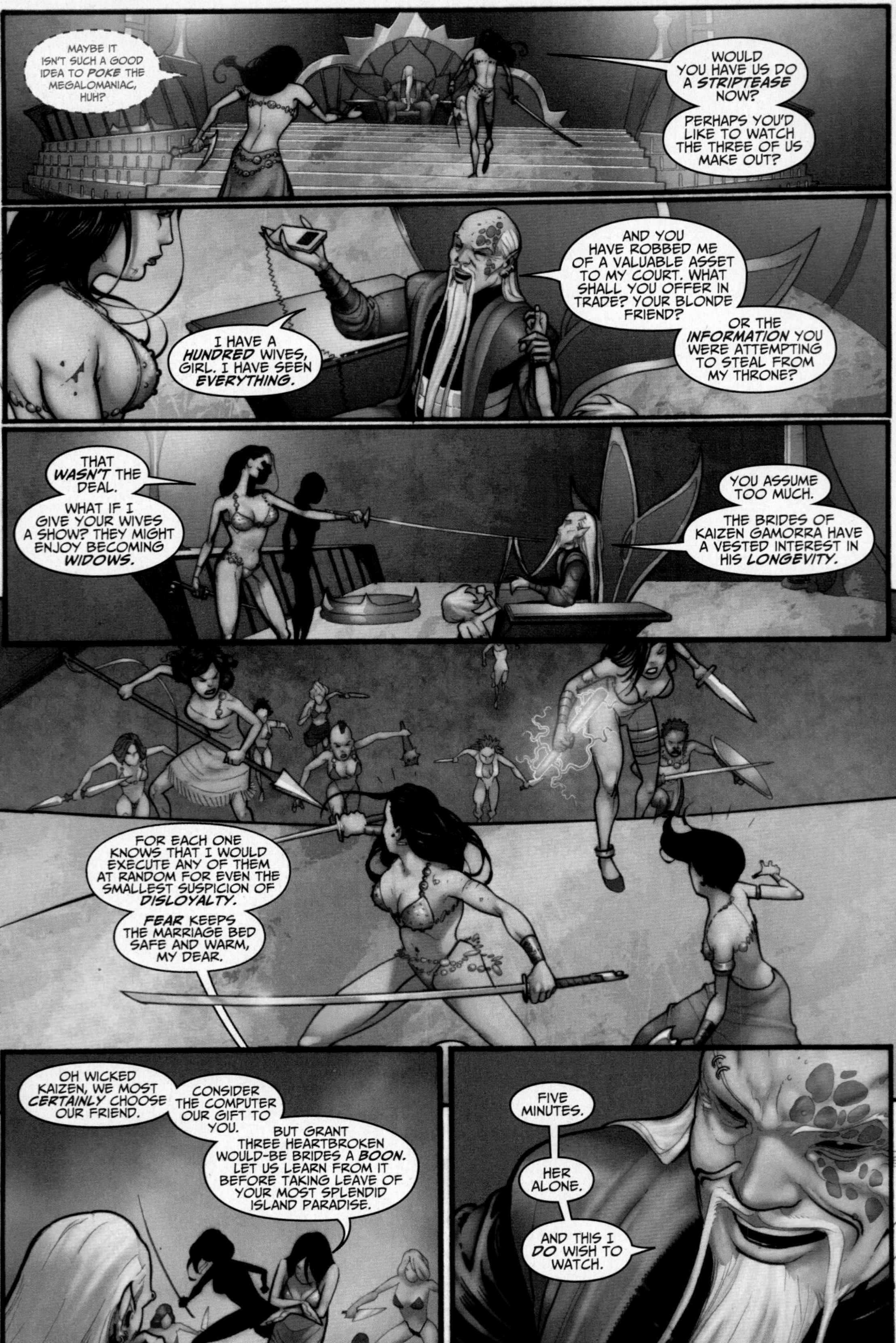
MAYBE IT ISN'T SUCH A GOOD IDEA TO POKE THE MEGALOMANIAC, HUH?
WOULD YOU HAVE US DO A STRIPTEASE NOW?
PERHAPS YOU'D LIKE TO WATCH THE THREE OF US MAKE OUT?
I HAVE A HUNDRED WIVES, GIRL. I HAVE SEEN EVERYTHING.
AND YOU HAVE ROBBED ME OF A VALUABLE ASSET TO MY COURT. WHAT SHALL YOU OFFER IN TRADE? YOUR BLONDE FRIEND?
OR THE INFORMATION YOU WERE ATTEMPTING TO STEAL FROM MY THRONE?
THAT WASN'T THE DEAL.
WHAT IF I GIVE YOUR WIVES A SHOW? THEY MIGHT ENJOY BECOMING WIDOWS.
YOU ASSUME TOO MUCH.
THE BRIDES OF KAIZEN GAMORRA HAVE A VESTED INTEREST IN HIS LONGEVITY.
FOR EACH ONE KNOWS THAT I WOULD EXECUTE ANY OF THEM AT RANDOM FOR EVEN THE SMALLEST SUSPICION OF DISLOYALTY.
FEAR KEEPS THE MARRIAGE BED SAFE AND WARM, MY DEAR.
OH WICKED KAIZEN, WE MOST CERTAINLY CHOOSE OUR FRIEND.
CONSIDER THE COMPUTER OUR GIFT TO YOU.
BUT GRANT THREE HEARTBROKEN WOULD-BE BRIDES A BOON. LET US LEARN FROM IT BEFORE TAKING LEAVE OF YOUR MOST SPLENDID ISLAND PARADISE.
FIVE MINUTES.
HER ALONE.
AND THIS I DO WISH TO WATCH.

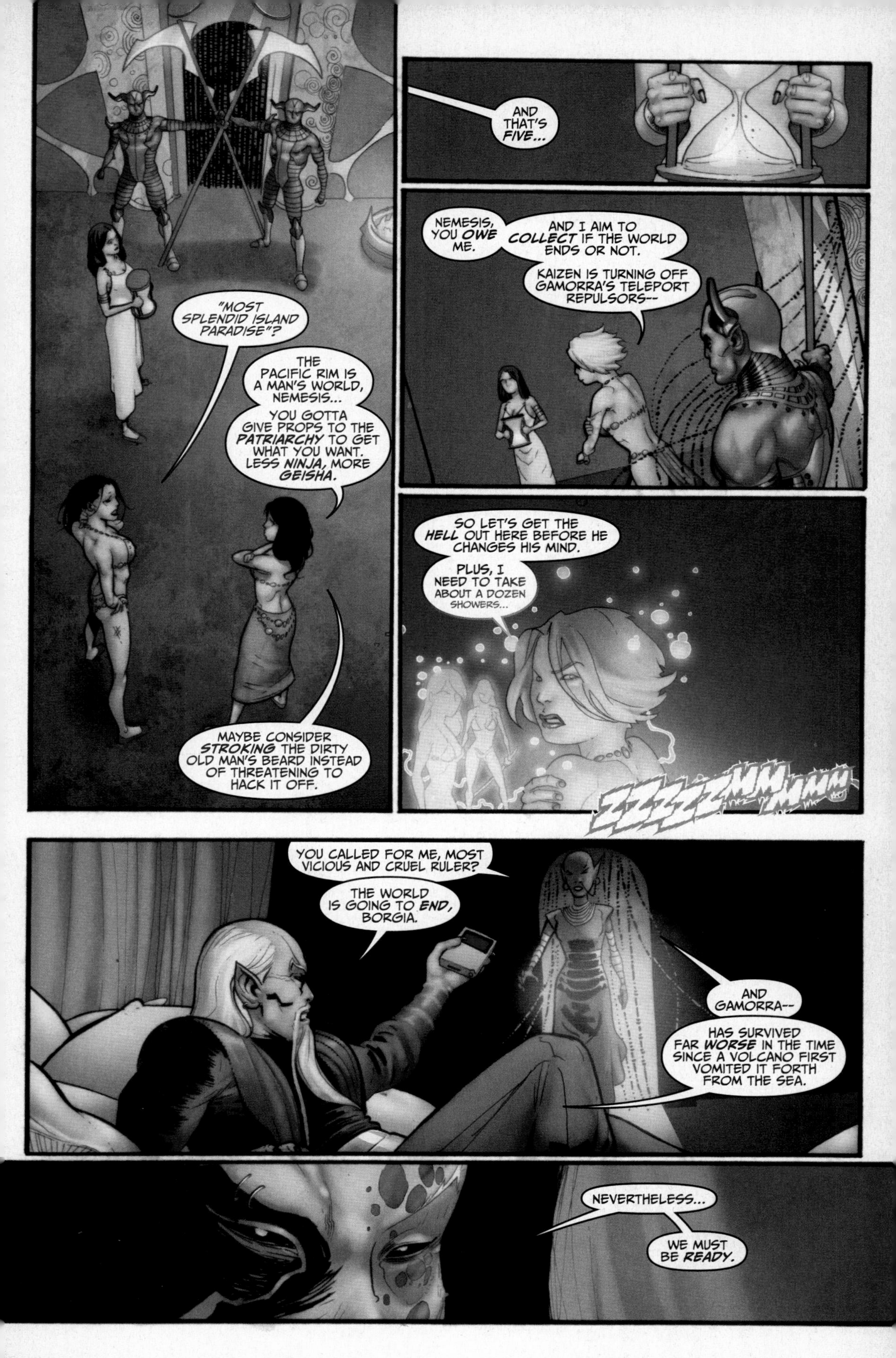

"MOST SPLENDID ISLAND PARADISE"?
THE PACIFIC RIM IS A MAN'S WORLD, NEMESIS...
YOU GOTTA GIVE PROPS TO THE PATRIARCHY TO GET WHAT YOU WANT. LESS NINJA, MORE GEISHA.
MAYBE CONSIDER STROKING THE DIRTY OLD MAN'S BEARD INSTEAD OF THREATENING TO HACK IT OFF.
AND THAT'S FIVE...
NEMESIS, YOU OWE ME.
AND I AIM TO COLLECT IF THE WORLD ENDS OR NOT.
KAIZEN IS TURNING OFF GAMORRA'S TELEPORT REPULSORS--
SO LET'S GET THE HELL OUT HERE BEFORE HE CHANGES HIS MIND.
PLUS, I NEED TO TAKE ABOUT A DOZEN SHOWERS...
ZZZZZZMMMMMM
YOU CALLED FOR ME, MOST VICIOUS AND CRUEL RULER?
THE WORLD IS GOING TO END, BORGIA.
AND GAMORRA--
HAS SURVIVED FAR WORSE IN THE TIME SINCE A VOLCANO FIRST VOMITED IT FORTH FROM THE SEA.
NEVERTHELESS...
WE MUST BE READY.

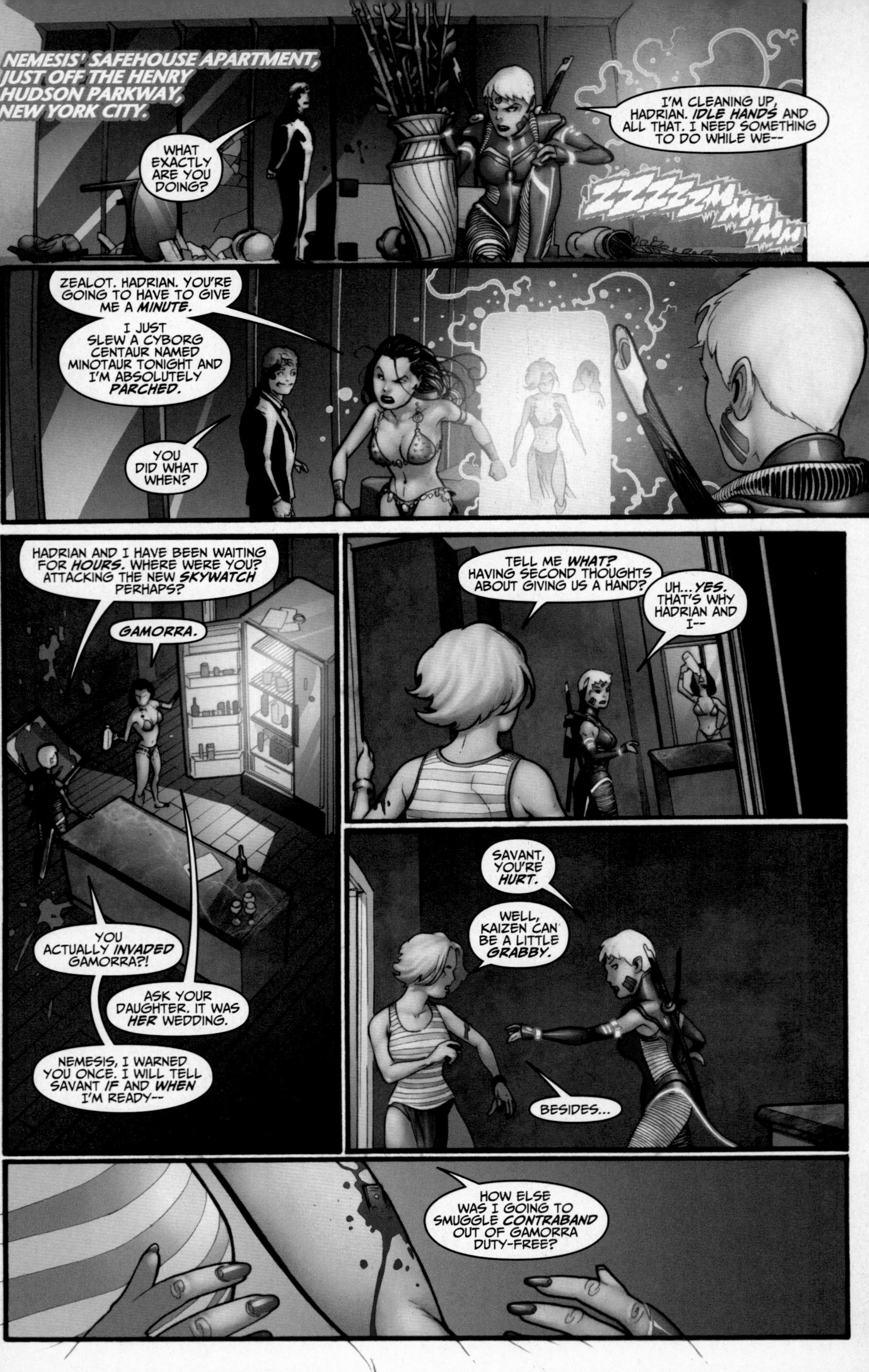
NEMESIS' SAFEHOUSE APARTMENT, JUST OFF THE HENRY HUDSON PARKWAY, NEW YORK CITY.
WHAT EXACTLY ARE YOU DOING?
I'M CLEANING UP, HADRIAN. IDLE HANDS AND ALL THAT. I NEED SOMETHING TO DO WHILE WE--
ZZZZZMMMMMM
ZEALOT. HADRIAN. YOU'RE GOING TO HAVE TO GIVE ME A MINUTE.
I JUST SLEW A CYBORG CENTAUR NAMED MINOTAUR TONIGHT AND I'M ABSOLUTELY PARCHED.
YOU DID WHAT WHEN?
HADRIAN AND I HAVE BEEN WAITING FOR HOURS. WHERE WERE YOU? ATTACKING THE NEW SKYWATCH PERHAPS?
GAMORRA.
YOU ACTUALLY INVADED GAMORRA?!
ASK YOUR DAUGHTER. IT WAS HER WEDDING.
NEMESIS, I WARNED YOU ONCE. I WILL TELL SAVANT IF AND WHEN I'M READY--
TELL ME WHAT? HAVING SECOND THOUGHTS ABOUT GIVING US A HAND?
UH...YES. THAT'S WHY HADRIAN AND I--
SAVANT, YOU'RE HURT.
WELL, KAIZEN CAN BE A LITTLE GRABBY.
BESIDES...
HOW ELSE WAS I GOING TO SMUGGLE CONTRABAND OUT OF GAMORRA DUTY-FREE?

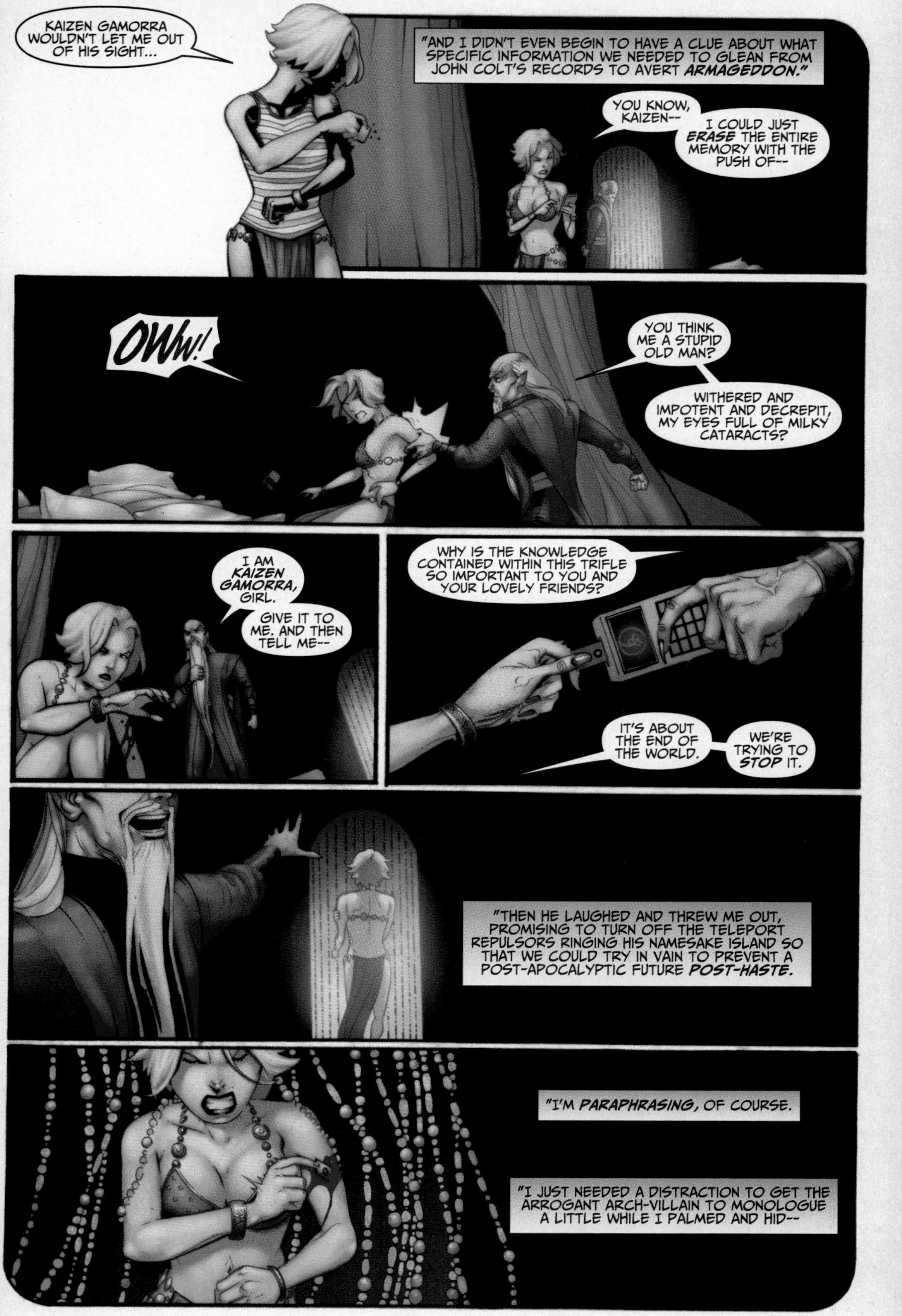
KAIZEN GAMORRA WOULDN'T LET ME OUT OF HIS SIGHT...
"AND I DIDN'T EVEN BEGIN TO HAVE A CLUE ABOUT WHAT SPECIFIC INFORMATION WE NEEDED TO GLEAN FROM JOHN COLT'S RECORDS TO AVERT ARMAGEDDON."
YOU KNOW, KAIZEN--
I COULD JUST ERASE THE ENTIRE MEMORY WITH THE PUSH OF--
OWW!
YOU THINK ME A STUPID OLD MAN?
WITHERED AND IMPOTENT AND DECREPIT, MY EYES FULL OF MILKY CATARACTS?
I AM KAIZEN GAMORRA, GIRL.
GIVE IT TO ME. AND THEN TELL ME--
WHY IS THE KNOWLEDGE CONTAINED WITHIN THIS TRIFLE SO IMPORTANT TO YOU AND YOUR LOVELY FRIENDS?
IT'S ABOUT THE END OF THE WORLD.
WE'RE TRYING TO STOP IT.
"THEN HE LAUGHED AND THREW ME OUT, PROMISING TO TURN OFF THE TELEPORT REPULSORS RINGING HIS NAMESAKE ISLAND SO THAT WE COULD TRY IN VAIN TO PREVENT A POST-APOCALYPTIC FUTURE POST-HASTE.
"I'M PARAPHRASING, OF COURSE.
"I JUST NEEDED A DISTRACTION TO GET THE ARROGANT ARCH-VILLAIN TO MONOLOGUE A LITTLE WHILE I PALMED AND HID--

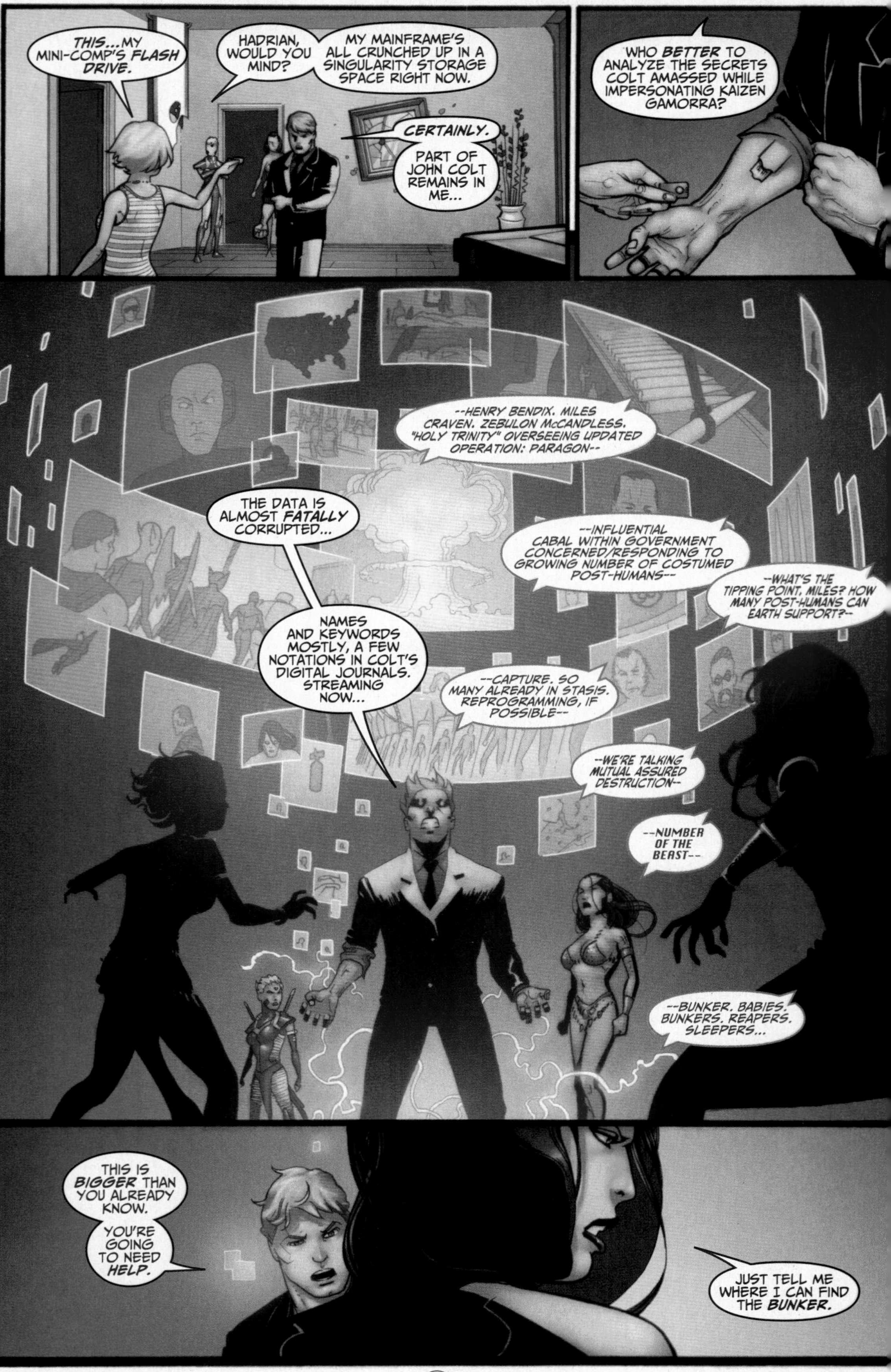
THIS...MY MINI-COMP'S FLASH DRIVE.
HADRIAN, WOULD YOU MIND?
MY MAINFRAME'S ALL CRUNCHED UP IN A SINGULARITY STORAGE SPACE RIGHT NOW.
CERTAINLY.
PART OF JOHN COLT REMAINS IN ME...
WHO BETTER TO ANALYZE THE SECRETS COLT AMASSED WHILE IMPERSONATING KAIZEN GAMORRA?
--HENRY BENDIX. MILES CRAVEN. ZEBULON McCANDLESS. "HOLY TRINITY" OVERSEEING UPDATED OPERATION: PARAGON--
THE DATA IS ALMOST FATALLY CORRUPTED...
--INFLUENTIAL CABAL WITHIN GOVERNMENT CONCERNED/RESPONDING TO GROWING NUMBER OF COSTUMED POST-HUMANS--
--WHAT'S THE TIPPING POINT, MILES? HOW MANY POST-HUMANS CAN EARTH SUPPORT?--
NAMES AND KEYWORDS MOSTLY, A FEW NOTATIONS IN COLT'S DIGITAL JOURNALS. STREAMING NOW...
--CAPTURE. SO MANY ALREADY IN STASIS. REPROGRAMMING, IF POSSIBLE--
--WE'RE TALKING MUTUAL ASSURED DESTRUCTION--
--NUMBER OF THE BEAST--
--BUNKER. BABIES. BUNKERS. REAPERS. SLEEPERS...
THIS IS BIGGER THAN YOU ALREADY KNOW.
YOU'RE GOING TO NEED HELP.
JUST TELL ME WHERE I CAN FIND THE BUNKER.

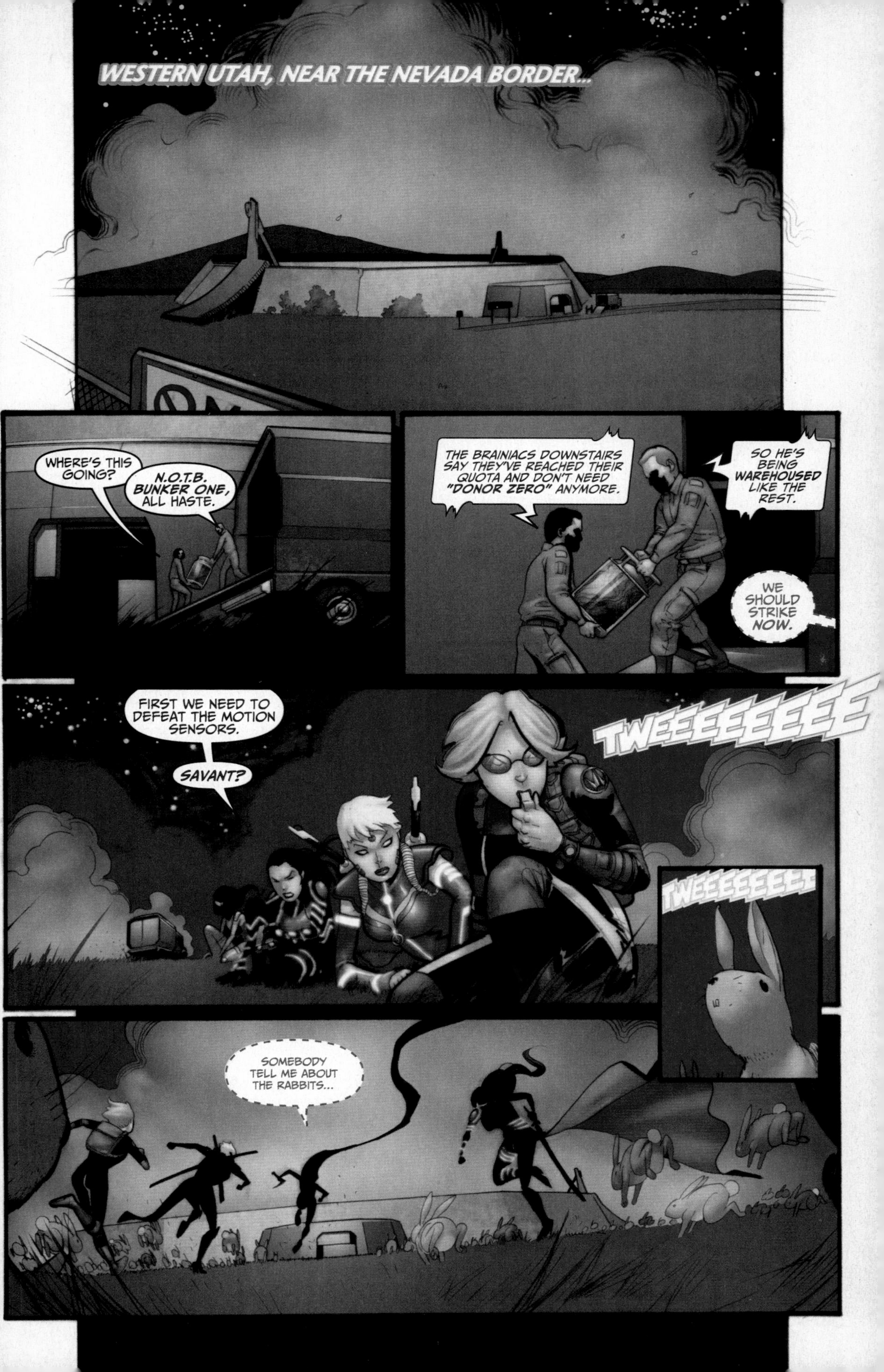

WESTERN UTAH, NEAR THE NEVADA BORDER...
WHERE'S THIS GOING?
N.O.T.B. BUNKER ONE, ALL HASTE.
THE BRAINIACS DOWNSTAIRS SAY THEY'VE REACHED THEIR QUOTA AND DON'T NEED "DONOR ZERO" ANYMORE.
SO HE'S BEING WAREHOUSED LIKE THE REST.
WE SHOULD STRIKE NOW.
FIRST WE NEED TO DEFEAT THE MOTION SENSORS.
SAVANT?
TWEEEEEEEE
TWEEEEEEEE
SOMEBODY TELL ME ABOUT THE RABBITS...

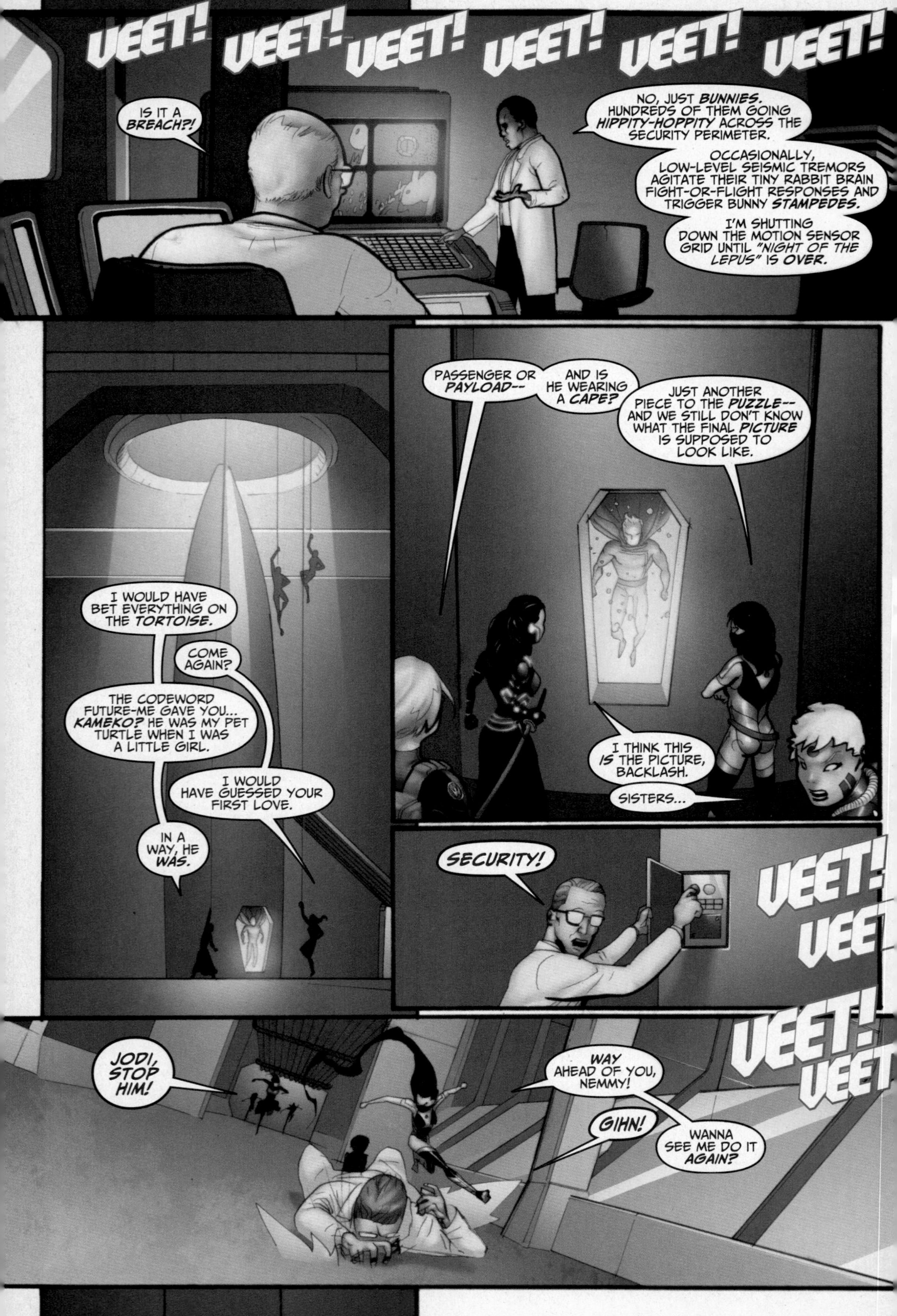
VEET! VEET! VEET! VEET! VEET! VEET!
IS IT A BREACH?!
NO, JUST BUNNIES. HUNDREDS OF THEM GOING HIPPITY-HOPPITY ACROSS THE SECURITY PERIMETER.
OCCASIONALLY, LOW-LEVEL SEISMIC TREMORS AGITATE THEIR TINY RABBIT BRAIN FIGHT-OR-FLIGHT RESPONSES AND TRIGGER BUNNY STAMPEDES.
I'M SHUTTING DOWN THE MOTION SENSOR GRID UNTIL "NIGHT OF THE LEPUS" IS OVER.
I WOULD HAVE BET EVERYTHING ON THE TORTOISE.
COME AGAIN?
THE CODEWORD FUTURE-ME GAVE YOU... KAMEKO? HE WAS MY PET TURTLE WHEN I WAS A LITTLE GIRL.
I WOULD HAVE GUESSED YOUR FIRST LOVE.
IN A WAY, HE WAS.
PASSENGER OR PAYLOAD--
AND IS HE WEARING A CAPE?
JUST ANOTHER PIECE TO THE PUZZLE-- AND WE STILL DON'T KNOW WHAT THE FINAL PICTURE IS SUPPOSED TO LOOK LIKE.
I THINK THIS IS THE PICTURE, BACKLASH.
SISTERS...
SECURITY!
VEET! VEE
JODI, STOP HIM!
WAY AHEAD OF YOU, NEMMY!
GIHN!
WANNA SEE ME DO IT AGAIN?
VEET! VEET

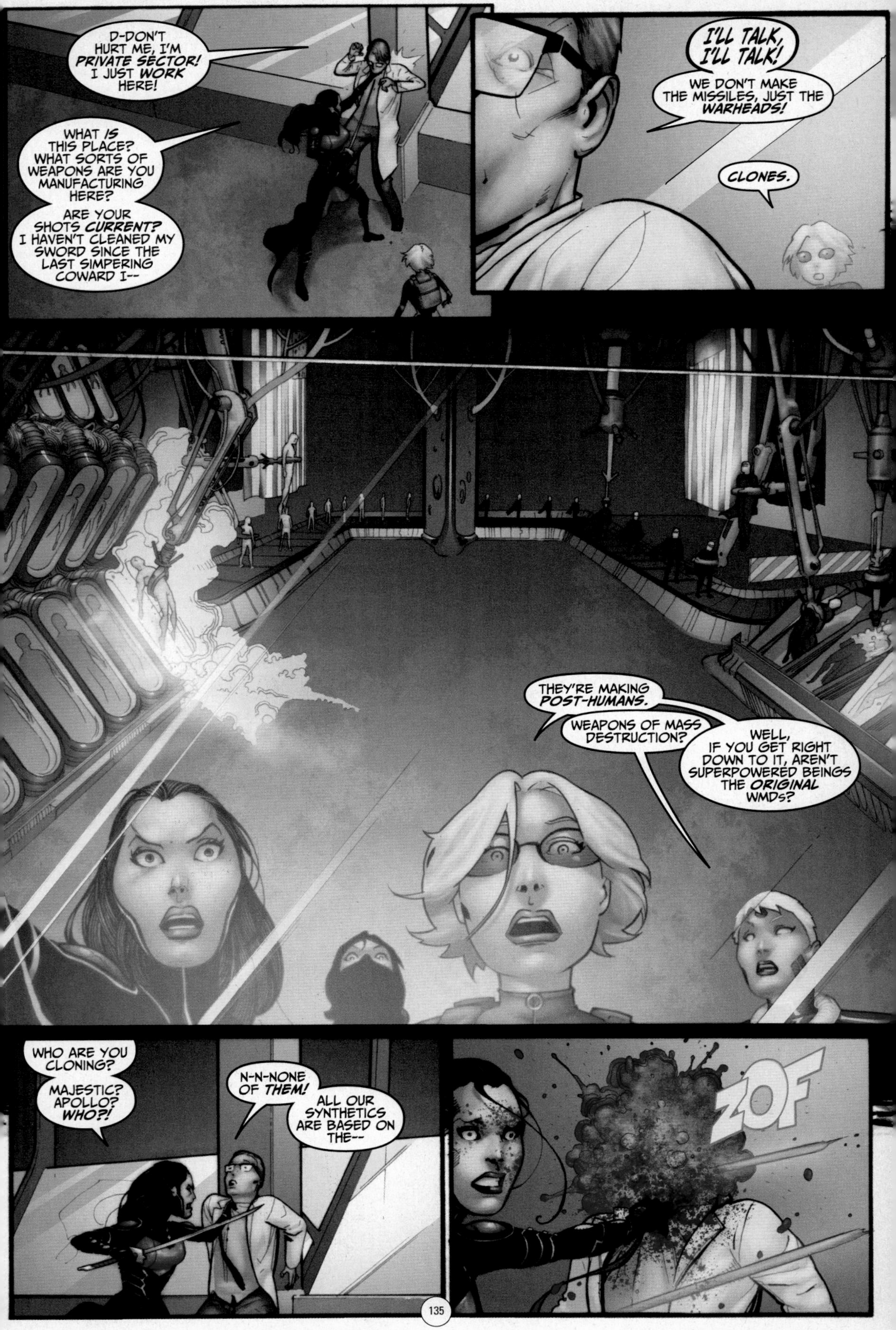
D-DON'T HURT ME, I'M PRIVATE SECTOR! I JUST WORK HERE!
WHAT IS THIS PLACE? WHAT SORTS OF WEAPONS ARE YOU MANUFACTURING HERE?
ARE YOUR SHOTS CURRENT? I HAVEN'T CLEANED MY SWORD SINCE THE LAST SIMPERING COWARD I--
I'LL TALK, I'LL TALK!
WE DON'T MAKE THE MISSILES, JUST THE WARHEADS!
CLONES.
THEY'RE MAKING POST-HUMANS.
WEAPONS OF MASS DESTRUCTION?
WELL, IF YOU GET RIGHT DOWN TO IT, AREN'T SUPERPOWERED BEINGS THE ORIGINAL WMDs?
WHO ARE YOU CLONING?
MAJESTIC? APOLLO? WHO?!
N-N-NONE OF THEM!
ALL OUR SYNTHETICS ARE BASED ON THE--
ZOF

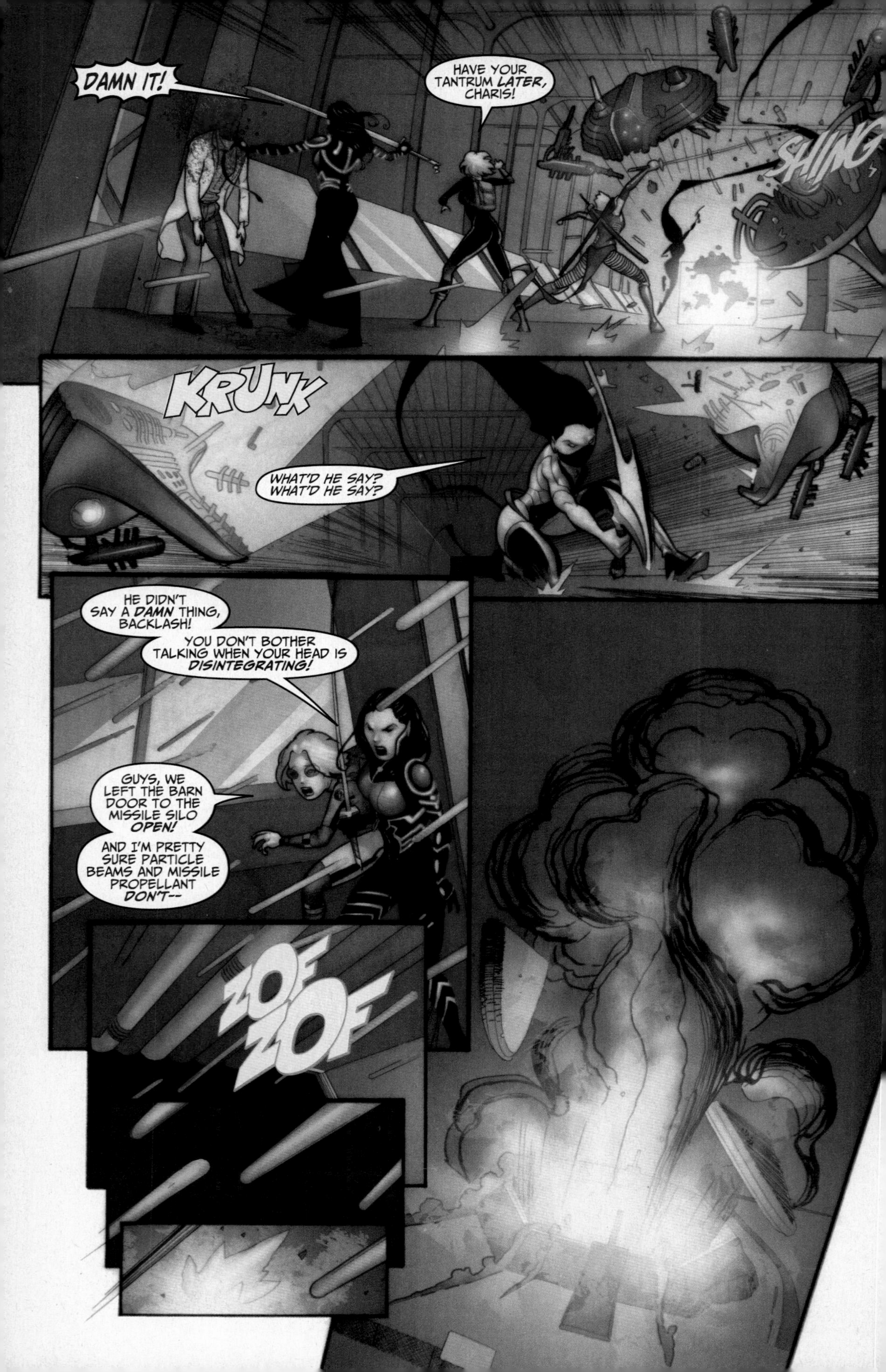
DAMN IT!
HAVE YOUR TANTRUM LATER, CHARIS!
SHING
KRUNK
WHAT'D HE SAY? WHAT'D HE SAY?
HE DIDN'T SAY A DAMN THING, BACKLASH!
YOU DON'T BOTHER TALKING WHEN YOUR HEAD IS DISINTEGRATING!
GUYS, WE LEFT THE BARN DOOR TO THE MISSILE SILO OPEN!
AND I'M PRETTY SURE PARTICLE BEAMS AND MISSILE PROPELLANT DON'T--
ZOF ZOF

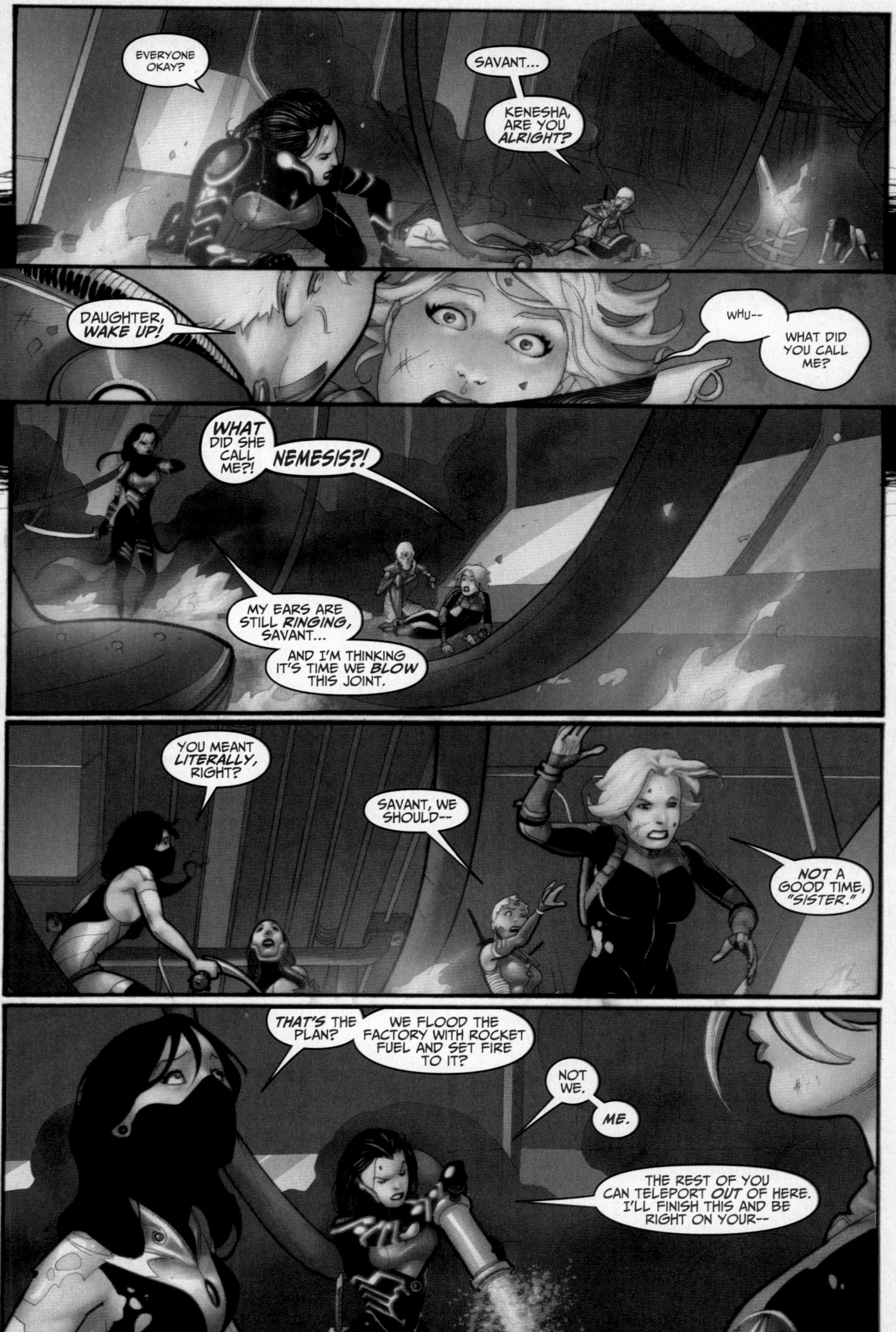

EVERYONE OKAY?
SAVANT...
KENESHA, ARE YOU ALRIGHT?
DAUGHTER, WAKE UP!
WHU--
WHAT DID YOU CALL ME?
WHAT DID SHE CALL ME?!
NEMESIS?!
MY EARS ARE STILL RINGING, SAVANT...
AND I'M THINKING IT'S TIME WE BLOW THIS JOINT.
YOU MEANT LITERALLY, RIGHT?
SAVANT, WE SHOULD--
NOT A GOOD TIME, "SISTER."
THAT'S THE PLAN?
WE FLOOD THE FACTORY WITH ROCKET FUEL AND SET FIRE TO IT?
NOT WE.
ME.
THE REST OF YOU CAN TELEPORT OUT OF HERE. I'LL FINISH THIS AND BE RIGHT ON YOUR--

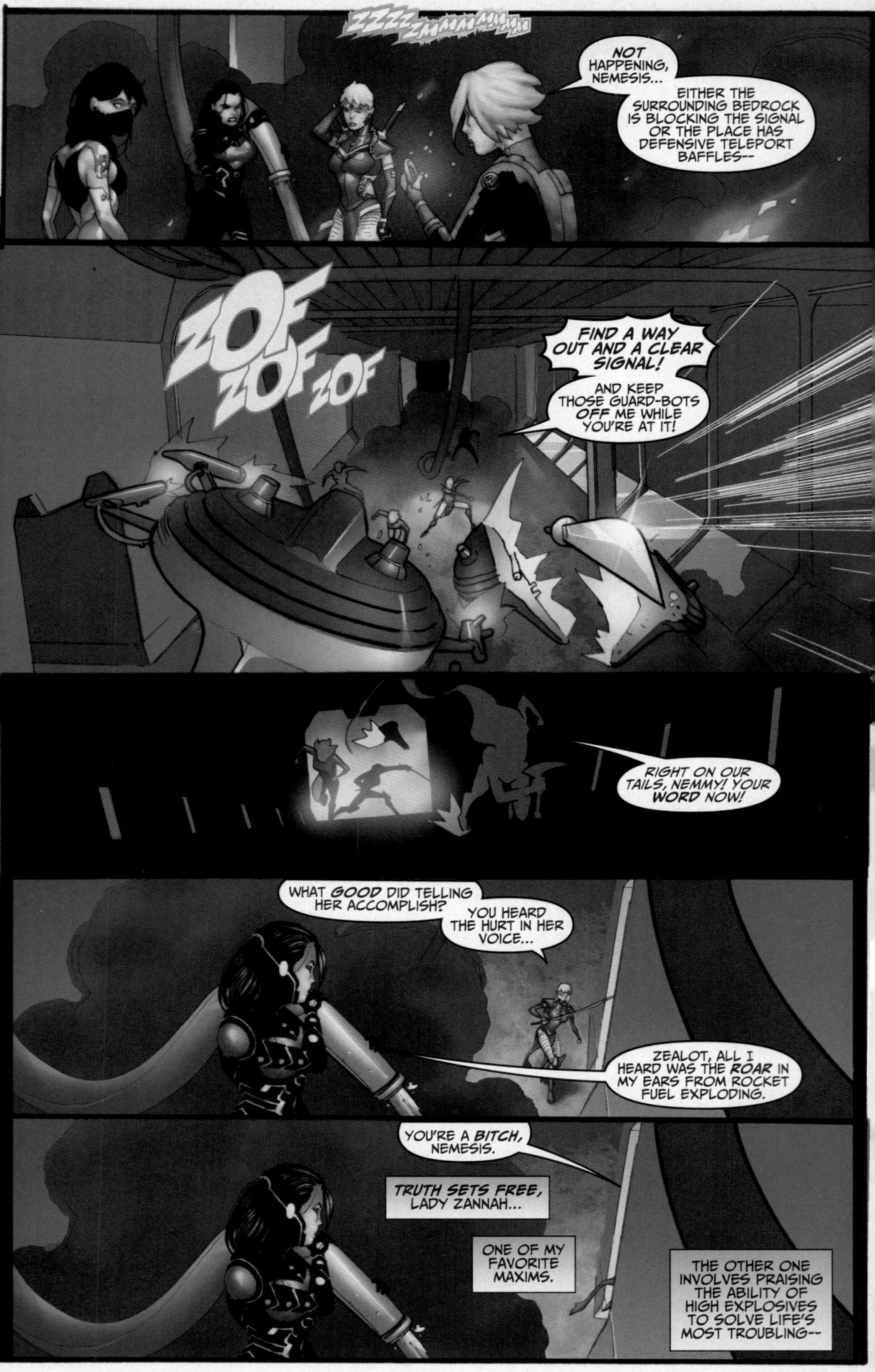
ZZZZZMMMMMMMM
NOT HAPPENING, NEMESIS...
EITHER THE SURROUNDING BEDROCK IS BLOCKING THE SIGNAL OR THE PLACE HAS DEFENSIVE TELEPORT BAFFLES--
ZOF ZOF ZOF
FIND A WAY OUT AND A CLEAR SIGNAL!
AND KEEP THOSE GUARD-BOTS OFF ME WHILE YOU'RE AT IT!
RIGHT ON OUR TAILS, NEMMY! YOUR WORD NOW!
WHAT GOOD DID TELLING HER ACCOMPLISH?
YOU HEARD THE HURT IN HER VOICE...
ZEALOT, ALL I HEARD WAS THE ROAR IN MY EARS FROM ROCKET FUEL EXPLODING.
YOU'RE A BITCH, NEMESIS.
TRUTH SETS FREE, LADY ZANNAH...
ONE OF MY FAVORITE MAXIMS.
THE OTHER ONE INVOLVES PRAISING THE ABILITY OF HIGH EXPLOSIVES TO SOLVE LIFE'S MOST TROUBLING--

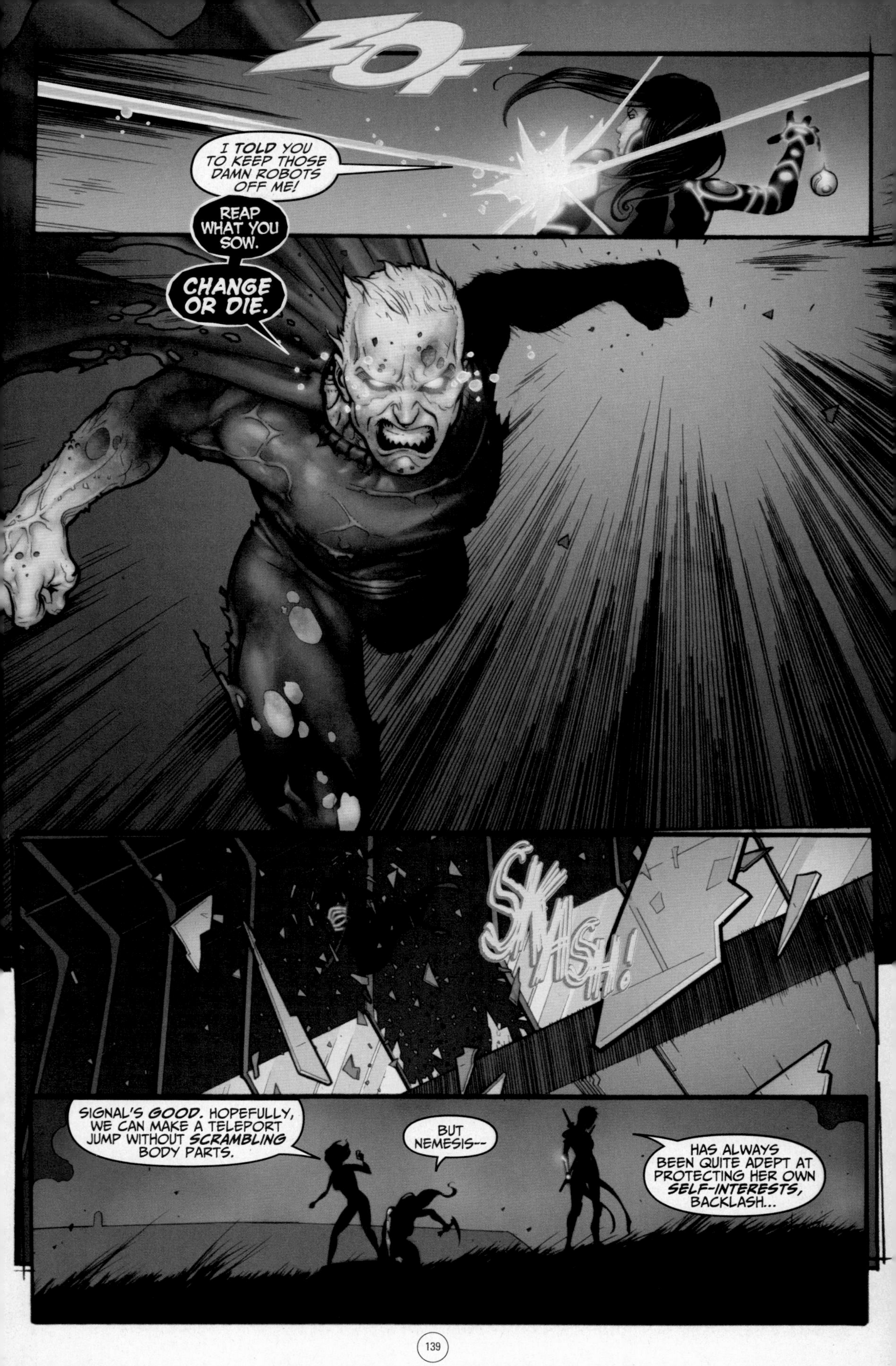
ZOF
I TOLD YOU TO KEEP THOSE DAMN ROBOTS OFF ME!
REAP WHAT YOU SOW.
CHANGE OR DIE.
SMASH!
SIGNAL'S GOOD. HOPEFULLY, WE CAN MAKE A TELEPORT JUMP WITHOUT SCRAMBLING BODY PARTS.
BUT NEMESIS--
HAS ALWAYS BEEN QUITE ADEPT AT PROTECTING HER OWN SELF-INTERESTS, BACKLASH...

I'M SURE SHE'S ALREADY SAFELY HOME AND DRAWING A HOT BATH RIGHT NOW.
YOU'RE HALF-RIGHT, ZANNAH...
REAP WHAT YOU SOW.
I HEARD YOU THE FIRST TIME, REAPER.
WHO ARE YOU MADE FROM?
WHAT IS YOUR TARGET?!
THAK
CHANGE
OR
DIE.

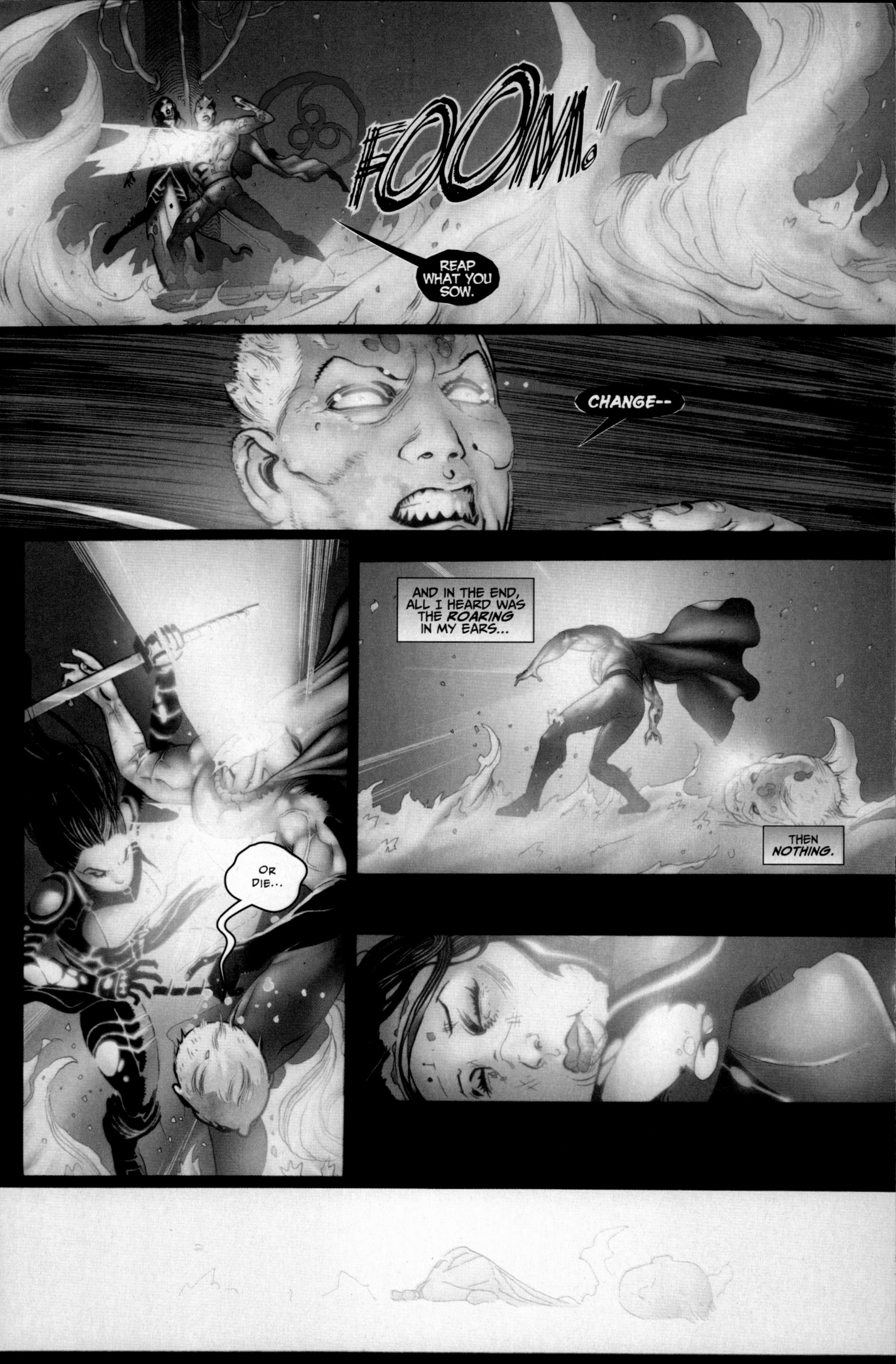
FOOM!
REAP WHAT YOU SOW.
CHANGE--
OR DIE...
AND IN THE END, ALL I HEARD WAS THE ROARING IN MY EARS...
THEN NOTHING.

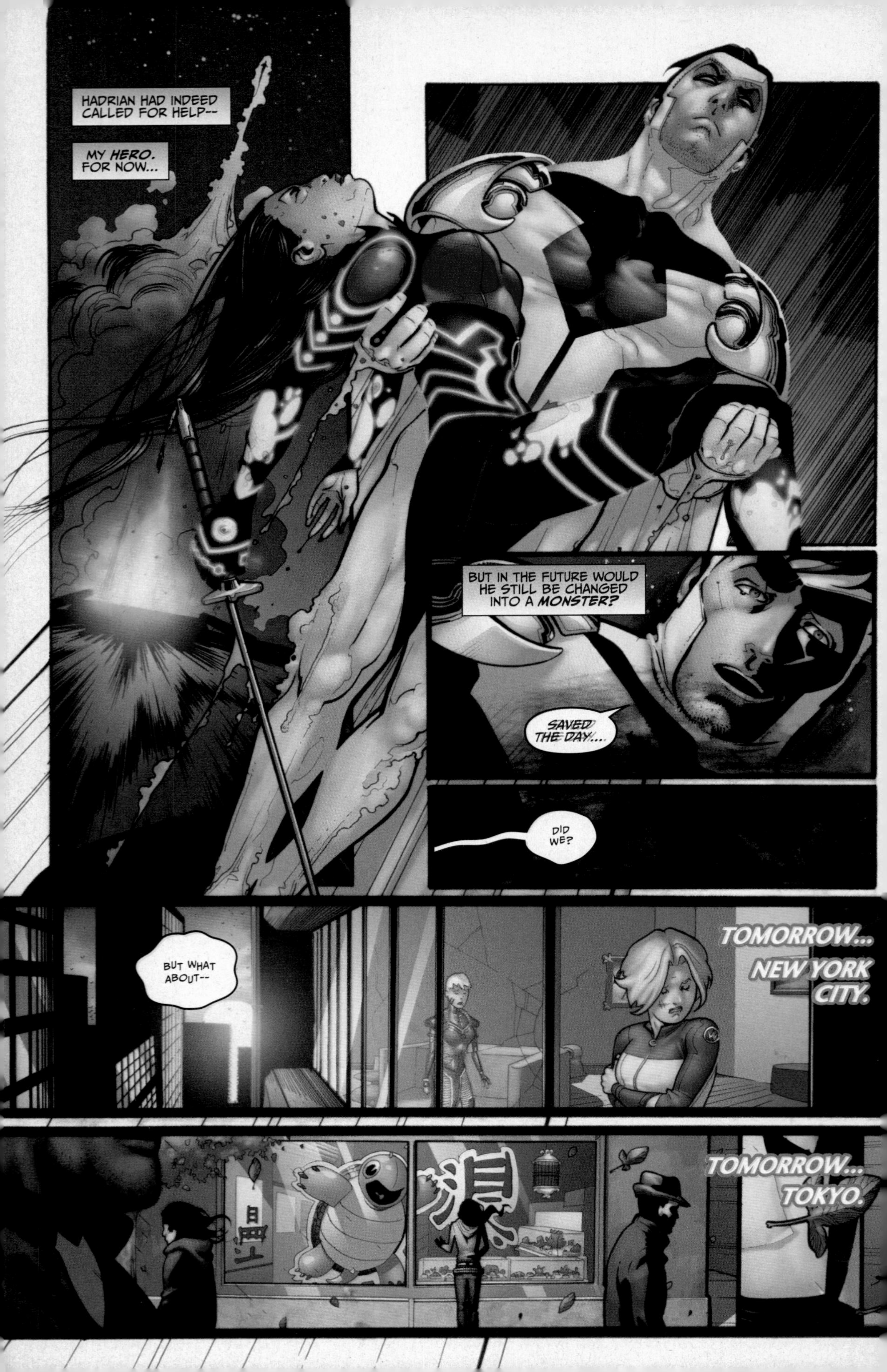
HADRIAN HAD INDEED CALLED FOR HELP--
MY *HERO.* FOR NOW...
BUT IN THE FUTURE WOULD HE STILL BE CHANGED INTO A *MONSTER?*
SAVED THE DAY....
DID WE?
BUT WHAT ABOUT--
TOMORROW... NEW YORK CITY.
TOMORROW... TOKYO.

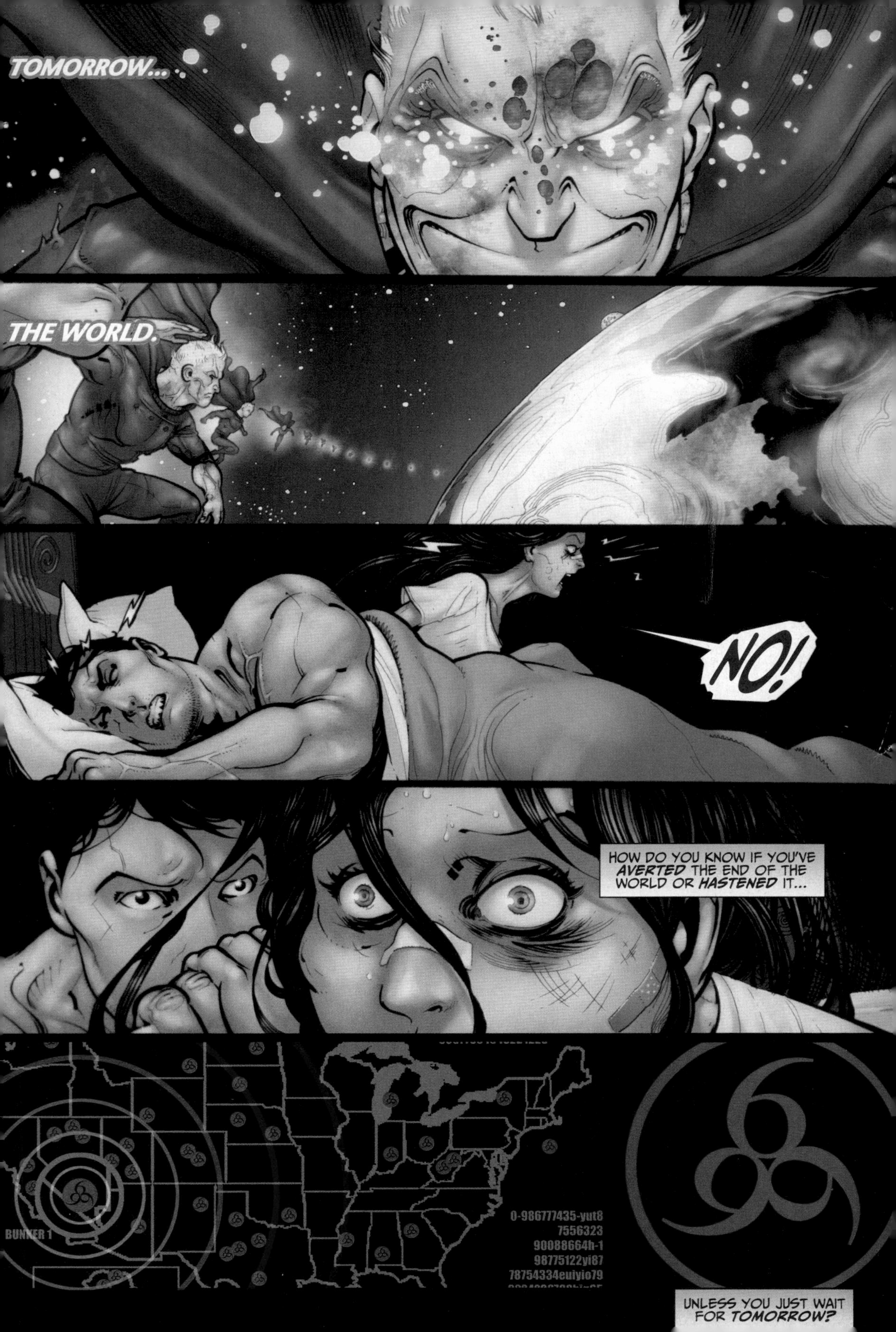
TOMORROW...
THE WORLD.
NO!
HOW DO YOU KNOW IF YOU'VE *AVERTED* THE END OF THE WORLD OR *HASTENED* IT...
BUNKER 1
0-986777435-yut8
7556323
90088664h-1
98775122yi87
78754334euiyio79
UNLESS YOU JUST WAIT FOR *TOMORROW?*

WANT TO KNOW MORE ABOUT THESE CHARACTERS?
START HERE!

W.I.L.D.C.A.T.S NEMESIS

WILDSTORM
W.I.L.D.C.A.T.S
NEMESIS
MORRISON CALDWELL DOMINGUES
BANNING SMITH

Framed for the betrayal and slaughter of the Kheran military forces on Earth at the dawn of mankind, rogue warrior Charis Adrastea embarks on an epic quest. Hunted by former friends and foes alike, she is determined clear her name and bring those responsible to justice. She'll soon discover a conspiracy that threatens the entire universe...but can one woman fight an entire war alone?

Robbie Morrison and artists Talent Caldwell and Horacio Domingues bring you this millennia-spanning adventure.

ALAN MOORE'S COMPLETE WILDC.A.T.S

ALAN MOORE'S
COMPLETE WILDC.A.T.S

MOORE • VARIOUS

STORMWATCH BOOKS 1-5

STORMWATCH
FORCE OF NATURE

ELLIS • VARIOUS

TEAM ZERO

TEAM ZERO
DIXON
MAHNKE
HOPE

DIXON • MAHNKE
HOPE

TO FIND MORE COLLECTED EDITIONS AND MONTHLY COMIC BOOKS FROM WILDSTORM AND DC COMICS

CALL 1-888-COMIC BOOK

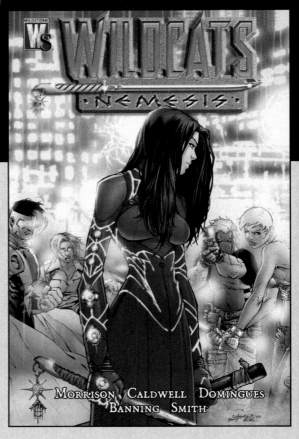

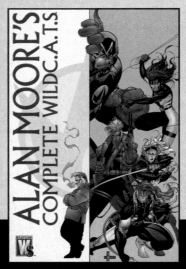

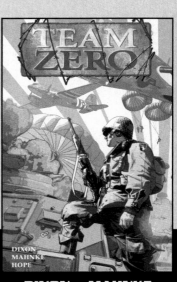